'Helen Hester and Will Stronge's excellent introduction to post-work thinking and politics is essential reading for anyone interested in the critique of work and in the possibilities of a life beyond work as we known it.'

Kathi Weeks, Author of *The Problem with Work* (2011)

'A devastatingly clear critique of what is wrong with the world of work, and a dizzyingly exciting, but never naive, guide to the possibilities that exist to create something much better.'

Andy Beckett, *Guardian* and *London Review of Books,* and author of *The Searchers* (2024) and *When the Lights Went Out* (2009)

'A thorough and accessible guide to post-work thinking, and a powerful challenge to our work-obsessed politics and culture. This book illuminates a path to a world in which we can live and breathe more freely.'

Daniel Chandler, author of *Free and Equal* (2023)

'*Post-Work* makes the case for a world in which work no longer dominates our lives. Hester and Stronge's incisive book shows how moving beyond the work ethic could improve the lives of everyone, as well as tackle political issues from climate change to gender inequality and disability discrimination. A compelling argument for work reduction as a key aspect of liberation.'

Alva Gotby, author of *They Call It Love: The Politics of Emotional Life* (2023) and *Feeling at Home: Transforming the Politics of Housing* (2024)

'Confident, lucid, and irresistible, *Post-Work* lifts all existing leftist policy discussions by the seat of the pants and gives them a tremendous shake. This book gave me the same excited feeling I experienced reading *The Problem with Work* by Kathi Weeks in 2011. Helen Hester and Will Stronge have given us a potent antidote to the anti-utopianism that hovers like a deathly miasma over our fearful, burnt-out and catastrophic times. A crystal-clear case for revaluing, redistributing and (above all) reducing work.'

Sophie Lewis, author of *Full Surrogacy Now* (2019) and *Abolish the Family* (2022)

'Hester and Stronge guide their reader towards an understanding of what is at stake in our "negative freedom," that is, our temporal freedom from the constraints of work. They care deeply about the ways labour changes our bodies, minds and ability to truly be with one another in meaningful and transformative ways. They want to rescue us from the work week. With clarity and precision, they show us precisely how what we will must be the driving force for any "post-work" future.'

Lola Olufemi, author of *Feminism Interrupted* (2020)

'A remarkable synthesis of post-work thought and a hugely significant contribution to the debate around our shared future.'

Amelia Horgan, author of *Lost in Work* (2021)

'Since the 19th century, nothing has signalled the victory of capitalism over those it exploits more forcefully than the recurring notion that work is something to be fought for, rather than against. In this landmark intervention, Hester and Stronge remind us that the fight for freedom can only be a struggle against work, while comprehensively surveying the field of contemporary post-work politics and making the case for its urgent indispensability.'

Jeremy Gilbert, Professor of Cultural and Political Theory, University of East London and co-author of *Hegemony Now* (2022)

'Post-work is the movement of our time. This is a super smart, accessible and comprehensive account of how to think about, implement and thrive in a society that is moving away from an outmoded work ethic to a new, more humane way of being. If you don't have time to read the many books being produced on this subject, just read this one. Essential reading for anyone worried about where we are going. Ideal for classes at all levels. And a must-have on the bookshelf. It's going straight onto my class reading list.'

Juliet Schor, Professor of Sociology at Boston College and author of *The Overworked American* (1992)

'I have waited a decade for a book like this to come along. With wide-eyed clarity, Hester and Stronge give the field of "post-work" the extended treatment and advancement it deserves. Bridging philosophy, labour history and policy debates, the book becomes more than a resource: it is a call for fresh forms of political intervention in a world where work is not working.'

David Frayne, author of The Refusal of Work (2015)

Post-work

*What It Is, Why It Matters and
How We Get There*

Helen Hester and Will Stronge

BLOOMSBURY ACADEMIC
LONDON · NEW YORK · OXFORD · NEW DELHI · SYDNEY

BLOOMSBURY ACADEMIC
Bloomsbury Publishing Plc, 50 Bedford Square, London, WC1B 3DP, UK
Bloomsbury Publishing Inc, 1359 Broadway, 12th Floor, New York, NY 10018, USA
Bloomsbury Publishing Ireland, 29 Earlsfort Terrace, Dublin 2, D02 AY28, Ireland

BLOOMSBURY, BLOOMSBURY ACADEMIC and the Diana logo are
trademarks of Bloomsbury Publishing Plc

First published in Great Britain 2025
Reprinted 2025

A catalogue record for this book is available from the British Library.

A catalog record for this book is available from the Library of Congress.

ISBN: HB: 978-1-3500-8997-6
          PB: 978-1-3500-8998-3
          ePDF: 978-1-3500-8996-9
          eBook: 978-1-3500-8999-0

Typeset by Integra Software Services Pvt. Ltd.
Printed and bound in Great Britain

For product safety related questions contact productsafety@bloomsbury.com

To find out more about our authors and books visit www.bloomsbury.com
and sign up for our newsletters.

Helen dedicates this book to Nick, Kit, Owen and Miles.
Will dedicates this book to Irene.

Contents

Acknowledgements

We would like to say thanks to all who fed into this work, directly or indirectly, including all of those who have passed through the Autonomy Institute and many many more. Thanks in particular are due to David Frayne, Deborah Fenney and Nick Srnicek for their helpful comments on the manuscript. Thank you also to Liza and the team at Bloomsbury for their patience, guidance and support.

On a personal note, Helen would like to thank the members, past and present, of the 'Gender, Technology and Work' research cluster at the University of West London, who provide an ongoing infusion of fresh thinking and intellectual energy. She would like to express her gratitude to Will Stronge, for bringing his sharp mind, easy charm and endless optimism to all elements of the writing process, and to all the caregivers (paid and unpaid) who maintain the people, spaces and things that enable her to think and to write. *Post-Work* could not exist without them.

Will would like to thank the team at Autonomy and its wider network, who he's been lucky enough to know during the years that this book developed. In particular, he would like to thank Phil Jones, Kyle Lewis, Julian Siravo, Maria Dada, James Muldoon, Philipp Frey, Seth Wheeler, Rob Calvert Jump, Ellie Mae O'Hagan, Cleo Goodman, Nic Murray, Andy Beckett, Matt Phull, Alice Martin, Charlie Clarke and Steve Howard (The Phull Set) for all the generative conversations. Thanks also to Sophie Lewis, Kathi Weeks, David Frayne, Nick Srnicek and Alex Williams for inspiring the book – and for all the other help along the way besides. He would also like to thank Helen, who has consistently forced him to raise his writing game across these years and whose sheer knowledge, experience and warmth have brought so much to the project.

Introduction: What we will

This book is a variety of things: it is a critique of how we organize work in our society, it is an introduction to a radical but perhaps lesser-known field of theory and politics, and it is an intervention into that field itself. Ultimately this is a book about the possibility of freedom from the burdens of work and the design of a world in which the role of work is minimized – a vision that many have had, and which we are yet to achieve. Throughout the chapters that follow, we hope to paint a picture of what 'post-work' is via the theories of some of its major proponents and advocates, but also to lend our own critical voices to this conversation. In this regard, the book seeks to serve not only as a resource for readers but as a provocation for people to reflect on, challenge and engage with. After all, doesn't everyone have an opinion about work?

Troubling time(s)

'Eight hours for work, eight hours for rest, eight hours for what we will!' So goes the famous slogan, taken from a popular nineteenth-century labour song. Time has long been a frontier of struggle for workers' movements, with demands for a shorter working day emerging alongside attempts to impose capitalist work discipline. In the pre-industrial era, boundaries between 'on the job' and 'off the job' were often blurry and hard to pin down. The division between working time and other sorts of time was less stark than we might imagine today, as specific tasks were often interrupted by unscheduled breaks, extended lunch hours and impromptu conversations. Indeed, from the seventeenth century onwards, the custom of skiving off at the beginning of the week was sufficiently well-established as to warrant its own nickname – 'Saint Monday'. Although still considerably constrained by social, religious and environmental forces, pre-capitalist workers had a significant degree of agency in terms of how they spent their hours and days, and how they met their needs; punctuality and productivity were evidently not the top priorities. This kind of laissez-faire approach to time, as we will learn in Chapter 1 of this book, was hardly ideal from the perspective of emerging industrialists, who often found themselves battling against the customs, traditions and ingrained expectations of the earliest factory workers.

As a demand 'eight hours for work, eight hours for rest, eight hours for what we will!' is remarkable effective, as punchy as it is commonsensical. Equal hours for work, rest and play – equal weight given to all human activities and needs. There is clarity and fairness in that. And yet, when we dig into these categories from a twenty-first-century perspective, we find that they raise as many questions as they answer – for while the imposition of work discipline on our daily routines is supposed to demarcate different forms of time, to split 'off the job' from 'on', the boundaries remain somewhat slipperier than one might suppose. Hours for *work* would appear to refer to time engaged in gainful employment; *rest*, to the necessary activities of regeneration and personal maintenance (most obviously, sleep); and *'what we will'*, to leisure – the free time necessary for human flourishing. But there are various activities that we would struggle to slot into this seemingly all-encompassing schema.

Where would we situate the exertions of caring for elderly relatives, for example? This is not (always) remunerated work, but it's clearly neither rest nor leisure. If our elders do not have access to other forms of support, then there is inevitably a degree of compulsion or obligation underpinning the care we offer (no matter how much we may value the person or people involved). If it is not a freely chosen pursuit, can we really consider it to fall beneath the banner of 'time for what we will'? There are other activities of this kind to consider, too, from changing nappies, to unblocking drains, to laundering bedsheets. What work is visible? Whose labour counts? And how do struggles against the dominion of work deal with these kinds of pursuits?

These may seem like marginal concerns, but their implications for how we think about work and (or *as*) life may be significant, not least from a feminist perspective. As the sociologist Wally Seccombe notes, at its 'inaugural congress in 1866, the International Workingmen's Association (the First International) took up the struggle for the eight-hour day. Their slogan was "les trois huits": eight hours of work, eight hours of leisure, and eight hours of sleep. In their eight hours of leisure, working men, even their socialist vanguard, were not thinking of doing much work at home'.[1] Without unpicking these dynamics, it is unlikely that people will ever enjoy temporal justice – equal access for all to time for what we will. Without careful attention, the famous slogan risks leaving many people out in the cold.

What *do* we will?

Perhaps some of this categorical confusion stems from the ambiguity of a demand framed around 'what we will'. From a certain perspective, this can be interpreted as a straightforward call for unstructured time reserved for unspecified (but freely chosen) activities. People must have time left over in their lives to do whatever suits their purposes or takes their fancy – a daily eight hours of one's own. What is at stake here is a negative freedom – temporal *freedom from* the constraints of work and personal maintenance.

In this light, time for what one wills is largely a demand for a protected remainder of time – a third of one's total daily hours, set aside from providing for one's most basic needs (be they economic or biological). It fails to take into account time spent providing for *other's* basic needs, perhaps in part because it draws upon and assumes a clear demarcation in terms of hours on and off the job (the conditions which facilitated the emergence of the three eights framework). One is either at work or not at work, living or labouring – when, in fact, for those with caring responsibilities or for whom the home is an unwaged workplace (or, indeed, for those who have recently been working from home during the pandemic or who otherwise find working life bleeding into their unwaged hours), there can be no such clear-cut demarcation. Clock time doesn't hold.

And there are various other categorical anomalies thrown up by the 'three eights' framework. How should one categorize commuting, for example? This is another activity we are compelled to perform, for which we receive no remuneration, and which certainly cannot be described as restful (no matter how many times we might accidentally nod off on the bus)! Do the hours we spend zoning out in front of the television after an arduous shift count as leisure, or are they rest? How should we think about time spent cooking a meal, updating our LinkedIn profiles or queueing at the benefits office? Of course, one can hardly blame the First International or the early short-time movement for failing to foresee these twenty-first-century mundanities, but how we classify work rest, and play – and whether or not we choose to use these categories at all – will nevertheless have a substantial impact in terms of our understanding of contemporary social organization and lived experience. This book will attempt to navigate some of this terrain, in the aim of putting forth a more inclusive conception of work and a more ambitious vision of its future.

While the task of increasing our free time is not as simple as 'les trois huits' would imply, this should certainly not deter us from pursuing it. Many before us have sifted through the changing or persistent features of our worlds of work, and there is thus no shortage of theoretical resources available to help us understand and change them. Post-work mobilizes these tools past and present to take on the challenge of *knowing work so as to put it in its place*. However, as a current of theory and politics, it is up against a deeply sedimented set of beliefs about work that function to valorize and protect it in the face of any and all critique: this is the so-called 'work ethic'.

Rejecting the traditional work ethic

The 'work ethic', in brief, is the idea that work is a good in itself, or is at least amongst the most virtuous pursuits a person can undertake. The modern work ethic – as it is commonly understood today – is a form of the 'Protestant

Work Ethic' (PWE) chronicled famously by Max Weber.[2] For Weber, this ethic emerged from Protestant and Calvinist teachings and was foundational to the modern period of culture and capitalist economics. It gave work a new and elevated significance:

> What characterised the Protestant ethos in particular was the ethical sanction for and the psychological impetus to work; ascetic Protestantism preached the moral import of constant and methodical productive effort on the part of self-disciplined individual subjects.[3]

The infraction of the PWE's rules is not to be understood 'as foolishness', Weber writes, 'but as forgetfulness of duty'.[4] One was prescribed to dedicate oneself to a life of 'organised worldly labour' not because it would guarantee one's place in an afterlife but because it would assuage the anxiety of not knowing whether you were one of the worthy elect or not.[5] Hard work was understood as part of faithful practice.

Today, in our secularized world, the work ethic has become stripped of its religious meaning in its everyday use and has become a justification in itself – no longer referring to a higher, transcendent purpose:

> Where [today] the fulfilment of the calling cannot directly be related to the highest spiritual and cultural values, or when, on the other hand, it need not be felt simply as economic compulsion, the individual generally abandons to justify it at all.[6]

This, Weber was keen to acknowledge, deepens the work ethic's incoherence. From the perspective of the Puritan worker then, the dominant position that our secular culture gives to work without end reveals a hollowness to our *'workaday* existence'.[7] Without a religious justification and context, the work ethic becomes an imperative to work for work's sake, hence the ease with which it has become open to multiple uses. Indeed, as Kathi Weeks notes, the work ethic has been and continues to be deployed in diverse contexts and from different perspectives. It can be mobilized by the rich to implore the poor to work harder, but has equally been wielded by workers' movements to slander the rich for not earning their living through hard graft – a trope that has become one of the purest symbols of virtuousness.[8]

Weeks traces the modifications undergone by the work ethic over the past half century – as our structures and methods of work morphed from the production line, pioneered by the likes of Henry Ford, to the deindustrialized service economy.

> Whereas Fordism demanded from its core workers a lifetime of compliance with work discipline, post-Fordism also demands of many of its workers flexibility, adaptability, and continual reinvention. If originally the work ethic was the means by which already disciplined workers were delivered to their exploitation, it serves a more directly productive function today: where attitudes themselves are productive, a strong work ethic guarantees the necessary level of willing commitment and subjective investment.[9]

Many studies have been written on today's peculiar form of work ideology – perhaps most famously Boltanski and Chiapello's *The New Spirit of Capitalism*, which documents the new approach to human management that emphasizes flexibility and self-expression.[10] Other examples include Arlie Russell Hochschild's study of modern service work, which illuminates how 'seeming to "love the job" becomes part of the job' itself,[11] or David Frayne's *Refusal of Work*, which powerfully critiques the pervasive 'company as family' discourse that attempts to garner consent from employees through instilling a sense of deep commitment and responsibility.[12] In various guises then, adaptability, flexibility and commitment to the job at hand are the subjective characteristics that we are supposed to internalize if we are to succeed in today's world of work: this is the latest form of the work ethic – one which can be hard to identify because it is so deeply embedded in our mode of thought. Once it has been identified, however, its ubiquity is quite evident.

The modern work ethic does not merely emerge from philosophical or religious texts, nor does it stem from spontaneous word of mouth. Historically, strong, institutional enforcement has been required in order to embed it into daily life. In its most direct and extreme form, the work ethic was an explicit ideological instrument driven by twentieth-century fascist states and their dictatorships. The Nazis had the 'Strength through Joy' organization (KDF), Salazar's Portugal had its 'Fundaçao Naçional para Alegria no Trabaljo' (National Foundation for Joy at Work), The Greek Ergatixi Estia (Workers'

Hearth/Home) was founded by the Metaxas regime and a similar programme was put in place under Franco's regime in Spain – with the Fuero del Trabajo (Charter of Work) organization.[13] Historian Victoria de Grazia has detailed Fascist Italy's iteration: the state-run Opera Nazionale Dopolavoro (OND – or national after work club). This involved a newly proposed *dopolavoro* (after work) culture, where various social clubs, leisure facilities and sporting institutions were 'called upon to perform double duty; as social mediator and disciplinarian of labor' – with the idea of replacing socialist social clubs and buttressing a strong, productivist culture amongst the working class.[14]

Each of these fascist institutions across Europe was installed to ensure 'better uses' of workers' time outside of their jobs and to quell discontent: materially enforcing a work-first hierarchy of values. Behind many of them was a fear of strong working-class movements and the ability to collectively determine life and work. For contemporaries in places such as Britain, tellingly, these authoritarians were doing what democracies dared not attempt: training the mob and beating a resistance to industry out of them.[15] Political and economic elites across nations in the early twentieth century were deeply concerned about the so-called 'problem of worker leisure', and there was a suspicion that, left to their own devices, workers would deteriorate into 'self-indulgence, sloth, social inefficiency, and a craving for unhealthy excitement'.[16] The European fascist states had taken action where elites in other countries – countries in which stronger worker movements were pushing for shorter hours and further concessions – were held at bay.

Today, the work ethic's institutional life continues, albeit in less overt forms – from government offices of social security that make you see any job as a *good* job through to the work visa procedures that regulate people across borders; from the 'love what you do' slogans draped everywhere in a WeWork office through to the 'jobs jobs jobs' slogans of major political parties.[17] It's common to see politicians occasionally singing the gospel of work – see Boris Johnson, for example, claiming that it was work that allowed Winston Churchill to overcome his depression, adding that

> what was true for Churchill is basically true for all of us: that to a very large extent we 'derive our self-esteem from what we do'. It is often from our jobs

... that we get that all-important sense of satisfaction ... as soon as someone leaves their job, and forsakes that selfdefining sense of purpose, they are at risk of entering a downward spiral of depression.[18]

Equally, anxieties about 'money for nothing' culture and 'welfare queens' reactivate older attitudes about worklessness, albeit under a disingenuous pretence of 'fairness' (in reality, little more than negative solidarity) and not explicitly out of a fear of working-class freedom as it was in the 1930s. Work propaganda is still very much a government strategy in most places in the world. As Chapter 2 will show, the work ethic ideology and rhetoric fused with the enforcement of wage labour upon the population so as to create the work-centred society that we know today.

The effects of the work ethic's ideological dominance are, of course, very tangible. It facilitates the stigmatization of those 'out of work'; it produces shame in individuals who understand themselves as falling short of the ideal, productive citizen; it can legitimate the physical and mental hardships that modern work imposes on us; it sediments traditional and oppressive family relationships; and its language is wielded by politicians as justification for labour market discipline or austerity measures. As AJ Withers writes: 'Those of us who violate the goal of striving for the ideal ... or who challenge our roles within the socio-economic system face consequences for our deviance.'[19] These consequences usually take the form of social and economic deprivation: an area that we will interrogate further in our discussion of welfare in Chapter 2.

Post-work thinking is keenly aware of the work ethic's presence in contemporary discourse around work and welfare, and a core tenet of post-work theory and politics is to push back against it in all of its iterations. Many post-work writers seek to point out its inconsistencies and violences, its anachronistic vision of virtue and its toxic vision of self-worth. And in its place, post-work seeks to install an altogether different disposition towards our labour.

Post-work ethics

As we shall see throughout this book, post-work is best understood as a variegated tendency, encompassing a range of different approaches, positions and politico-philosophical orientations. In our understanding, however, the post-work ethos can be best characterized by three general principles regarding labour:

1. Reduce
2. Redistribute
3. Revalue

Reduce

Despite the variety within post-work discourse, there is broad agreement that labour must be framed as a problem rather than a solution, and that we must seek to be emancipated *from* (rather than *through)* our labour. In the words of Andre Gorz, the 'emancipation of individuals, their full development, the restructuring of society, are all to be achieved through the liberation *from* work'.[20] Perhaps the most obvious component of post-work, then, is its call to *reduce* the amount of time we spend working.

Very broadly speaking, this means reducing all forms of work that are experienced as being imposed from 'the outside' – impinging on our 'discretionary' time, or the time wherein we might direct our energies elsewhere. While different authors take different forms of work as their object of critique, and target of reduction, the most comprehensive approach today would include both employment (wherein we exchange our labour for money) and the unpaid but necessary work of reproducing ourselves and others (wherein we do what we *must* rather than what we *will*). Overall, the broad push is for greater control over our time use, rather than accepting that capitalism should foreclose in advance the question of how we spend most of our lives.

Reducing our working time is thus instrumental to increasing our freedom, and it is no surprise that it has been a concern of humanity for centuries – particularly of labour movements since the onset of industrialization, as Chapter 1 details. But the more exciting and utopian edges of post-work seek to go beyond the relatively arbitrary demands of these movements, as suggested by our discussion of the 'Three Eights' above. The call for eight-hour shifts may well fit neatly into clock-time conceptions of the twenty-four-hour day – and does indeed have the rhetorical advantage of clarity and simplicity

– but there is no objective rationale for making this the final destination of our political imaginaries. Why should a third of our lives be unquestioningly ceded to (whatever counts as) work? Why is time that is not centred on dealing with basic bodily and financial needs crammed into a paltry eight hours a day? If we accept the framework of the three eights, or cease to make time the object of our political organizing, we risk mistaking a mutable state of affairs for a transhistorical inevitability and thereby limit our political horizons.

A more radical return to the idea of working time reduction would see us orient ourselves towards seizing the *whole day* for what we will. This, we proffer, is the ambitious call of radical post-work theorizing. As we shall see in Chapter 5, this is not an attempt to deny the inevitable role of necessity within human existence – we will always need to take some action to collectively meet our basic needs and to provide for our own subsistence, just as we will always be somewhat constrained by the physical processes via which we regenerate ourselves (on both a daily and generational level). Instead, it demands to be seen as a relentless endeavour to maximize freedom in light of, as well as in spite of, necessity. It is a call for the wholesale restructuring of life – a move that sees emancipation as bound up with temporal sovereignty, and that sees freedom as a matter of fitting systemic socioeconomic forces around the needs of people and communities, rather than the other way around.

Redistribute

In order to achieve the reductions in work that post-work demands, ways and means must be found. This could, as Chapter 3 explores, be achieved by automating away certain labours – but mechanisms need to be in place to make sure that this benefits workers, and this will require sufficient power in the workplace, in politics and across civil society more generally. Besides, there are some forms of work that do not lend themselves readily to automation, or which we might actually *wish* to pursue via more labour-intensive means (childcare being one obvious example). Beyond tech augmentations, a staple proposition of post-work has been around the redistribution of necessary work so as to lighten the load for individuals. Our labour markets (in the Global North, particularly in the UK and United States) are plagued by overwork for some and a scarcity of paid hours for others; by redistributing work across the paid workforce, we can achieve sufficient waged working hours for all, while reducing the working week for each. Redistribution isn't just applicable between workers in the labour market, however: it is also needed between workers within households too. As many studies have shown, there is a stark asymmetry between the amount of unpaid housework carried out by women versus men;[21] post-work seeks a fairer distribution here too, and this can be achieved in various ways – not only through a fairer resharing of work and free time between individuals in the home but also via the use of new public or common facilities wherein household labours can be more efficiently carried out.

The question of redistribution thus begins to broach the question of *who* is going to be doing any remaining work: Who is going to, in principle, have their heavy workloads carved up and redistributed? Who will do the arduous jobs that are hard to automate, who will get to do the fun stuff and for how many hours a day? Who will empty the bins after the revolution? Even outside of a hypothetical, totally planned economy, these questions of distribution can guide us to more equitable and just outcomes.

Finally, redistribution as part of the post-work ethos also applies to wealth (which is, under current conditions, also a matter of freedom, time and free time). Post-work's interest in universal basic income and labour-saving public infrastructure means that it should be situated within a wider redistributive economic framework: it is not just free time that is to be redistributed but also income and investment in common resources.

Revalue

If post-work advocates reject the modern work ethic as a toxic dogma, more often than not wielded as a cudgel with which to beat workers and non-workers alike, we should not assume that this equates to immediately rejecting all forms of work as worthless. Quite the contrary: post-work opens up the *question* of work's value. In place of the 'any job is a good job' dogma, or the exaltation of the 'labours of love' of the household, we proffer post-work as an approach that seeks to *revalue* different kinds of work. Currently, as Chapter 1 will make clear, certain kinds of work – and worker – are ranked higher than others, along class, race and gender lines. As David Graeber once noted, arguably the most important jobs such as social care, waste collection and teaching are amongst the lowest paid, most exhausting or largely overlooked in policy terms – while many of the highest-paid jobs are in destructive industries such as fossil fuels, or of dubious societal benefit such as public relations.[22] Stepping back even further, it is also clear that paid work is recognized far more than unpaid work, be that intrafamilial domestic labour or other forms of so-called 'shadow work' that we all do every day. Post-work theory cracks open this unequal system of valuation to draw attention to its inequalities and negative consequences.

Using post-work's critical stance as a kind of tool for thinking, we can start to distil which work is actually necessary, which work we *want* to be doing (the work that we *will*) and which kinds of work are damaging and should be either modified, automated or abandoned altogether.[23] In concrete terms, this inevitably leads (productively, we think) to questions of value, of pay and of working conditions. Are we remunerating health and social care workers enough? Should jobs that are created merely to provide personal services to the elite exist at all? Is child rearing as important an activity as the work of engineers in the tech industry – and how do we recognize that in practice?

Alongside the pursuit of the reduction of work, in part via its redistribution across the population, post-work approaches have thus broached questions of *which* labours should be carried out in the first place. This is of course a healthy debate to re-open, given the apparent emerging capacity of tech to replace certain human tasks (wherein we might be happy to be free of the load!) and given the unfolding climate crisis (wherein inevitably some jobs will have to be discontinued in order to shift towards more sustainable production). Crucially, the question of revaluation is also of practical benefit for workers, who should not simply accept their work as a good in itself but as something to be *justified* insofar as it is taking up their scarce free time.

Of course, there is plenty of work that we might accept *needs* to be done – for example, in healthcare, in building and maintaining our energy systems, in education, in food production, in logistical systems; the list is long. Plus, there is a lot of work involved in ensuring that many of life's *pleasures* are provided for too – our entertainment, our creative endeavours and our various excesses.

But this is precisely why the question as to how we as a society *value* this work – in terms of pay as well as in terms of how much of our personal energies we dedicate to it – is so important. Instead of letting the market 'decide' – via demand and supply – what work we value, post-work raises the question to a *political* level.[24] By posing the simple, general but radical question 'why work?' we can start to give strong responses with solid justifications and turn those into real world changes.

The task of revaluing our work could start from a number of angles, but a cursory list might include: workers' experience and subjective evaluation of the labour, the objective working conditions, the overall purpose of the work (what or whose end does it serve?) and perhaps how pivotal it is to key shared goals. A more explicit framework for what counts as 'good work' might in fact help us bring work and autonomously chosen activity (or "free time") closer together – as maximizing the former would likely mean more people enjoy their work, no longer experiencing it as an oppressive (if necessary) burden but as something enjoyable, useful and only one part of their lives. This question of value and revaluation thus returns us to the ambiguity at the heart of the demand for time 'for what we will'. While, as we've seen, this demand could simply be read as time for whatever one wants, it also lends itself to a more purposive or volitional interpretation – one with greater ties to a framework of collective political desire.

∗∗∗

Note that the above post-work principles rely upon and complement each other thoroughly: we can *reduce* the amount of work in each of our lives by *redistributing* it across the population, or perhaps by *revaluing* some of it as worthy only of automated machinery or not worthy of doing at all;[25] we can *redistribute* work based on our *revaluations* of necessary versus harmful, or desirable versus inherently arduous, work. Plus, once we've *reduced* some people's working weeks, then they will be free to take on tasks from others – thereby *redistributing* work in consequential ways; finally, we might start to be able to *value* some forms of work more – at the level of desire – if the working week is drastically *reduced* and *redistributed*: we might enjoy teaching more when we're not exhausted by its demands and we will likely get more out of whatever craft it is we pursue, or whatever people-facing role we currently perform, should we know that it is not so time-consuming as to envelop our whole being every week; revaluing, redistributing and revaluing our work are perhaps all necessary for the full pursuit of each. Of course, specific proposals or individual tracts of post-work theory rarely manage to capture or articulate all three – but by our account, they will always embody at least one.

Post-work variations

Material under the post-work umbrella falls along a spectrum, ranging from analyses primarily grounded in the critique of existing conditions to those which are more speculative in imagining a new social order. Even amongst avowedly left-wing thinkers, there is notable variety; writers suture their perspectives on life after work to differing political ambitions, be they anarchist, communist or social democratic.

As such, there is no single post-work canon but rather a wide range of more or less closely related projects looking at the changing circumstances surrounding labour via a range of different lenses (from automation, to the work ethic, to the inequitable distribution of specific forms of paid and unpaid work). Post-work is more of a family of resemblances than a strict genre, as it were. Although post-work projects each have their own distinctive flavour, they nevertheless have certain key ideas in common. They respond to changing labour conditions, often seeking to confront rising inequality, the erosion of autonomy and ever-more precarious working arrangements. They typically critique the idea that work is capable of delivering prosperity, purpose and social equality, and argue instead that the left needs to resist wage labour (and the work ethic) as part of a proactive response to social and economic crises.

As this book will demonstrate, post-work also draws from a number of adjacent fields of research and theory – extended theories of mind, utopian studies, xenofeminism, value-form Marxism and more. In what follows, we draw out some of these proximities and introduce a few novel connections of our own. We incorporate innovative theory from places such as disability studies, welfare sociology, histories of the science-work intersection, genealogies of the medicalization of work and cyborg feminism. While it is the porosity of post-work as a body of discourse that makes it such an interesting space, it also requires rigour and attention to detail on the part of its readers in order to discern the differences and continuities that abound.

The structure and scope of the book

As we have suggested, this perspective on post-work is not one that is universally shared. Amongst both its critics and supporters,[26] post-work is often understood not according to the interlocking principles of the 'three Rs' via which *we* characterize its ethos but in terms of three programmatic demands, which will be discussed in detail over the course of this book:

1. A shorter working week

2. Universal basic income

3. Automated production (the use of productivity-enhancing technologies to reduce the need for human wage labour).

This interpretation of post-work is, to our minds, unduly narrow, placing an arbitrary and unrepresentative limit upon what this discourse can concretely posit. This is not to deny the significance of these three factors, however. Working time reduction, UBI and automation do indeed all have their place within different strands of post-work thinking. However, as we shall see, post-work is much more expansive than these three policies would suggest. Not only do different approaches to post-work make different demands or rely on different tactics but the tendency as a whole is about *ends* rather than just *means*. That is to say, it is founded on ambitions to perpetually strive towards a better world rather than being wedded to particular routes via which to achieve this.

In order to demonstrate this point, we have structured our text around both the concrete political demands that are common amongst post-work thinking *and* the broader philosophical framework that we think should underpin them. The first part of the book adopts a tripartite structure reflecting the three demands that our version of post-work sometimes incorporates but always exceeds. With chapters loosely themed around working time reduction, basic income and technologization, we seek to explore the nuances and complexities contained within each of these seemingly simple demands, asking how they interact with the principles of reducing, redistributing and revaluing work. At the same time, however, we will insist that post-work should not be reduced to a policy programme.

The second part thus tackles two related elements of a post-work tendency. Firstly, it considers freedom and the crucial (indeed, the defining) role it plays within post-work imaginaries. Of what does freedom consist? How does freedom relate to work? What does freedom look like under capitalism and what might an alternative to this look like? This leads us to our final chapter, which explores post-work utopias. Here, we will consider the specific content of post-work utopias, the use of utopianism as a *method* and the critical role played by the idea of utopia as part of the DNA of post-work politics. Ultimately, we will argue, post-work cannot be reduced to the programmatic proposals often ascribed to it. Rather, it opens up, and helps develop, discussions of strategy and of the place of work, care, technology and incomes in our visions of better worlds. Most of all, it demands to be seen as an approach to freedom, to the future and to a labour politics commensurate with a wider post-scarcity agenda.

While the issue of work is universal – and while, we would argue, the 3 Rs framework might have purchase across multiple historical and geographical contexts – the focus of this book is on work (and resistance to it) across the Anglosphere, and most particularly in the UK and United States. Thus, the empirical and theoretical resources upon which we draw emerge from these regions. These are countries that have been globally significant in terms of forming the agenda around capitalist cultures of work, and which have successfully exported these to many other countries via both directly colonial means and the operations of cultural hegemony. This lends them a particular significance in some ways. Nevertheless, however, this is a consciously parochial project rather than the definitive account and should be understood as such. More needs to be done in terms of articulating a truly international post-work imaginary; the global history of post-work thought and practice remains to be written.

1

Shorter working weeks

One of the most prominent ideas found within post-work discourse is that of reducing working hours. The 'four-day week' – referring here to paid work time – is now a prominent topic of discussion in the mainstream media, in such places as The World Economic Forum and in the mouths of politicians the world over. In Norway, Spain, Wales, Scotland and New Zealand, to take prominent examples, governments have declared that working time is firmly on their political agendas.[1] Even some of the world's largest firms including Microsoft and Unilever are piloting – or outright adopting – shorter working weeks for their staff. We ourselves have been involved in running pilots in private and third sector organizations, analysing the results and taking note of implementation designs.[2]

To risk hyperbole for a moment, as we approach the second quarter of the twenty-first century we might well be witnessing a sea change in the culture around working hours – within Global North countries in particular. This shift has no doubt been accelerated by the Covid-19 pandemic and the industrial and governmental responses to it, with furlough schemes essentially paying (some) workers for time where they are not at work and with whole sectors of the economy switching, *en-masse*, to remote working.

Stepping away from the world of party politics and corporate adoption, in this chapter we set out how working time reduction operates within post-work theory and politics. We offer a contemporary critique of working time, both within and beyond our jobs, to underline just how much of our time is spent working – and why post-work authors identify ours as a 'work-centred society'.[3] We then situate post-work theory within wider philosophies and political struggles around working time. We offer a brief history of how our working hours have been shaped over the course of capitalism's lifespan and of how the move towards reducing the working week has been conceived by a whole range of thinkers. All of this serves to make the case for a reduction, redistribution and revaluation of working time.

Time well spent? A critique of work and free time

Let's scope in on the issue in question: working time. This seemingly simple concept gets to the heart of many things in our society. A post-work perspective asks, how much of our time can legitimately be called free? And – on a related but not identical note – how much of our time is taken up by work? Of course, both of these questions presuppose a definition of work (and its difference from free time) that should be made clear from the outset.

When we talk about work here, we are referring to purposive activities, be they paid or unpaid, which are means to an end rather than an end in themselves. As we will discuss in more detail in Chapter 4, work is understood as something undertaken in circumstances of relative 'unfreedom' – that is to say, as something that we *must* do. This unfreedom might relate either to biological survival and self-reproduction or to social requirements (on the understanding that these are not distinct but rather mutually inflecting categories). Under capitalism, the impersonal domination – or 'mute compulsion' – of our economic system is a key part of what drives this unfreedom, endeavouring to impose work activities on everyone, everywhere.[4] But there are other forms of domination (both personal and impersonal) which might render a pursuit un- or less-free, such as those related to the structural oppressions of race, gender and sexuality, which can exist outside of capitalist frameworks. Such a characterization makes clear that, to the extent that it can be called work, an activity is unfree and thus undesirable. Work, therefore, deserves to be understood as a political and social (i.e. collective) *problem*.

This is clearly not a universal understanding of what constitutes work, and we'll be reckoning with several different approaches to the topic over the course of this book. With our own definition in mind, however, we can begin by considering work in its most widely and immediately recognized form: employment – our jobs. We might define a job as the selling of our time, skills and energy. More precisely, we could say that a job is an arrangement in which we *rent* ourselves out to somebody (given that, unlike slavery, it is understood by all parties that we retain formal ownership of *ourselves*). The first, perhaps most obvious, point to note here is that our jobs constitute a certain kind of relationship: one in which we hand over control of a portion of our time to another person and/or organization so that they can use us to pursue specific ends of their choosing (within legal boundaries). Hence why mainstream economics considers a job to be a 'disutility' – a sacrifice that someone decides to make in order to gain a beneficial 'utility' (in this case, an income).[5] This chimes with common sense: we work to live rather than live to work. Jobs are primarily means to ends, mechanisms via which we obtain cash in order to pay for our necessities and our luxuries. We give up our freedom – in the form of our time – in order to be able to survive, and, if we're lucky, to have some cash left over to pursue our interests. In one of his more succinct formulations, Marx points out that 'all economy is finally reducible to the economy of time',[6] gesturing to the crucial fact that everything from a national government's labour market policy to the everyday experience of our jobs ultimately concerns prescribing how time is to be spent. Understanding how we distribute free and unfree time via the allocation of work and its rewards can help us assess and evaluate our current society. From a post-work perspective, it also helps guide us towards a shared, desired future.

Despotism at the office

In 2017, a poll asked the British public 'How much [money] would you want to never work again?'[7] More than 70 per cent of respondents knew exactly how much they would want for immediate resignation and only 12 per cent of people said that no amount of money would be sufficient. Fascinatingly, 35 per cent of people said that they would ask for £500,000 or less to never return to a job in their lifetime; this would only amount to £25,000 a year, over a twenty-year period – much less than the national average income. Such a thought experiment helps us understand something crucial: we often talk about jobs as if they are unquestionably good – ends in themselves, even – but if we were offered sufficient material security, the vast majority of us would drop them in a heartbeat. The dream of early retirement looms large in the cultural imagination.[8] In a seemingly unrelated situation, the United States is reportedly experiencing a hidden but creeping 'Male Flight from Work', wherein working-age men are leaving the workforce and abandoning the search for work in their millions.[9] Such a phenomenon sends a similar message to our reported desire to retire early: that even in our relentlessly work-centred world, employment fails to be universally appealing, and many of us would reject our own jobs given half a chance, even if that meant accepting a more austere lifestyle.

Submitting to waged work does not indicate a freely made choice, then, so much as a lack of opportunity to live otherwise. Unless you own property or possess vast sums of wealth, jobs can scarcely be refused and opting out is all too rarely an option. Yet despite this reality, we still tend to think of ourselves as free agents, insofar as every new job is a voluntary contract between employee and employer of supposedly equal standing. In this understanding, working for a wage represents a just and equitable exchange of our time and energy for cash.[10]

However, even if the labour market was a place of freedom, this pretence ends once one signs that contract and enters what Marx calls the 'hidden abode of production'. Here, two people enter as equals – one buying another's time and the other selling it freely – and yet the very process of entering into such a relation leaves both parties profoundly changed. As Marx puts it, as these two, once equal, parties step into the roles of employer and employee

> we think we can perceive a change in the physiognomy of our dramatis personae. He, who before was the money-owner, now strides in front as capitalist; the possessor of labour-power follows as his labourer. The one with an air of importance, smirking, intent on business; the other, timid and holding back, like one who is bringing his own hide to market and has nothing to expect but – a hiding.[11]

In the actually existing workplace then, you must leave ideas of freedom and equality at the door.

To give a frank illustration of what a workplace really is, Elizabeth Anderson invites us to engage in a provocative thought experiment:

> Imagine a government that assigns everyone a superior whom they must obey … Orders may be arbitrary and can change at any time, without prior notice or opportunity to appeal. Superiors are unaccountable to those they order around. They are neither electable nor removable by their inferiors … There are multiple ranks in the society ruled by this government. The most highly ranked individual takes no orders but issues many. The lowest-ranked may have their bodily movements and speech minutely regulated for most of the day … Everyone lives under surveillance, to ensure that they are complying with orders. Superiors may snoop into inferiors' e-mail and record their phone conversations …
>
> … The economic system of the society run by this government is communist. The government owns all the non-labour means of production in the society it governs. It organises production by means of central planning. The form of government is a dictatorship. In some cases, the dictator is appointed by an oligarchy. In other cases, the dictator is self-appointed … This government mostly secures compliance with carrots. Because it controls all the income in the society, it pays more to people who follow orders particularly well and promotes them to a higher rank.[12]

Would you call such a society free? Probably not. And yet, many of us find our lives organized in such a manner every day. Anderson is, of course, describing the typical American workplace – a domain of strong hierarchy, unquestioned managerial control and a distinct lack of democracy.[13,14] Of course, not all workplaces are as dominating as Anderson's portrayal would suggest – and indeed, different workplace dynamics and styles of management can make a meaningful difference to people's working lives – but the point here is that the legal and structural setup of modern companies *allows for* such maximal domination, should a particular employer wish to operate that way. Anderson is drawing the boundaries of workplace power, which are one and the same as the possible constraints upon employee freedoms.

There is of course a reason for why such workplace domination is prevalent and it can be understood if we view organizations within the context of a competitive, capitalist economic system: firms need their workforces to be pumping out as many widgets, serving as many customers, cleaning as many homes, delivering as many meals or making as many calls as possible in order to make their profits. In order to achieve the required level of productivity, many firms need to keep workers under strict supervision to make sure there is no slacking or deviation from the tasks at hand. An extreme example of this kind of quasi-totalitarian practice can be found in Amazon's 'fulfillment centers' (their Orwellian name for warehouses).[15] Workers there are fitted with digital trackers while they work, allowing managers to keep tabs on whether each individual is functioning at the expected speed (if you are too slow you get warning beeps).[16] Workers are actively prevented from speaking amongst themselves, and even toilet breaks are heavily discouraged. In effect, Amazon's system of control is trying to eliminate any and all possible discrepancies; their workers are kept 'on the rails', as it were, expected to perform with the regularity and efficiency of automatons.

No one would choose these conditions voluntarily and companies like Amazon only get away with it because workers often have no other viable choice. But we should pause to ask a simple question: Are other places of work really so different? In which industries are workers' spared a rap on the knuckles for arriving late or taking too long on their lunch break? Who hasn't felt the presence of a manager looming over their shoulder, making sure they are keeping to task? Many of us will know somebody who has been scolded at work – reprimanded for not meeting sales targets, using the wrong tone of voice, missing a scheduled delivery or making a mistake in the intense heat of a restaurant kitchen.[17] External control, lack of freedom and unequal, managerial power seem to be present in the vast majority of jobs today – it's just the level at which these are experienced that differs. Sometimes the pay is good enough to sweeten the pill, sometimes you find ways of resisting or navigating around those uncomfortable pressures, but there is typically no way of eliminating them altogether. In this sense there is no such thing as the 'perfect job', and, if we keep all of the pressures of competitive production in view, there are rarely even such things as 'good jobs' – just better or worse forms of being told what to do.

Power and control in the workplace are widespread and undeniable facts, then – part of the way in which many firms within capitalism *have* to function if they are to squeeze as much out of their workforces as possible in the pursuit of profit. But however 'necessary' this state of affairs may be, we should not lose sight of the crucial point it reveals: jobs are not necessarily conducive to human freedom or happiness. Let us be perfectly blunt about this: the activity that many of us spend the majority of our days, weeks and working lives doing (if we're 'lucky' enough to have full-time work) is one in which we simply are not free, one in which we're probably not doing what we think is most meaningful and one in which we may even be helping to build a worse, rather than a better, world.

Post-work arguments are premised on these realities. When discussing jobs, the labour market and the workplace, post-work perspectives point out that we too often think about these things in their idealized form – 'jobs give us our purpose in life', and so on – and rarely do we consider them as they really are.[18] Post-work rejects 'job romanticism' and instead adopts a sober analysis of what it means to work in a market-driven world. If we want a more free and equal society, then we should start by reducing the time we spend at work.

But aren't there good things about jobs?

Let's pause here for a moment to tackle a common criticism of post-work – one which, in her short book on the topic, Amelia Horgan urges us to take seriously.[19] It usually takes the following form: Are we not throwing the baby out with the bathwater? By being so critical of jobs, and wanting to reduce the time we spend in them – are we not missing some of the *good* things about them (beyond their income-generating role)? Many would extoll the virtues and pleasures of work, or even the claim that there are aspects of our employed lives that are fundamental to our human nature. Jobs can provide us with the opportunity to meet new people and start new relationships outside of our home lives. It's undeniable, too, that many people find it extremely fulfilling to work with others in a team, towards a common purpose. If part of your job is to support and produce something with colleagues, there is a certain enjoyment that comes from mutual achievement and from feeling *useful* above all else. Being part of, say, a fire rescue team, a design studio, a hospital ward or even just part of an everyday office environment could no doubt bring these kinds of pleasures – the pleasures that come with collective coordination.

We should acknowledge these possible benefits, and yet remain suspicious that common work dogmas – the pernicious 'work ethic' – might be playing a part here. We can ask a number of simple but incisive questions in response to the pro-job agenda. Firstly, are the positive experiences that we *sometimes* – but by no means always – get from employment, exclusive properties of jobs? Can we not, for example, find the meaningful collaboration that we desire in other, non-employment-based activities? Many of us will have felt the buzz of being part of a team, whether that be in sport, or through organizing an event, or while preparing a meal with friends; none of these things are less satisfying just because they are informal or unpaid. Equally, learning new skills can be very fulfilling, but this is not an activity that must be carried out under an employment contract. On the contrary, as Marx, Adam Smith and many other analysts of the division of labour often point out, the vast majority of jobs under capitalism only develop human skills to the extent that they become useful to the employer. You learn to type and use software so that you can send those emails and format documents; you learn how to make coffees in just the right way solely in order that they can be sold more effectively; you learn to drive a forklift so that you can move goods more efficiently across a warehouse; your interpersonal skills are cultivated primarily to lubricate the day-to-day running of the firm. It is incredibly rare for workers to have the chance to develop themselves in a manner of their own choosing, with company finances, on company time.[20]

Secondly, we might ask whether focusing on the (sometimes pleasurable) experience of waged work can prevent us from seeing the wider system of which we are a part. The labour market is rife with inequality, and our jobs are the wheels that keep the whole thing moving. Very few of us are aware of the precise differences in pay packets across our workplaces – between the CEO and upper management on the one hand and average employees on the other. We may also be unaware of the vast returns that go to shareholders, the questionable investments that the firm makes and so on.[21] Equally, we have very little control over the purpose or impacts of the organizations we work for: our job might be enjoyable on a day-to-day level, while also playing a part within a wider, morally dubious entity, such as a fossil fuel company, for example, or a lobbying firm that gives big corporations unfair advantage. Even if our job counts as a 'good one' in terms of our personal experiences and working conditions, then, it may nevertheless be part of a rotten and corrupt enterprise which wreaks a negative effect on society.[22]

Thirdly, while we might occasionally expand and enrich our social lives via employment, perhaps making new friends or meeting romantic partners at work, the *opposite* can also be the case. In our jobs we're often lumped together with people that we don't get on with at all – or worse still, we might find ourselves in an abusive relationship with our colleagues. This is much more likely if you're a woman or an LGBT person: a 2023 survey conducted by the Trades Union Congress found that in the UK, 58 per cent of women have been subject to some form of bullying or harassment while working, with more than three in five women reporting that they've experienced more than three separate incidents of bullying at work; 68 per cent of LGBT people reported at least one type of sexual harassment.[23] If we really want to give everyone the possibility of pursuing a meaningful and enjoyable social life, perhaps the labour market isn't the best mechanism via which to enable this. In lieu of other possible means by which we can congregate and socialize, employment admittedly remains one of our only options – but this doesn't necessarily make it a good one.

Finally, even if we accept that employment does bring some fundamental benefits to our health and well-being – so long as we don't have a toxic working environment – does it follow that the more hours we work, the healthier we feel? In a project dedicated to this topic, researchers at Cambridge University set out to answer a very similar question: 'How much paid work is needed for mental health and well-being?'[24] Using data gathered from over seventy thousand individuals over a nine-year period, they used a survey with various metrics relating to mental health, life satisfaction and working time in order to gauge the link between hours on the job and individual well-being. Their conclusions? Individuals receive important well-being effects with just eight hours a week of employment (roughly one day's work). Remarkably, beyond these eight hours of employment, the researchers found that we receive no significant benefits for our mental health and well-being. The often-touted mantra that 'a job is good for you' is apparently only partly true: even as things stand, with a whole array of social experiences being provided primarily via wage work, it seems that we need only a small dose of it to get our fill.[25]

Precarity and time: Despotism on demand

Even in the case of 'good' work, then, a little goes a long way. But much of the employment on offer today is far from good. As post-work theorists have been noting for decades, the well-unionized, secure and well-paid jobs of the mid-twentieth century have increasingly given way, not necessarily to mass unemployment but to impoverished working conditions.[26] Our era can be characterized by a steady and alarming increase in so-called 'precarious' forms of work, for example – jobs with very temporary contracts, uncertain hours or bogus 'self-employed' status (thus stripping them of benefits such as sick and holiday pay). 'Clearly new jobs are being created', Stanley Aronowitz, Dawn Esposito, William DiFazio and Margaret Yard write in their 1998 *Post-Work Manifesto*.

> But it would be a huge error to mistake the quantity of new jobs for the substance and quality of enjoyable, lucrative and secure jobs that can allow us to relax about our futures. Rather, it is more likely for people to become engaged in piecemeal and subdivided jobs which are likely to be worse paying, and which offer sharply fewer benefits, than the jobs most people held before.[27]

Guy Standing's work on the 'precariat' – a portmanteau of 'precarious' and 'proletariat' – has usefully drawn attention to the new characteristics of the people working such jobs.[28] The precariat has distinctive relations to production (its labour is insecure, unstable and casualized), to distribution (it relies almost entirely on money wages and has very little access to the secure benefits of standard employment) and to the state (it has few economic, political and cultural rights to leverage).[29] Finally, and crucially for the purposes of this chapter, Standing remarks that the precariat's struggle is also a matter of control over one's time. Despite the apparent differences between the usual 'nine to five' and emerging precarious occupations, time domination is common to both – albeit in different forms.

In his ethnographic study of work time within contemporary capitalism, Benjamin Snyder tracks the experience of those working in jobs characterized by disturbances to linear or predictable rhythms. Increasingly, people have to work *on demand* – taking opportunities *whenever* work turns up.[30] This existence not only disrupts us on a day-to-day, week-to-week basis, crashing our free time with work we can't turn down, but it also disrupts our grasp of other temporalities such as the future. By living in a constant limbo between (standard) employment and unemployment – balanced precariously on the promise of the next gig around the corner – the precariat are 'prisoners of the middling future', with nothing certain except uncertainty.[31]

The flexibility of 'flexible capitalism', in other words, cuts predominantly one way. Of course, very temporary contracts technically afford the freedom to take or refuse work at short notice, but in the context of a low-wage market, this means that most workers are forced to jump from gig to gig indefinitely in order to make a living; freedom on paper does not translate to freedom in actuality.[32] For employers in this context, flexible contracts afford the freedom to pick up and use workers for precisely the time they need them – which works well for the company balance sheet, but creates periods of 'limbo', or stasis, time for workers. This is not 'free' or disposable time but rather a time of waiting, or indeed searching, for the next chance to earn some cash.

Paul Apostolidis suggests that people with fragmented working lives are 'out of time' in three ways:

1. They lack the time to do much apart from working, or going to and from whatever jobs they have at that moment;

2. They must perpetually carve out time in the midst of their present work-lives to find and prepare for the next job they will need when the one at hand expires;

3. They are 'out of synch' with 'normal society' insofar as their disrupted and time-poor work lives dissipate usual ideas of long-term careers, the usual work week and general social mobility.[33]

The 'suffering produced by this temporal drain and arrhythmia imposes itself on the working population at large through generalised syndromes of anxiety'.[34] As Apostolidis goes on to note, the temporal drain imposed by precarious work disproportionately falls on the shoulders of women, who typically undertake the majority of unpaid (and under-valued) work in the home and the wider community, often alongside paid activity.

Beyond the wage: The family, the commute, the never-ending job application

Post-work theory is quick to identify the structural inequalities and experiential unpleasantness associated with a lot of paid work (precarious and otherwise). It does not stop at the office door or the factory gates, however. A number of post-work thinkers are keen to recognize that work goes beyond paid employment, and to argue that anyone seriously engaging with 'work', theoretically or practically, must consider the plethora of other forms it takes as part of our day-to-day existence.

To this end, philosopher Ivan Illich sought to define a subfield of study: shadow work. In his book of the same name, he defined shadow work as 'the unpaid work unique to the industrial economy'.[35] More recently, Craig Lambert defines shadow work as including 'all the unpaid tasks we do on behalf of businesses and organizations'.[36] Consider the self-checkout machines common to today's supermarkets: the work of scanning and packing is now increasingly allocated to consumers, rather than to employed cashiers; *we* now do this necessary work, which 'shadows' our shopping. In what follows, we unpack three examples of shadow work that stand out in the contemporary world and consider how they impact our 'free' time.

The family-household

The broadest (and perhaps most crucial) form of shadow work is housework and care work, which reproduces us as humans ready to engage in the labour market in the first place. The bulk of such work today occurs within the family-household, where a great deal of time and energy is expended. Indeed, the way in which we currently organize this work demands a massive duplication of human effort. As Ruth Schwartz Cowan puts it:

> Out there in the land of household work there are small industrial plants which sit idle for the better part of every working day; there are expensive pieces of highly mechanized equipment which only get used once or twice a month; there are consumption units which weekly trundle out to their markets to buy 8 ounces of this non-perishable product and 12 ounces of that one.[37]

Furthermore, Cowan tells us, this work has proved to be remarkably stubborn, barely decreasing at all between the 1870s and the 1970s.[38] This is particularly remarkable given the developments in labour-saving technologies that occurred during this period. Considerable infrastructural innovation (in gas, water and electricity, as well as in things like waste management) and the introduction of new devices (novel forms of cooking and cleaning equipment, for example) appear to have had little to no impact on the time being spent in unwaged domestic work.

In part, this can be attributed to a concomitant rise in standards – the expectation of more complex forms of home cooking, for example, or the idea that clothes should be laundered more regularly. But it was also due to changes in the approach to and social organization of this labour. Not only do we see decreasing reliance on a domestic servant industry in many of the wealthy nations in the early twentieth century (not least because fewer people were willing to perform this work), but we also witness a shift away from certain forms of collective provision. The labour of washing clothes, for example, ceases to be a matter of paid labour undertaken in a dedicated laundry, and becomes instead a matter of work being performed within the family home. Here, new technologies are part of a shift of domestic labour into private households and onto the shoulders of individual household members – particularly women, who have, throughout much of the twentieth century, been positioned as the family-household's reproductive specialists.[39]

This is not merely a historical inequality, given that the family continues to embody a marked gendered division of labour. Women continue to provide the bulk of unwaged work in the home, even as their hours in the waged workplace have been increasingly brought in line with men's. In fact, for every country in the world for which we have data, women spend more time than men on unwaged work – on average 3.2 times as much.[40] As this would suggest, women across the world almost always enjoy less leisure time than men – on average, nearly four hours less per week.[41] It is of little surprise, then, that 40 per cent of full-time working mothers in America report feeling rushed *all the time*.[42]

And free time is only decreasing for parents, with women bearing the brunt of the loss.[43] For instance, American mothers have seen their free time decrease from a high of 37.7 hours per week in 1975 to 31.4 hours per week in 2008. Fathers saw a similar decrease from 35.7 hours to 32 hours over the course of the same period.[44] Predictably enough, we find that lone mothers are particularly burdened, with around thirty hours a week less discretionary time than those in childless dual earning households.[45] In short, primary carers within the family are typically women and they're typically exhausted.

On the one hand, conditions around wage work continue to have a profound shaping influence here, and the demand for a shorter working week is key; women are amongst the most obvious beneficiaries of working time reduction given that they represent a group that is particularly time poor. As we have noted elsewhere, the opportunity to spend less time engaging in waged work with no loss in income would no doubt be particularly welcomed by those currently most harried and depleted by the delivery of unpaid care (namely, those who are not rich, white, male, healthy, able-bodied and dependent-free).[46]

On the other hand, however, such measures are unlikely to be sufficient on their own. The introduction of a four-day week, concentrating as it does upon the sphere of waged work, cannot fully account for entrenched temporal inequalities in the domestic sphere. As Elizabeth Lawson put it in 1956, in the context of the trade union struggles of the twentieth century:

> While the labor movement fights for a working week of less than forty hours …, a large section of our population regularly, without vacations and with no days off, puts in 100 hours a week or more – a longer working day than that against which American workers revolted more than a century ago … They are housewives.[47]

Clearly, we don't want a situation where collective energy is targeted only at work in the sense of paid employment, leaving a massive (and highly gendered) sphere of drudgery untouched and implicitly naturalized. Therefore, the push for shorter hours in the waged workplace demands to be understood as but one part of a wider post-work struggle – one which factors in those kinds of work that too often remain in the shadows.

The commute

Commuting is another good example of shadow work that needs accounting for in our analysis of labouring society today. What kind of activity is commuting exactly? It isn't employment strictly speaking – as we are not yet at our workplaces, on the job.[48] And yet, it isn't free time either – after all, we *have* to get to our workplace: we wouldn't choose to be on that packed train or bus if it was up to us. Commuting fulfils important economic functions – not just for the commuter/employee (facilitating them earning a wage) but also for the business/employer that benefits from its workforce coming to work.[49] Workers coming to their place of work is, from a business perspective, analogous to a key component of the production process being delivered to the firm; the cost of this travel can be construed as a business expense – albeit one not paid for by the firm, but by the commuter.

Most immediately, though, commuting is unpaid effort that puts pressure on the wallet and the physical and mental well-being of the worker. Before the pandemic, the average UK worker was spending twenty-seven days per year commuting to and from the workplace – which is roughly the same amount they receive in terms of annual leave.[50] It is no wonder, in this regard, that since Covid, a great many workers are finding remote work (working from home or another convenient place away from the office) to be a cost and time-saving positive.[51] Commuting is therefore, as Illich and others have noted, 'very expensive, time-consuming shadow work' – or what economist Joseph Stiglitz calls a 'hidden tax'.[52]

The never-ending job application

To round out our initial list of shadow work, we should also add a time-consuming activity that has only grown to prominence particularly in the last two or three decades: employability. Working on becoming 'employable' is now a common imperative for workers across the job spectrum. Working on our CVs, our personal statements and 'brands' as they are occasionally described; building our educational achievements; and re-writing our work histories so as to project an ideal profile to actual and potential employers: all of these activities involve time that no one would describe as freely chosen and which therefore should be accounted for as part of our 'working weeks'.[53]

But identifying employability activities as a form of work is not merely about measuring our working hours more accurately: it also helps us understand in particularly stark terms what we *are* vis-à-vis employers in the labour market. Who is this shadow work for? What position does it force us into and what can it tell us about work within our economies?

Employability is peculiar to a form of economic reasoning that has its roots in the neoliberal dogma around jobs as 'investments' in an individual's future (or sometimes, 'human capital').[54] This reinterpretation of jobs as *opportunities* was embodied in Third Way political projects such as New Labour in the UK at the end of the twentieth century.[55] Instead of job creation, or the state-simulated growth that might lead to it, governments instead focused on the subjective capabilities of workers themselves. Individuals, within this mode of economic policy, are expected to be 'employable', if not necessarily employed.[56]

To put it more bluntly, we might say that employability indicates a set of capacities or traits that are required of the labour-power sold (i.e. of us) by its purchaser (i.e. our employers): essentially a spec of what they are buying – not dissimilar to the blurb on the back of a ready meal at the supermarket. In this sense, being 'employable' can quite literally mean rendering and presenting ourselves as desirable to those who might pay for our labour.[57] As this practice of employability occurs before the purchase and use of labour power – that is, before we're actually on the job – cultivating employability means fashioning ourselves as potentially commodifiable. This temporal stance towards ourselves (in which we are always anticipating employment) means that the power relationships we find in paid work (i.e. between employee and employer) effectively begin even before we sign the contract.

In contrast to the disciplinary power of the workplace, which is enacted when the individual has already entered into an employment relation, employability culture requires that the individual is always already influenced or affected by future employment. As Phoebe Moore writes:

> The worker who can demonstrate employability has begun a relationship of
> subordination to capital before even necessarily being employed, meaning
> that capitalism is successfully becoming integrated into increasing levels of
> people's everyday lives.[58]

Ciara Cremin identifies this process of becoming-employable as a form of 'reflexive exploitation', in which we are involved in an 'ongoing reflection of the self as an object of exchange'.[59] That is to say, this demand upon bearers of the ability to work enforces an internalization of the demands of our potential employers; an internalization that subtly, and not without resistance, moulds our everyday subjective existence. The lived time of employability is often tinged with desperation (to find work), deferred promises (of a good job) and uncomfortable self-selling: a dystopian eclipsing of non-work elements from our lives that Mareile Pfannebecker and Jason Smith describe with the neologism '*lifework*'.[60]

Noting how work culture – being a 'good employee' – has infected our lives beyond our jobs is one of post-work's important interventions. In precisely the opposite direction to those approaches celebrating the 'dignity of labour', promoting up-skilling as the secret to success, or the blunt valorization of 'jobs jobs jobs',[61] post-work demands the rejection of an employment-centric culture full-stop and a reversal of its associated work-creep. The dogmatic valuation of employment and 'hard work' in general – even from an ostensibly worker-friendly perspective – sits uncomfortably close to the self-branding language of recruitment firms or the human-capital-centric elements of education, which encourages the consideration of our employment prospects to seep into our everyday consciousness as much as possible. Employability is toxic, and yet it is work that we do for employers, whether real ones or merely imagined, for free. Only by rejecting such an approach, and by expecting a lot more from jobs in order to consider them worth doing, will we be able to get to a future of work that we want.

***

In this critique of actually existing free time, we have articulated an expanded definition of work and with it a more robust accountancy of work vs non-work activities within our scarce time resources. By unpacking work into a number of categories, we can understand what we mean by the 'work-centred society' and identify what Danaher refers to as the 'problem of temporal colonization', wherein, 'most of our mental and physical effort is taken up with preparing for, performing, or recovering from work'.[62]

Working less: Philosophies and historical legacies

To be a productive labourer ... is not a piece of luck but a misfortune
KARL MARX[63]

Shortening the working day is not a new concept – and certainly not one invented by recent post-work authors. The demand to work less and the vision of a world with little-to-no work have a long and rich history. In the classical works of the ancient Greeks, for example, we find that labour is deplored as fit for only animals or slaves. Aristotle and Plato, for instance, famously saw the toil of everyday life as the lowest rung on the hierarchy of human functions – far below the higher capacity for politics and philosophy that humans uniquely exercise. Consigning slaves and women to the care of the *oikos*, or household, a clear separation was maintained between the reproductive functions of life and its higher purpose (of fulfilling our potential in thought and in the social-political life of citizens).[64] Such a definition of labour as a lower form of activity has been widely maintained ever since – leaving distinctive marks on our conceptual vocabulary. In her historical overview of the subject, Andrea Komlosy plots the linguistic distinction between 'work' and 'labour' in various European languages, showing the lines drawn to distinguish creative (work) versus toilsome (labour) activity that have left their trace on our speech today.[65]

Interpreting these distinctions for the modern era, philosopher Hannah Arendt points out that artists can produce *a work*, for example (creative production), while women can go *into labour* (toil).[66] Note also that the French word *travail* and the Spanish *trabajo* both stem from the Latin *tripalium* – a three-pronged stake that was used to torture non-compliant slaves; the very words we use for labouring imply that it is a form of punishment.

Shorter work weeks in modern history

Working time took on a specific significance for working people with the emergence of industrialism in the early nineteenth century. Historians such as E.P. Thompson in the UK and Benjamin Hunnicutt in the United States have documented in detail the role that struggles around working time played for the birth of organized labour movements, as they emerged in reaction to the economic changes underway.[67] Roediger and Foner demonstrate that reducing working time has been no less than 'the central issue raised by the American labor movement during its most dynamic periods of organisation':[68]

> The reduction of working hours constituted the prime demand of the class conflicts that spawned America's first industrial strike, its first citywide trade union councils, its first labor party, its first general strikes, its first organization uniting skilled and unskilled workers, its first strike by females, and its first attempts at regional and national labor organization.[69]

Before waged employment became the standard mode of labour in the late nineteenth century, task work, or 'piece work', was the dominant form of earning a living. We can understand this kind of work as the original form of what we now call the 'gig economy': one completed a task for an agreed sum, as opposed to taking an hourly amount via a wage. This essentially meant that employers were primarily concerned with the *product* of the work, rather than how the worker went about it.

Deep into the nineteenth century, many workers in the Global North were still carrying out this piece work,[70] but with accelerated industrialization and centralization, the wage and factory system of employment finally became the predominant form of capitalism across nations. A shift from tasking towards set periods of work, that is, from output-based labour to submitting one's time to another's instruction throughout the day, was gradually achieved. This established new parameters for employer-worker confrontations: *time* became the resource to struggle over.

> The first generation of factory workers were taught by their masters the importance of time; the second generation formed their short-time committees in the ten-hour movement; the third generation struck for overtime or time and a half.[71]
>
> (Thompson, p. 86, 1967)

Once the *time* of work – as compared to the product strictly speaking – became so important to employer's calculations, workers had a clear terrain to fight on.

They had accepted the categories of their employers and learned to fight back within them. They had learned their lesson, that time is money, only too well.

(ibid.)

Sometimes this struggle was quite literal. In 1830s America, it was commonplace that employers would slyly add thirty minutes to the working day by manipulating the clocks – which only they owned – that marked their beginning and end. In response, artisans in Rhode Island raised money to build a town clock by which the working day of all could abide, insisting that no longer would 'the clock … be figured to suit the owner'.[72] Similarly, in New York, carpenters fashioned the 'Mechanics Bell' that would come to be known as the 'Ten-Hour Bell' that kept the bosses honest. Labour activist George McNeill wrote, '[a]s the "Liberty Bell" [representing freedom from British tyranny] rang out the proclamation of liberty from monarchical control, so the "Mechanics' Bell" proclaimed the liberty of leisure for the sons of toil.'[73]

These early stirrings of conflicts around working time presaged an age in which trade unions would play a pivotal role – particularly in the early decades of the twentieth century. Indeed, a closer look at the long list of achievements of trade unions – achievements that many of us still enjoy today – reveals that a great many of these involve facilitating freedom from work in one form or another: paid holidays, maternity/paternity leave, shorter working hours, retirement, pensions and, of course, the weekend. Those two days at the end of the working week are arguably our most precious, precisely because they are *ours*: time for what we will.

'Wage slavery'

Many worker collectives in nineteenth-century America were fighting for more time for themselves, explicitly as a rejection of arbitrary authority. Leaders within the labour movement, as well as associated intellectuals, put forward radical, republican arguments around the inalienable right to freedom belonging to individuals, which must be respected at work. This freedom was defined as 'mastery over the self … the absence of interference by others … [and] freedom as non-mastery or … non-domination': reduced working time and increased leisure time was one obvious route to protecting this liberty.[74] The arbitrary power of factory-owners was seen as a direct threat to such republican freedom – and if this control over workers is inherent to the workplace under capitalism, then reducing the time within such an environment becomes an ethical imperative.[75] There was thus something deeply and persistently uncomfortable about the contradiction between the ideal of an independent workman and the realities of the wage system. While Abraham Lincoln was trying to cling on to the idea that 'there is no permanent class of hired labourers among us', the economic world was being restructured such that the majority of his compatriots were becoming just that: 'hirelings'.[76] And as the population fell more and more into the grip of the wage, many thousands 'flocked into the labour unions filled with hopes for a shorter working day'.[77]

It is no coincidence, either, that shorter hours movements in the United States were given a jumpstart off the back of the Civil War, with anti-slavery arguments dovetailing with anti-work sentiment.[78] For campaigners and returning soldiers alike, there were broad similarities apparent between the forced labour of the slave and the 'free labour' imposed on people for a wage in order to live.[79] Indeed, the often close proximity – both physically and in terms of status – between slaves and wage labourers is an uncomfortable yet revealing truth of capitalism's history.[80] Most obviously, the system of slavery held millions of the workforce in the most unfree and horrific conditions imaginable, and served as a disciplinary tool – and sobering comparison – for those who lucky enough to be doing 'free', waged work:

> The existence of slavery … gave working Americans both a wretched touchstone against which to measure their fears of unfreedom and a friendly reminder that they were by comparison not so badly off.[81]

There is always a worse form of work. But the contemporary debates around slavery versus the wages system are interesting for the home truths that they surfaced about industrializing America more broadly.[82] As part of their self-serving discourse, proslavery advocates put forward various criticisms of the emergent labour market, pointing out the daily indebtedness to an employer that a wage system produces (as compared to the supposed 'security' of the livelihoods of slaves).[83]

Northern abolitionists would point out the fallacies in these latter claims and counter with arguments based upon philosophical defences of freedom from exploitation and arbitrary authority – imagining the North, by contrast, as a 'society of hardworking and economically independent farmers, mechanics, and tradesman, defending the cause of a worker's freedom against the inroads of the Southern master-servant economy'.[84] What the pro-slavery position, in its cynically disingenuous self-defence, sought to capitalize on was what the abolitionist position sought to ignore or cover up: that America was not the land of entrepreneurship, independence and autonomous craft but increasingly a land of wages, factories and daily servitude. As Rodgers puts it:

> If the North should produce its own class of permanent hirelings – if there should turn out to be a grain of truth to the argument advanced by both the Southeners and a generation of labor spokesman that there was not a great deal of difference between bond slavery and slavery of wages – where then would be the victory?[85]

Indeed, as if spurred by this troubling question, many ex-slaves, now emancipated from one form of domination, fiercely resisted the wage system's unique oppressions. Frederick Douglass, for instance, who had escaped slavery and later entered into the wages system, knew well the differences but also the similarities between the two:

> Experience demonstrates that there may be a wages of slavery only a little less galling and crushing in its effects than chattel slavery, and that this slavery of wages must go down with the other.[86]

Indeed, the emancipation of slaves later served as a concrete inspiration for the labour movement's campaigns: movement leader Ira Steward would continuously refer to abolitionist arguments and themes in his fight for shorter hours as the 'first steps' towards labour's goal to 'wholly emancipate itself'.[87] In this way, 'labor's freedom followed from Black liberation', thus challenging the idea that White and Black liberation from arbitrary masters constituted a zero-sum game.[88]

The radical stance of emancipated slaves towards waged work – as just another form of bondage – is mirrored outside of the United States, too. Witness the expressions of Welsh miners a few decades later, decrying employment as only another form of drudgery, better than slavery but nonetheless part of a world to be overcome.[89] The forms of toil of various different oppressed groups throughout ancient, feudal and now capitalist work regimes have been dehumanizing, violent and ultimately should be abolished for a life of abundance:

> The weary sigh of the over-driven slave, pitilessly exploited and regarded as an animated tool or beast of burden: the medieval serf fast bound to the soil, and life-long prisoner on his lord's domain, subject to all the caprices of his lord's lust or anger: the modern wage-slave, with nothing but his labour to sell selling that, with his manhood as a wrapper, in the world's market-place for a mess of potage: these three phases of slavery, each in their turn inevitable and unavoidable, will have exhausted the possibilities of slavery, and mankind shall at last have leisure and inclination to really live as men, and not as the beasts which perish.[90]

The end of work, deferred

One is struck, reading these historical documents today, by how radical and indeed *confident* these worker collectives were concerning the reduction – perhaps even the eradication – of wage labour. Such radicalism would not remain, however. As mass movements won battles against slavery, female subjugation and long hours practices, the early decades of the twentieth century also saw failed revolutions, economic depressions, world wars and anti-communist campaigns that for various reasons tempered labour movements' ambitions.

A new concept of citizenship also emerged at this time, based on notions of 'independence' from old masters and other forms of bondage. Nancy Fraser and Linda Gordan trace this pivotal shift:

> Changes in the civil and political landscape of dependence and independence were accompanied by even more dramatic changes in the economic register. When white workingmen demanded civil and electoral rights, they claimed to be independent. This entailed reinterpreting the meaning of wage labour so as to divest it of the association with dependency.[91]

The significant and long-lasting gains achieved by workers in these periods had led to an affirmation of their independent identity, and power, but *as waged workers*.

> Radical workingmen, who had earlier rejected wage labour as 'wage slavery', claimed a new form of manly independence within it … Their collective pride drew on another aspect of Protestantism: its work ethic, which valorized discipline and labor. Workers sought to reclaim these values within the victorious wage labor system; many of them – women as well as men – created a new kind of independence in their militancy and boldness toward employers.[92]

As the twentieth century moved on, the strength and leverage of labour movements increased, but within a new container: the post-war social democratic compromise. In the United States, legislation such as the Fair Labor Standards Act and the Taft-Hatley revision of the National Labor Relations Act (both in 1947) severely curbed the militant union tactics that were utilized most successfully in shorter hours campaigns.[93] This taming of shorter hours campaigns also became inflected with Cold War competitive rhetoric: in a 1960 speech, then senator John F. Kennedy countenances the prospect of a 32-hour working week, but neutralizes the idea in favour of a productivist logic:

> My own feeling is I would prefer a different solution. I would prefer the solution of this economy going ahead at such full blast that in 40 hours a week we barely produce what we can consume, that at the time when we have a productive race with the Soviet Union, at a time when we need all the steel we can get to take care of a population which is increasing and which will double in 40 years, I would like to see economic and fiscal policies by this Government will be directed toward stimulating the economy so that the steel industry works full time and so your people go back to work … I feel before we move to 32 hours that we should try an administration which is dedicated to full economic growth, which wants our people and our country working.[94]

The contemporary trade union counterpart to this sentiment was summed up with *The Machinist* magazine's headline: 'Will the Soviets cut THEIR

Overtime?'[95] Anti-communist purges drove the more radical members out of the movement, reinforcing the perception and reality of trade unions as 'cooperating with management in maintaining shop floor discipline'.[96] The demand for shorter hours lost its way in amongst this more conservative drift, replaced by claims on higher wages and paid vacation – with some notable exceptions.[97] Perhaps most symptomatic of this was the United Auto Workers' Walther Reauther's transition from a pro-shorter hours position to one where he could accept that while auto factories may indeed be sweatshops, they would be 'gold plated sweatshops' – that is, workspaces with well-paid, intensively worked staff.[98]

Movements towards shorter and shorter hours elsewhere in the Global North suffered similar fates. In short, they stuttered through the compromise between industry, government and organized labour to compel compliance of the workforce, within an atmosphere of anti-communist reformism. This institutional, conservative turn was accompanied, as we have seen via Fraser and Gordan, by an unfortunate adaptation of the work ethic for dubiously 'progressive' or 'pro-labour' ends. Historian Daniel Rodgers notes how for the labour movement's institutions, this ideology 'turned necessity into pride and servitude into honor; it offered a lever upon the moral sentiments of those whose power mattered. But in the process, a work-immersed culture exacted its due from its largest body of rebels'.[99]

With the benefit of hindsight, we can say that the merits – or at least, the fortunes – of this approach are somewhat questionable. While understanding the extant pressures, we can lament the gradual accommodation with the labour market as the new route for working people's betterment – closing off, as it did, the more ambitious critique of wage labour as fundamentally inimical to human freedom. As a result, the shortening of the working week – once one of the most radical and prominent aims of the labour movement – fell down the list of priorities and the genie was, to a large extent, put back in the bottle.

The consequences of this pivotal turn away from shorter hours campaigns, to cut a very long story short, are all around us today: a world of mass overwork amidst trade union decline and the erosion of work-life boundaries. If one does even the most cursory research on working hours in modern Global North history, one will no doubt confront a graph showing that, across countries, the average number of hours worked has been in consistent decline throughout the twentieth century.[100] New industrial technologies – including forms of automation – were developed and trade unions achieved gains in the workplace and in politics; the lines in the graph are firmly aimed downwards until the Second World War. In the latter half of the century, as trade union radicalism declined and campaigns for shorter hours became less common, the decline in hours plateaued; the lines on the graph tend to level out. Overall this picture gives us some indication of the missed opportunity. In the UK, for example, research suggests that, had we continued on our pre-1980 trajectory, we would have *already* achieved a thirty-two-hour week by now, and would be well on course for a thirty-hour week by 2040.[101]

However, these graphs still tell a misleading story. If we factor in increased female participation in the workforce across the latter half of the century, the picture drastically changes. Between 1951 and 2018, the number of women in the UK workforce increased by nearly 2.5 times.[102] In the United States, the increase was around 30 per cent.[103] With this many new entrants to the labour market, we might expect a reduction in the amount of hours needed to be worked *per person*, as the existing work could then be shared out – and yet no such reduction is apparent during this period.[104] Instead, industry expanded, and output and profit increased: all that extra labour was put to work. After the Second World War, we may have *each* been working gradually shorter working weeks (up until around 1980), but *collectively* we were working more; that is to say, total paid hours in employment across the working population (and indeed within individual family-households) is likely to have significantly increased.

Both the continued time domination of housework and the plateauing of working time reduction should give us pause when considering notions of progress, technological labour-saving and more besides. Despite the speed-up of work, the outsourcing of manufacturing work to the Global South, the mechanization of industrial production, the introduction of household labour-saving devices and the huge amount of wealth that has been created over the decades, we are still putting in vast amounts of hours in both paid and unpaid work. The ideal of working less feels like an ever-more distant dream as we wade deeper into the twenty-first century – and at the same time, for this very reason, post-work politics feels more urgent and necessary than ever before.

Shorter working weeks revived

Struggles for working time reduction are not simply a matter for history textbooks, then – and indeed, we are now seeing the reemergence of working hours as a site of campaigning. To take a handful of examples, the steelworkers trade union, IG Metall in Germany, the PCS union in Scotland, the Communication Workers Union across the UK and – once again – the UAW in the United States have all led the way in new negotiations and industrial action in pursuit of shorter working weeks, with various other unions taking steps down this road too. As modern working conditions degrade even further, and time poverty becomes more acute, we suggest that the struggle for shorter working hours will grow in prominence amongst organized labour, and the flashes of campaigning here and there will become more regular features of the industrial relations landscape.

In this sense, post-work thinking around working time is a theorization – and reactivation – of a historic demand of working-class movements the world over. It can be seen as the response, in theoretical and strategic terms, to today's working woes and the possible routes towards overcoming them. For a post-work perspective, the history of struggles around working time – and the incontrovertible importance of what was achieved – gives a *directionality* and a guiding focus to today's approaches to work.

Today's post-work thinkers tie together these historical lessons with philosophies of work drawn from a variety of influences. The historical struggle for shorter hours can thus be read as a push to expand human freedom and maximize the development of collective potential (an idea we shall be returning to at various points over the course of this book). As Karl Marx remarked, in a particularly Promethean register:

> Time is the room of human development. A man who has no free time to dispose of, whose whole lifetime, apart from the mere physical interruptions of sleep, meals, and so forth, is absorbed by his labour for the capitalist, is less than a beast of burden.[105]

Such aspirations for the fullness of human capacity would also later motivate the English philosopher Bertrand Russell's calls for more free time. In this defence of idleness from 1935, he writes:

> In a world where no one is compelled to work more than four hours a day, every person possessed of scientific curiosity will be able to indulge it, and every painter will be able to paint without starving, however excellent his pictures may be. Young writers will not be obliged to draw attention to themselves by sensational pot-boilers, with a view to acquiring the economic independence needed for monumental works, for which, when the time at last comes, they will have lost the taste and the capacity. Men who, in their professional work, have become interested in some phase of economics or government, will be able to develop their ideas without the academic detachment that makes the work of university economists often seem lacking in reality. Medical men will have time to learn about the progress of medicine, teachers will not be exasperatedly struggling to teach by routine methods things which they learnt in their youth, which may, in the interval, have been proved to be untrue.[106]

As such comments suggest, and as we shall see in later chapters, freedom itself is crucial to understanding the full philosophical and political significance of the idea of free time for all.

In later post-work literature, these themes have been repeated, emphasized and given new content. David Frayne draws on Gorz's notion of a 'politics of time', calling for 'a concerted, open-minded discussion about the quantity and distribution of working time in society, with a view to allowing everybody more freedom for their own autonomous self-development'.[107] For Frayne and Gorz, one of the most important aspects of a shorter working week is its circumscription of the economic sphere – the space where 'economic rationality' dominates; in this sense, post-work is about putting work in its place – recognizing it as something to be distributed and managed but not allowing it to continue to dominate life as it does now.

Other authors, such as Pfannebecker and Smith, are wary of overly prescriptive accounts of the uses to which our free time might be put.[108] Weeks agrees, arguing for the importance of leaving the particular use of our free time wide open. Expanded free time is, in her view, 'time to reinvent our lives, to reimagine and redefine the spaces, practices, and relationships of nonwork time'. The aim is therefore not merely to enhance capacity for meeting existing needs and demands – as important as that is – but also to engender 'a process of creating new subjectivities with new capacities and desires, and, eventually, new demands'.[109] Free time is time for experimentation, where our seemingly rigid identities, structured as they are by our current schedules, begin to loosen up. Weeks pauses on *les trois huits* – the slogan of the eight-hour movement with which we began this book: 'eight hours for work, eight hours for rest and eight hours for what we will':

> Does time 'for what we will' refer to time for what we want, or time for what we will to be? In other words, is it more about getting what we wish for or about getting to exercise our will? Is it a matter of being able to choose among available pleasures and practices, or being able to constitute new ones? Both, I think, are crucial goals that the demand for shorter hours should articulate and advance: more time to partake of existing possibilities for meaning and fulfillment, and time to invent new ones.[110]

Famously, for the twentieth-century economist John Maynard Keynes, this radical openness to the possibility of free, non-working time was both an inevitable stage of progress but also nothing less than an existential problem for humanity.[111] As a follower of Plato and Aristotle, however, he also fervently believed – at least in principle – in the pursuit of 'the good life'; the suggestion that, for the mass of people, less work would be a challenge, rather than an opportunity, betrays an elitist bent in this thought.

Apostolidis' ethnographic work on day labourers in the United States, *The Fight for Time*, asks questions of these workers' desire and the forms of community they build through their struggles.[112] In these settings, Aposolidis finds a kind of post-work sociality and desire springing from the harsh precarity of an unregulated working life – alongside, and in tension with, a contradictory work ethic. Even in perhaps the most precarious of work contexts, there exists 'inchoate potential encoded in the generative themes of ordinary day labourers' to refuse bad work, and to come together to make convivial environments (worker centres) within which to socialize and to educate themselves.[113] It is here, perhaps – in the shelter from more brutal working lives – that we can catch a glimpse of what a life beyond work might be built from.

Despite post-work's continuity with modern thought and worker action around working time reduction, the shorter working week is conspicuously absent, or downplayed, in many of the critical engagements with post-work arguments.[114] While automation and universal basic income are often discussed (and rejected) in detail, and taken as reasons to dismiss the post-work project as a whole, working time reduction more often goes unremarked. This is remarkable, as the reduction of working time – as we have now seen – might in fact be the ultimate aim of most post-work theorizing. Indeed, we would argue that it is the demand that best identifies texts as relevant to any idea of post-work in the first place. Post-work is first and foremost about decentring the burdens of work within our lives, as part of a project of extending human freedom.

After all, we might ask, why would post-work advocates demand things such as full automation if not in order to ultimately reduce the prominence of drudgery and toil within human life? Equally, what drives post-work's continued interest in a universal basic income if not to materially facilitate the capacity to refuse bad work and to engage in more freely chosen activities? These obvious connections between demands frequently pass unnoticed or unreferenced in critical literature on post-work discourse, which can instead latch on to the shortcomings of celebrations of automation or calls for UBI.[115] For those of us who view post-work as a framework for practically oriented research and for advancing political demands, rather than as mere theory, such relationships are crucial.

Conclusion: Reduce, revalue, redistribute

Reduce

First and foremost, then, post-work thinking and practice is about reducing our time spent at work and maximizing our free – or 'discretionary' – time.

Defining what the work *is* that is to be reduced is difficult, given that we are used to a narrow definition of work as employment. But, as this chapter has shown, it is crucial that we widen the scope of what counts as work, given that this definition, as slippery and non-exhaustive as it may be, has real consequences. The employment-only definition, the most common, leaves a lot of unpaid care work, general domestic work and the various forms of shadow work imposed on us unaccounted for and thus invisible. If we are to reduce the burden of these labours, we must first recognize them for what they are.

Post-work's call to radically reduce work stands at odds with approaches – whether Marxist, liberal or conservative – that see the problem of work as merely one of *transforming* work so as to be more in line with a given notion of what is right, or human, or meaningful. While it is of course essential that working conditions are improved so as to better the situation of those carrying out their labours, we argue that such an initiative would be best served by *also* reducing the time people need to spend on work. Not only should working hours be considered one of the primary metrics of the quality of a job (and indeed one's life), and not an external factor, but also a shorter working week can be conducive to the all-round improvement of the other aspects of one's work. As Frayne, drawing on Gorz, points out, a 'renewed appetite for autonomy, developed outside work, might help to rejuvenate traditional labour struggles by encouraging people to be "more exacting about the nature, content, goals and organisation of their work"'.[116]

Post-work's principle of work time reduction is thus sensitive to both 'good work' and its irreducibly unfree nature too: its time and energy burdens and its misalignment with our personal goals. Danaher's post-work position, for example, is one we could call 'labour market pessimism', where work in the labour market is diagnosed as 'structurally bad' – that is, set up in such a way as to reproduce the same plethora of negative outcomes for people, again and again. Danaher is sceptical about the possibility of reforming this system:

It is important to appreciate the enormity of that task. It would require significant changes across several dimensions of our current social system, and those changes would in turn require significant cooperation and coordination.[117]

Danaher is of course correct that radically changing our world of work will require a daunting amount of ambition and scaled action – particularly given the ideological dominance of employment in the eyes of not only mainstream politicians but also of progressives and some labour movement leaders. We are, however, more optimistic about possible change vis-à-vis limiting and reducing the 'bads' of work – not least because we have seen precisely the kind of significant cooperation and coordination necessary to shorten the working week in the past (as detailed in this chapter).

Nonetheless, we agree with Danaher that in some fundamental sense, some of the deeply sedimented burdens of modern work (paid and unpaid) will persist, in some form at least, for the foreseeable future: some form of work will be necessary, for example, to run a healthcare system, to teach younger generations, to care for the elderly and to maintain our built environment. All of the work in these areas will still involve factors that limit our freedom, that require us to follow orders and that will dominate our time quite tangibly. Post-work thinkers such as Gorz are attuned to this fact – and we shall engage with his arguments about freedom and work more fully in Chapter 4.

If work as an activity cannot be abolished completely, then – despite the importance of 'reduce' as a post work principle – its more equal redistribution, to lighten the load of the work for all, is key: this is the second principle to which we now turn.

Redistribute

Today we live in a society marked by severe overwork but also by what is known as 'underemployment'. This is evidently a loaded term – after all, what does it mean to define someone as *lacking* a certain amount of employment? This would be better understood as 'underpayment', as it pertains to being in a state where the hours you work, or your hourly rate, are not sufficient for life. By redistributing work, more people can go 'up' in paid hours so as to reach the new shorter working week, while others can go 'down' in order to reach it.

> One of the functions of a politics of time is precisely to share out savings in working time following principles not of economic rationality but of justice

> … The political task is to redistribute them on the scale of society as a whole so that each man and woman can benefit from them.[118]

In various places across his work, Gorz sketches how such a redistribution might be possible – and how it could be planned democratically.

> The obvious effect of such a [planning] policy would be to mobilize the whole of society towards an outcome that concerns everyone. It will not be possible to determine and carry out the different policy programmes and their objectives technocratically, by issuing decrees from above. The elaboration of these programmes will have to call upon imagination, co-operation and the capacity for innovation and self-organisation at all levels, in the workshops, offices, schools, local council services, trade union branches, quality circles, works committees, parents' association meetings and so on.[119]

For Gorz, redistribution should come also with work *standardization* – a position that, while seemingly counterintuitive (from a humanist point of view), speaks to what we could call a post-work ethics of alienation or abstraction.[120]

> The emancipatory character of work in the economic [paid] sense derives from this: it confers upon me the impersonal reality of an abstract social individual, as capable as any other of occupying a function within the social process of production.[121]

Here, standardizing and sharing productive work around would give each role a purely functional, socially useful meaning – avoiding the possibility of toxic moralizing and individual identification with one's work as a 'calling' or as the 'meaning' of one's existence (as the modern work ethic would have us do).

> Precisely because what is involved is a *function* which is impersonal in its essence, which I occupy as an interchangeable person among others, work does not, as is generally claimed, confer a 'personal identity' upon me, but the very opposite: I do not have to engage the whole of my person, the whole of my life in it.[122]

By recognizing a lot of work as simply *work* that needs to be done, and perhaps cannot be automated away (or needs a specifically human eye), we can minimize its burden on each by distributing it as universally as possible. We are under no illusions – this is definitely necessary, unfree *work* – but its planned distribution now recognizes it as such, and we can each lead our autonomous lives outside of these (now minimized) periods of labour.

So much for redistributing and de-individualizing *paid* work – but what about the huge amounts of unpaid work that takes up so much of our discretionary time today? As we argued above, modern domestic life is designed to be particularly inefficient when it comes to sharing and reducing household labours.[123] The key to this problem is to go in the other direction: collective infrastructure to ensure that the labour of the home doesn't fall on only a few pairs of hands. Free childcare centres, long-term care centres for the elderly and public kitchens for shared meals:[124] these examples of seemingly basic demands would have hugely transformative effects for the nature and extent of unpaid work in our society.

For more radical post-work thinkers, such as M.E. O'Brien and Sophie Lewis, it is the family itself, as an idea and a practice, that needs challenging in order that the, currently unequally distributed, labours of household units be transformed into collective care, from gestation through to death. We'll encounter these ideas again in our final chapter on the value of post-work utopianism.

Revalue

Then there is revaluing work. This should have two senses: revaluing in the sense of *re-labelling* kinds of activity *as* work – revaluing as recognition, and revaluing in terms of placing a higher ethical and financial value on certain kinds of work (and thus giving those workers carrying it out better working conditions). We've already noted that more work needs to be valued as such, but, as we remarked in our introduction, revaluing work so as to maximize or minimize it is a crucial component of the push to reduce work in an equitable way. If we were to value care work much more – in terms of social estimation but also in terms of pay – then it is likely that the paid care sector would improve its delivery of care and that workers would be more inclined to take on these jobs to begin with; it might mean that that we'd find it easier to share unpaid care, where that is desired, amongst more people too – thus reducing the work for each. There is of course a danger that, in the process of revaluing work such as care, we risk sedimenting gender norms (if it is so great, then we should venerate and thank women for their honourable service – which they can't now give up because it is so crucial). We return to this theme in our final chapter, where post-work visions provoke us to think concretely about how to avoid this situation.

Redistributing and revaluing work in order to ultimately reduce it is a dominant theme in post-work discourse, and it will crop up in all of the chapters in this book; here we have presented a spread of arguments in its favour drawn from post-work thinkers but also from a basic analysis of work relations within a capitalist economy. In the next chapter, we will focus on another common proposal found within post-work – albeit one that touches on working life from a quite different angle: unconditional cash for all.

2

Unconditional, universal income

Introduction

This chapter detours from the waged workplace to focus on a different issue that is taken to be characteristic of post-work positions: unconditional cash for all, or as it is most commonly known – universal basic income (UBI). This is a policy proposal wherein people are guaranteed a regular cash payment, irrespective of their work status or living situation.[1] There can be different levels of payment for children versus adults, but beyond that this is a flat rate that replaces any existing welfare payments that require job searching or other behaviours mandated by state services.[2] In its purest form, a basic income should be sufficient for individuals to live on – but many, including some post-work authors, see a 'modest' or 'introductory' basic income of lower payment amounts as the gradual first step towards this.[3] A basic income scheme could be funded in a number of ways, but the more concrete proposals rely on a mixture of progressive taxation on income and wealth.

UBI – as a concept, a demand and/or a policy – appears across much of the post-work literature. Srnicek and Williams list it as one of their core demands, alongside shorter working weeks, full automation and a shift away from the modern work ethic.[4] Kathi Weeks lists basic income and shorter hours as her two feminist-utopian post-work demands. Elsewhere, Peter Frase has made the case from a labour movement perspective, factoring it into a response to creeping automation:

If pushed by progressive forces, the UBI would be a non-reformist reform that would also quicken automation by making machines more competitive against workers better positioned to reject low wages. It would also facilitate labor organization by acting as a kind of strike fund and cushion against the threat of joblessness. A universal basic income could defend workers and realize the potential of a highly developed, post-scarcity economy; it could break the false choice between well-paid workers or labor-saving machines, strong unions or technological advancement.[5]

Rutger Bregman makes a convincing case for a basic income in his hugely popular *Utopia for Realists*, basing his argument on previous experiments.[6] Andre Gorz endorsed various forms of basic income in his post-work writings: perhaps most intriguingly, he often discusses an 'income for life' which could complement a 'quota' of hours of work that individuals might, one day, be able to distribute over however many days/months/years they please.[7]

It is by no means universally endorsed by authors in the post-work lane, however. Martin Hägglund, for example, argues against the policy, as does Aaron Bastani – the former because basic income does not, in his view, have the potential to affect productive relations in the same direct manner as, for example, shortening the working week does, and the latter because basic income is expensive and not as effective, in its aim, as free public services would be.[8] We argue in this chapter that these perspectives tend either to misconceive of labour relations as confined to employment, or else express a scarcity mindset – the austere terrain of fiscal conservatives and neoliberal economists.

Basic income is a favourite focal point for post-work's critics. While most criticisms of an unconditional income have come from conservatives (who fear its radical consequences) there are also left-wing critics who employ misguided or obfuscatory accounts of the concept and its history. It is simply misleading, for example, to portray basic income as an idea that has supporters on the left and right of the political spectrum in equal measure. In truth, the idea has for centuries been expressed overwhelmingly by progressives – from Thomas Paine to Bertrand Russell, from guild socialist G.D.H. Cole to Martin Luther King Jr, and from John Stuart Mill to the Black Panther movement – a fact obscured by many accounts that offer a false 'two sides' portrait.[9]

While in our age there has been the occasional expression of support for UBI from billionaires looking to jump on an exciting 'new' idea, it is unlikely that they would continue to be so enthusiastic if they were confronted with the taxation scheme required to actually fund and deliver the policy.[10] Equally, while some neoliberal intellectuals have flirted with similar ideas, such as Milton Friedman and Friedrich Hayek, they didn't tarry for long and have written against such proposals in equal measure.[11] In the neoliberal era of politics, as we shall see, the trajectory of government policy in the United States and UK – and in many other countries – has been in the opposite direction: that is, *against* expanding cash benefits and *against* loosening welfare conditionality. If basic income is a 'neoliberal plot' or Trojan horse, as some have claimed, then no one has informed the actually existing neoliberal politicians of the past forty years, who have overseen a tightened grip on welfare conditions and the stigmatization of those receiving cash support.[12] In contrast, today's campaigners, politicians, policy outfits and academics actively pushing for basic income around the world are almost exclusively progressive. Nonetheless, as with any policy or demand, the emancipatory potential of basic income will be dependent on the specific form it takes if and when it is deployed, which in turn is subject to social and political pressure.[13] Post-work thought and politics, in this regard, aims at steering basic income in as emancipatory a direction as possible.[14]

It is also worth noting here that none of the post-work authors that we know of see basic income as a silver bullet, or as *the* method by which we can achieve a new socio-economic system or post-work world. Much more needs to be done, on many sides, including shortening the working week, changing ownership structures of key industries, building new care and energy infrastructure and so on and so forth. It is not for nothing that this book takes basic income as but one of *three* core post-work policy demands – demands which (as we are at pains to demonstrate) are insufficient on their own to capture the full radical potential of a post-work project. Primarily we see basic income as a very useful *mechanism* for extending freedom and for ameliorating the worst aspects of a work-centred society such as our own.[15] In this chapter we'll give the general case that advocates tend to make around this particular demand, before drawing on key moments in theoretical and activist histories to make the case ourselves, from a specifically post-work perspective.

Stepping back for a moment, a reader might be tempted to ask: What *do* cash transfers, or upgraded welfare payments, have to do with work – or even a *post*-work future? Don't these things change very little when it comes to work, precisely because they concern the distribution of income *outside* of the wage, to everyone, regardless of whether they are working or not? In other words, isn't UBI about distribution, rather than production? Such a myopic approach to issues of income, employment, work and their interrelationships is precisely what post-work seeks to push back against. We argue, in this chapter, that the world of work in modern capitalism cannot be properly understood without grasping the past and present of what has come to be called 'unemployment'. The question of unemployed life – its conditions, the resources available for it and the extent of people's ability to live freely in this situation – is of crucial importance when considering what a better future of work will look like in general.

The general case for basic income

The general case for a universalized income, in the form of a 'basic income' policy, has been well-made by many. Daniel Chandler, for example, makes a strong, liberal case, drawing on the philosophy of John Rawls.[16] Wealth economist Thomas Piketty has become an advocate of the idea as a new mechanism for combatting rampant inequality.[17] Equally, in the spirit of Beveridge, former ILO economist and welfare expert Guy Standing argues for a basic income in response to eight new giant evils of our time (inequality, insecurity, debt, stress, precarity, automation, populism and extinction).[18] We'll be drawing on these arguments in order to sketch out the 'general case' for some form of basic income before moving on to the more specific reasons why many post-work theorists support it.

Slashing inequality and poverty

Perhaps the most obvious impact that a basic income would have would be a significant redistribution of cash from the wealthy to middle and lower income groups. The UK and the United States in particular have incredibly unequal distributions of wealth and wage incomes, which lead to a plethora of well-documented negative social and economic effects.[19] Basic income would be a very efficient mechanism to direct cash away from the rich (via taxation) and into the budgets of everyone else.

In some of the more robust studies, the reductions in poverty that could be achieved by even low levels of UBI payments are remarkable. In a 2022 study, researchers found that even providing just £63 per week for adults and £40 for children would more than halve child poverty in the UK and would reduce working-age poverty by just over a quarter.[20] On slightly higher levels (£225 per adult per week) you would almost wipe out poverty altogether. When it comes to economic equality, nothing of this order of magnitude can be achieved, in such a short time period, by any other comparable policy: not by better education, nor early years interventions, not even by the creation of thousands of jobs or more skills training. Such a rebalancing of income and wealth flows should be supported by any progressively minded person.

There is an important gender equality element to basic income's impact too. Controlling the household's cash – its use and quantity – is a common strategy of abusive partners. A 2018 UN report revealed that 58 per cent of all female homicides that year had been at the 'hands of intimate partners or family members';[21] the household is often far from a safe place, and as Silvia Federici puts it, 'if we are short of money we will always be vulnerable to domestic violence'.[22] Traditional welfare payments can shore up asymmetries of power in this zone, as they have historically been allocated to the 'head of the household', rather than individuals within it – facilitating a concentration of power that is conducive to abuse. By providing a guaranteed source of cash directly to individuals, UBI loosens the financial grip of abusers. As UK Green Party politician Amelia Womak writes:

> Enabling women to independently rebuild their lives should be at the core of domestic abuse policy. UBI could help survivors escape with guaranteed income that could ultimately help them find a new home – or even just provide train fare money to friends or family.[23]

Guaranteeing cash makes an exit from abusive relationships a lot more viable (though certainly not easy) and as such it would be a demonstrable boost for women's equality.

Ensuring security

As a floor below which no one can fall, a basic income fulfils a function of social responsibility that governments are, depending on how one looks at it, obliged to carry out – or are at least best placed to. There were similar principles behind Roosevelt's Depression era reforms as well as the Great Society policies that followed – not to mention Beveridge's model in Britain post-Second World War. In the latter case,

> the state would limit the risk of adverse events – shocks – and provide contributions-based insurance (mainly paid by employers) to enable people and families to cope with them better and to recover from them sooner and more easily.[24]

In today's era, where states have been, at best, shrunk down to dysfunctional points of contact for the public, and, at worst, mechanisms by which to facilitate value capture by the most powerful private entities, it is no surprise that insecurity and deprivation have run rampant. As Standing notes, today's insecurity is as much about widespread *uncertainty* as it is about risk of negative shocks: uncertainty of working hours, uncertainty of contract length and ultimately uncertainty of income.

> With uncertainty, you just do not know. There are 'unknown unknowns'. No actuarial calculation of probabilities can be made and it is hard to develop a social insurance system as an adequate response.[25]

Basic income – guaranteed at a certain level, as a right – would be a key pillar of such a response: a step in precisely the opposite direction to these emergent employment practices and social precarities. The security offered by basic income is a 'superior kind of public good', most importantly due to its universalism: as everyone is receiving it, the benefits for society get compounded. Collective, everyday life might not feel so competitive and abrasive, abject poverty would reduce, and communities would likely feel greater trust in public institutions as mechanisms that work in their interests.[26] In many relevant, real-world experiments, public health has improved too, such as in the Mincome experiment in Canada – a scheme very similar to a basic income – where researchers noted a significant drop in hospital visits for those receiving unconditional payments.[27]

Basic income will also likely become more necessary as a security measure in the face of various incoming crises. As this century progresses, it is realistic to expect a string of cascading and interlocking shocks to our economies: from new epidemiological threats to resource scarcity, from ageing populations and care shortages to financial collapse, from geopolitical conflict to climate volatility and breakdown. All of the above phenomena will disrupt economic activity and labour markets in some way – putting livelihoods (and national economies) at risk. In this scenario, it makes little sense to still force people to look for work in order to receive income support, or have conditional welfare systems in place that incur lengthy waiting times for payment. As we saw during the onset of the Covid-19 pandemic, getting support cash to people as quickly as possible is a priority in times of crisis; having the circuitry of unconditional income already in place during times of relative stability makes us more ready and resilient in the face of disruption. A basic income can be a lifeline that can efficiently increase the incomes of households, directly and quickly, when necessary; given that it is likely that the state will need to be more interventionist, and 'higher spend' as the climate crisis deepens, such a mechanism could be essential to the economic planning we require.[28]

Clearing some 'cognitive bandwidth'

Creating some financial security that we can rely on – unlike the whims of an employer we have to satisfy for a wage – has huge effects on our mental health also. Here, behavioural economist Sendhil Mullainathan and psychologist Eldar Shafir's now famous work on scarcity is relevant to the basic income conversation.[29] Across various studies, they showed that with meagre resources – and the acute awareness of this precarity – people's cognitive capacity to problem solve and navigate day-to-day financial situations is greatly reduced: living in scarcity is like a computer running an intensive programme that sucks up all of your processing power. This is why Standing marks stress as one of the 'giant' evils of our time: everything from precarious work, to huge amounts of private debt, to lack of access to decent housing demonstrably increases our stress levels and disables our ability to plan ahead and make time to think. Having an income that you know will come through on a regular basis – and will also come through for your friends and loved ones – will help assuage the scarcity mindset and provide at least some solid ground to stand on. This cognitive benefit is a largely hidden but nevertheless crucial consequence of the kind of income security that a guaranteed and unconditional income can uniquely provide.

The unique capacity of cash

Basic income is often counterposed to what is sometimes called 'universal basic services' (UBS) – what are in effect extended and updated public services which would be free at the point of use.[30] We think this dichotomous framing is a mistake. First and foremost, posing a zero-sum game between decent public services and more substantial cash benefits strays too close to a reactionary, austerity-oriented position.[31] No progressive seriously argues, for example, for a free health service *instead* of social security or jobseekers' benefits, and nor should anyone argue for free bus services or housing (UBS) *instead* of an unconditional cash floor for all (UBI).

Secondly, and more technically, we need to consider the distinct affordances that services offer versus cash in the pocket.[32] Some UBS-only positions involve an implicit (sometimes explicit) assumption that these services are sufficient replacements for – or are like for like equivalents of – cash when it comes to meeting people's basic or necessary requirements. Let's consider for a moment what precisely we refer to as 'necessary' (or 'basic') when we pose this opposition.

When looking at what people's basic requirements are, we enter a debate about criteria and definition: What do we use to measure basic needs and how are these needs decided and defined exactly? This debate also pertains to the question as to what exactly constitutes deprivation/poverty, should a basic standard of living not be met. The definition of poverty and deprivation has always been a controversial and ever-changing one. Over the years, however, we have generally moved from 'absolute' definitions of poverty (the lack of shelter and food, etc.) to 'relative' definitions based on the needs of a particular society at a certain point in history.[33] This idea has had strong support in the history of economics – from classical liberals like Smith to Marx to post-Keynesians such as J.K. Galbraith.[34]

Since the 1980s, robust surveys have given indication as to the changing nature of public needs, the relative material threshold of deprivation and thus the detail on what constitutes a 'basic' standard of living – according to the public themselves.[35] So, for example, the public consistently think that well-heated, non-damp housing is a basic necessity, as well as a winter coat – but attitudes have changed as to how necessary meat is in our diets, or how important access to the internet is (in the 1990s it was an emergent technology, by 2012 it was perceived as fundamental).[36] What is most relevant for our discussion here is that many basic requirements for contemporary life – as reported by the public – require individual choices to a large degree, both in terms of practicality but also desirability. For example, people probably care less about which kind of bus comes to collect them than they do about what they eat and which clothes they wear – matters of taste, personal preference and even creative expression. People would probably have no qualms about having only one choice of internet service as long as it performed well, whereas they would experience the external prescription of specific kinds of holidays or specific treats and toys for children very differently (and possibly negatively). Even if a UBS programme could issue the entire set of basic items we need and cater to all everyday activities, it would simply not be desirable for those choices to be taken automatically out of people's hands.

As progressive as it might sound then (in the face of dysfunctional neoliberal privatization of everyday life), we simply cannot – and should not – cater to every need with a state- or locally run service. It follows that if services are a poor fit for meeting a significant chunk of the basic needs of modern life (while at the same time being perfect for meeting some of these needs), a basic income would by contrast be much more dynamic. Money is, of course, the universal equivalent, meaning that (at least under a system predicated on monetary exchange) it can be exchanged for anything. As such, it in theory offers those who have it access to an extensive consumption basket. If this money was not provided in exchange for labour but was given as a right, unconditional upon anything, then it would become a secure, flexible resource that people could allocate to whatever items or activities they (and no one else) defined as necessary. As political theorist David Calnitsky summaries in his excellent article on socialist arguments for basic income:

> the needs and preferences of poor and working-class people are deeply heterogeneous – the needs of a young man living in a small rural town, a single mother in a large city center, and an older suburban couple are inescapably diverse. On these grounds, money, a highly fungible good, can better satisfy diverse needs and subjective preferences than even a fairly comprehensive suite of specific goods and services.[37]

Basic services and basic income are each very good at meeting different needs: services make more sense for commonly used, necessary infrastructures such as transport and health, while an income floor would allow people to acquire the basic – and less basic – items of everyday life in the twenty-first century and fully participate in social life.

It is this difference and complementarity that is missed by theorists such as Nancy Fraser, for example, who argues that there is no need for a basic income in a more equal and democratic society, as there will be no markets for 'the bottom' set of basic goods and nor will society's wealth be marketized 'at the top' of the distribution steam.[38] Fraser too quickly brushes over the nuances of our 'basic' needs, not distinguishing between shelter, clothing, food, leisure, transportation and breathable air – all of which we would agree should be 'provided as a matter of right',[39] but precisely *how* they should be made accessible is an important and sensitive issue. Interestingly, beyond the basics, Fraser argues that there likely *should* in fact be a market for a 'middle' set of activities and goods within a post-capitalist world. We should

> [i]magine the in-between as a space for experimentation with a mix of different possibilities: a space where markets could find a place, along with cooperatives, commons, self-organised associations, and self-managed projects ... Once the top and bottom [of our economies] are socalised and decommodified, the function and role of markets in the middle would be transformed.[40]

If there are indeed markets for some things in post-capitalism, then surely we don't want to make access to them dependent solely on the size of one's wage packet. Would it not be more generative of equality and freedom if some form of guaranteed cash made it possible for all people to access beyond-basic goods and services in this transformed market? The gaps in Fraser's arguments here are thus useful vectors through which we can tease out some of the conceptual misunderstandings and undesirable conclusions that vex the income versus services debate.[41] For as long as there remains a money system, we must consider how to distribute money in the most equitable fashion possible.

In summary, there are important ways in which cash and services are not equivalent and each policy affords different sets of freedoms. Deployed together, they would be a powerful mechanism for eliminating poverty and taking people out of a scarcity lifestyle (with all of the material and psychological consequences that involve). Crucially, understanding the specificities of basic income – the uniqueness of cash and unconditionality – can help us understand its place in moving to a more equal, emancipated society.

The post-work case for basic income

A lot of post-work theorists will endorse some or all of the above arguments – recognizing the overlaps between basic social democratic principles and the radical ambition of post-work visions. Here, however, we are interested in specifically why unconditional or universal income floors have regularly found their way into post-work texts, sometimes becoming core demands. We want to situate basic income in the history of life outside of the labour market within capitalism – what was called 'relief' and now is called 'welfare'; by situating basic income within core tendencies of capitalist society, we can see how powerful a tool it can be for changing our system of work today. We also want to open up the discussion to arguments about the distribution of value in capitalist economies and why basic income helps revalue non-employment activities in a material and cultural sense. To make the case, alongside theoretical interpretations and empirical evidence from the United States and UK, we draw attention to two campaigners in particular from the history of welfare activism, and draw lessons from their legacies; finally, we make arguments as to why basic income dovetails with post-work's ethos, acting as a crucial lever in shifting our work culture irreversibly.

Basic income runs against the historical tendencies of capitalist work-welfare regimes

In the previous chapter, we saw how one can grasp the modern history of our societies – of capitalist economies – through the lens of working time; this meant looking at the different, competing interests involved in controlling the use of time and ultimately considering how much of our time we can really call our own. In this section, we want to show that it is just as revealing of our system to consider its history through the perspective of life *outside* of the formal labour market.[42] In short, let's understand the development of modern capitalism through the experiences of 'unemployed' life and how 'we' (or rather, the governments ostensibly representing us) treat those who, for one reason or another, do not engage in wage labour.[43]

In the following potted history, while there are of course various twists and turns, we want to hold onto some distinct continuities – namely, punishment for unemployment and coercive mechanisms used to push people into the labour market. These constant and ongoing features are important contexts for understanding just how much of a sea-change something like basic income would bring about with regards to the world of work.

Punish the idle: From the Poor Laws to Beveridge

Punishment of 'the idle' preceded modern capitalist societies. At times, denigration of the 'workless' built on earlier, draconian laws involving human slavery, such as those introduced in England in 1547:

> In light of complaints of idleness and vagabondrie it is therefore enacted that if any man or woman able to work should refuse to labour, and live idly for three days, that he or she, should be branded with a red-hot iron on the breast with a letter V, and should be adjudged the slaves for three years of any person who should inform against the said idler.[44]

In 1641, leading intellectual Samuel Hartlib expressed what today is a fairly commonplace demonization of those 'not working'. What was needed, in Hartlib's view, was 'a godly and politick government; that the godly and laborious poore may be countenanced and cherished, and the idle, and wicked poore supprest'.[45] Indeed, as Elizabeth Anderson notes, the work ethic contained the seeds of an 'epistemology of suspicion about the poor' from its conception,[46] and such attitudes have been typical of elites and their mouthpieces ever since. By this analysis, poor relief is in fact 'unjust, because it puts the interests of the undeserving dependent poor ahead of the worthy, hardworking, independent poor'.[47]

Maintaining the labouring poor precisely as that – poor and labouring – was an explicit strategy for creating wealth as capitalist economic relations became established. The point of the 'New Poor Laws' of 1834, for example, was to maintain levels of poverty and deprivation at such a level so as to coerce the population into working for a wage for a master. Edwin Chadwick, an architect of this infamous system, was quite clear:

> Poverty … is the natural, the primitive, the general and the unchangeable state of man; that as labour is the source of wealth, so is poverty of labour. Banish poverty, you banish wealth. Indigence, therefore, and not poverty is the evil, the removal of which is the proper object of Poor Laws.[48]

The Poor Laws also baked in racial categories and enforced particular forms of family relations from an early stage. Robbie Shilliam has demonstrated that the debates around rural populations outside of industrial centres, and particularly populations not amenable to the imperatives of industrialism, were connected with colonial rule and thus racialized others – namely, slaves from English plantations abroad. The 'undeserving' poor in England – those who refused work – were 'blackened' insofar as they were portrayed as akin in their laziness to unproductive slaves.[49] In other arguments, 'the idle' were portrayed as always, tragically, at risk of becoming 'like slaves' insofar as they had no regular work and were thus unable to achieve independence. Blackness, and its racialized specifications, was perceived as a creeping threat amongst the unemployed: a discursive thread that runs through US and UK social security history up until this day. Equally, the ability to receive resources has long been tethered to the obligation to perform gendered familial roles. The original Poor Laws themselves enforced the idea of 'family responsibility – that relatives had a duty to and should be compelled to support their relations before public monies would be handed out', while later forms of relief were targeted specifically at those imagined to be 'excluded from the work relationship' (such as widows and mothers).[50] Unemployment policy has essentially always been a tool for division and tight regulation of people's lives, through (the threat of) impoverishment.[51]

This is the context we must always keep in mind: unemployment regulation systems – what we now call welfare – consistently discipline a population into being proto-labourers, even if employment doesn't always manifest. Nothing represents this better than the workhouse:

> The 19th century workhouse as a space of internment was explicitly premised on the idea that life outside of work (and life inside the workhouse itself) must be demonstrably worse than life in waged labour.[52]

As Anderson remarks, throughout 'their entire history, workhouses were unprofitable, despite the wretched food, clothing, housing, and other goods they provided their inmates. It was always much cheaper for parishes to provide relief with cash.'[53] The punishment is the point; work might be bad, but being without it is – by design – even worse. Later, a system of 'labour exchanges' – the forerunner of job centres – would add a new function into this system. Winston Churchill, then the president of the Board of Trade, was clear as to what this was to be:

> It is not possible to make the distinction between the vagrant and the loafer on the one hand and the bona fide workman on the other, except in conjunction with some elaborate and effective system of testing willingness to work such as is afforded by the system of labor [*sic*] exchanges.[54]

Such a distinction between the 'vagrant' and the 'legitimate' job-seeker, so common to the history of poor relief and social security, will recur through the creation of the post-war welfare state and into today's 'workfare' projects.

There is no question that the Beveridge reforms (from 1942 onwards) represented an exceptional moment in welfare statemaking.[55] They put in place an infrastructure by which people could live their lives more easily whether they had a job or not – taking one's fate outside of the pure, blind play of market forces. What are today known as 'work-first' conditions (support tethered to a commitment to find a job) were in this sense loosened, marking a modest change in the discursive disposition towards industrial life – acknowledging that destitution and poverty are not always the fault of individuals but rather are common to modern, capitalist societies in general. In part, its emancipatory edges were due to the efforts of radical social campaigners such as Eleanor Rathbone – as we shall see in sections below.

At the same time, and this is a mark of continuity with the above history of punishment, the expansion of the structure for out-of-work regulation also constituted an increase in state involvement in individual lives, including their physical and mental health, in 'order to adapt them to the requirements of the capitalist economy'.[56] As Pfannebeckerr and Smith point out, 'even as they offered new protection to those out of work, [post-war] welfare regimes naturalised the idea that truly belonging to their citizenry meant being in waged work.'[57] This was an age in which the male breadwinner norm was entrenching its hegemonic status and finding increasing acceptance as a cultural standard. One of Beveridge's more negative legacies in this regard is his claim that 'idleness' – the condition of non-participation in employment – is one of five 'giant' obstacles on the road to prosperity. This, as is obvious from our sketch of historical attitudes to welfare, is a view repeated by those irritated by the concept of a non-labouring poor – both in centuries past and in more recent years (such as conservative decriers of 'welfare queens' and 'scroungers'). In contrast to these long-standing dogmas and moral panics, leading social policy experts are more often of the opinion that 'idleness' is not – and probably never was – the problem: rather, unfavourable jobs markets and overly complex welfare systems are much larger factors in persistent unemployment.[58] Arguably, 'idleness' only appeared as such a towering problem for Beveridge as a result of centuries of targeted, aggressive, and stigmatizing policy and political discourse.

This history also teaches us something important about 'relations of production' (the precise relationships between workers and their employers); we cannot consider these relations in isolation, cut off from wider coercive pressures on workers. In *Capital*, Marx himself spends a number of chapters drawing on the emergent regime of violence against work-resistant populations – the so-called 'primitive accumulation' that underpins capitalist economic relations. It is coercion on the part of state (or parish) authorities – horrifically violent in the first couple of centuries of capitalism's development – that ensured participation in the world of work as we know it today. Because unemployed life has become intolerable, workers 'freely' choose to submit to the discipline of their employers.

Against neoliberal thought and practice

Jump forward a few decades from Beveridge's intervention and, via the Great Society Reforms of the 1960s, welfare universality in the United States was arguably approaching its peak, though not without the persistent, underlying DNA of work ethic dogma and stigma. More and more people were being supported by federal assistance programmes such as Aid to Families with Dependent Children (AFDC), including Black American families – and yet campaign groups, leftists and liberals were pushing to go even further, towards a guaranteed or basic income.[59]

This era in the United States marks a pivotal moment of policymaking and economic rationality – wherein ever more influential neoliberal economic actors dovetailed with conservative fears about the threat that welfare 'dependency' and decadence posed to traditional family models. As Cooper's *Family Values* details in-depth, these forces of counterrevolution served to reinstate the work of the traditional home and family on the one hand and curb the resistances to labour market discipline on the other; to do this, welfare was to be a primary target.

What neoconservatives, for their part, fearfully perceived in the Great Society before them (particularly in the ADC/AFDC but also Nixon's Family Assistance Plan) was the facilitator of New Left countercultures: a post-work generation in the making, as it were, that questioned both the family and the work ethic simultaneously.[60] Julian Vaïsse, historian of neoconservatism, summarizes this anxiety as an animosity towards an emergent working and middle class with too much 'time and money to spare'.[61] Neocons would spend the ensuing decades lumping in welfare, Black radicals, single parents and countercultural destabilization as one homogenous enemy in their arguments.[62] Neoliberals, for their part, largely agreed with the importance of traditional family as an economic vector, but would also argue that welfare was an unaffordable burden and that too much of it would distort optimal market mechanics. It became economic orthodoxy to claim that welfare spending was one of, if not *the,* main causes of the inflation crises of the 1970s – despite amounting to a small fraction of overall budgets.[63]

Milton Friedman's trajectory as one of the leading thinkers of the period is instructive for understanding the extent to which basic income challenges neoliberal positions on welfare.[64] Cooper documents a shift in Friedman's position from 'pragmatic' accommodation with expanded welfare provision to aggressive opposition to said reforms and a retrenched family oriented traditionalism that would endure for the rest of his political career. In 1972, Friedman was central to the melting pot of influences that would feed into the US government's ambitious guaranteed income plan – the nearest the United States has come to a basic income – having drafted the concept of a 'negative income tax' which would form the basis of President Nixon's proposal. This was a unique moment in welfare, and indeed US policy history, wherein libertarians, neoliberals, left-wing welfare campaigners and old New Deal advocates united around what would arguably have been the most expansive and transformative welfare policy in modern history.[65]

But this unique and unsteady coalition would not last, with Nixon's eventual (much diluted) policy decision proving unpopular on a number of fronts. By the 1980s, as Cooper documents, Friedman had turned distinctly against redistributive welfare, and would renounce his support for any form of guaranteed income. His accommodation of guaranteed income proposals was, he admitted on reflection, always held with a view to demolishing the welfare state and reinstating familial orthodoxy;[66] when the effects of expansive welfare were in fact operating in the opposite direction – and non-normative, non-family life was seemingly *encouraged* by this loosening of welfare conditionality – Friedman would abandon his previous position. *Too* redistributive welfare policies, he would write, 'weaken the family; reduce the incentive to work, save and innovate; reduce the accumulation of capital; and limit our freedom'.[67] Once again, elite opinion returns to the work ethic and the ever-present threat of the 'lazy poor'.[68]

Other neoliberal intellectual leaders and their policymaking counterparts continued steadfastly down this path back to quasi-Poor Law governance, and, as Stuart Hall noted at the time, 'under the guise of monetarist orthodoxy, the attempt to dismantle the welfare state has now received the cloak of respectability'.[69] The Social Security Act of 1989 in the UK made a significant step up in requirements for support: those who are in receipt of unemployment benefits were not permitted to turn down jobs on the grounds of inadequate pay or because it did not align with their experience.[70] It was now a state-enforced requirement that you had to be 'actively seeking work', no matter the quality or quantity of the jobs actually out there. In the United States, the neoliberal clampdown was consolidated when Clinton replaced AFDC with the 'Temporary Assistance for Needy Families' plan (TANF) – which he boasted represented 'the end of welfare as we know it'.[71]

By the end of the century, the now neoliberal Labour Party in the UK followed suit. Peter Mandelson's restatement of the Poor Laws' ethos was clear:

> It is a crucial New Labour commitment that society must accept a serious obligation to find work for the young unemployed … In these circumstances the young unemployed themselves have to accept obligations too … It is not right that some people should collect the dole, live on the black economy, and then refuse to cooperate with society's efforts to reintegrate them into the labour market … In circumstances where new opportunity is being offered and refused, there should be no absolute entitlement to continued receipt of social security benefits … *Such a tough discipline is necessary to demonstrate the seriousness of the government's efforts and break the culture of hopelessness, idleness and cynicism.*[72]

The result, as Jamie Peck has demonstrated in detail, is neoliberal 'workfare' regimes across both sides of the Atlantic.

> [T]he unemployed themselves are no longer portrayed, in the Old Labour convention, as the unfortunate victims of deindustrialisation and job loss, but as active agents in a dysfunctional economy of benefit dependency,

fraud, and illegal work; it is seen as axiomatic that the unemployed should be 'obliged' to 'cooperate'.[73]

By the dawn of the millennium, any deviations represented by the Beveridge system in the UK or the Great Society policies in the US were largely erased, and welfare was put on track to a new era of neo-Poor Law misery. Today's welfare or 'social security' systems are descendants of this history: conditionality, 'targeting' (non-universality) and stigma characterize a system of regulation that continues to function as a stick with which to beat those outside of the labour market and a threat for those who are within it. There is by now broad academic agreement that welfare conditionality *as such* has failed – it is 'counterproductive, ineffective and unethical'.[74] Our systems enact a paternalist work-welfare regime of 'counterproductive compliance'.[75]

This is the tide that basic income swims against: making life intolerable outside of employment is a long-standing crutch of modern breadwinner-focused regimes and the fight against it is a fight for fewer conditions, greater universality and guaranteed security.

Decommodifying ourselves

The above history of the emergence of welfare as an instrument of regulation and discipline, coercing populations into paid work and punishing those who resisted, is also a story of how our societies became organized around markets. As Ellen Meiksins Wood notes, markets have existed for centuries, across different types of social systems, but predominantly as an 'opportunity' for the seller to improve their lot.[76] Within capitalist societies, by contrast, the market exists as an 'imperative'; exchanging commodities on the market has become non-optional, essential to survival (in other words, crucial to the reproduction of human life).

The history of the encroachment of markets into many facets of our lives is thus the history of commodification – giving (almost) everything a price and letting it be influenced by the ebb and flow of the market. This is true of land and housing, of resources like gas and coal, and of people: it is a labour *market*, involving the exchange of human *resources*. From Karl Polanyi to Marx to today's value-form Marxists and more autonomist theorists, we can glean that the core of life in modern capitalism revolves around the fact that survival is best filtered through the selling of our time and energy – our lives – in a scenario of buyer and seller (where the seller has nothing to fall back on).[77]

At their high point, in their most emancipatory form, welfare states have been engines of *de*commodification. They've taken the direct cost of medicine, of travel and of housing out of the daily life of the population by providing free or very cheap public services. Equally (and even more radically) though, cash benefits have allowed people to have some choice as to if and how they sell their time, as a worker, to a boss.[78] In other words, welfare states can allow us to be less of a commodity – a body that labours at the behest of someone else – depending on the standard of benefits we receive.[79] This is a key point from a post-work point of view, then: cash benefits have the capacity to weaken the hold of labour commodification.

In some countries, such as Sweden in the 1980s or Finland, Slovenia and (to some extent) Germany today, cash benefits are offered at much higher levels, offering a more robust safety net than that available elsewhere.[80] Yet these systems often still rely on a contribution model – workers have to pay in to get the support – thus reinforcing the traditional deserving (they've toiled enough) versus undeserving (they've not put in the hours) dichotomy so familiar in the history of capitalism. What post-work finds interesting about basic income is precisely how it explodes this distinction and the arguments it stands on: income is a guarantee, not based on what people put in but justified insofar as it enables greater freedom from the discipline of work, from the desperation of the job hunt and the precarity of labour markets in general. A welfare system based on unconditional and universal – or near universal – income floors would therefore be historic for all nations: for the first time, punishment of the 'idle' and planned destitution would no longer be the flipside – the constant threat – of a prescribed world of work.

By universalizing cash payments, at a level of common denominator, basic income would drastically reduce the threat of stigmatization – based as it is on our willingness or ability to have our labour power be sold as a commodity. The categories of 'deserving' and 'underserving' would lose their material component, given that everyone – rich or poor, working or not working –

would receive the same. As we've seen, in the UK and US this pernicious distinction between 'skivers' and 'strivers' has also been threaded with racialization for hundreds of years, precisely at the same time as humans and their labour were being turned into commodities at scale; thus a universalizing, non-discriminatory cash benefit system would also go some way in loosening and blurring these pernicious categorizations. As we will see in sections below, activists for guaranteed incomes have recognized this emancipatory potential.

The wage don't fit: Moving towards post-capitalist income

Another case for basic income put forward by post-work theorists is rooted in an analysis of how value circulates – and how people are rewarded for their work – in our societies. In this line of argument, post-work authors have questioned whether anti- and post-capitalist movements should be so attached to the individual wage as an adequate channel of remuneration, given the long and well-documented list of inadequacies and detrimental features of this mechanism; not least amongst these, from a post-work perspective, is the fact that the wage has numerous strings attached, with a boss at the other end. Given the bloody history of the imposition of wage labour, and given Marx's famous call to 'abolish the wages system!' perhaps we should countenance what, ultimately, might constitute our exit strategy from said system.

Many figures in socialism's history, for example, have pointed to basic problems of accountancy, particularly to the specific sources of the value of each product, and the perverse cul-de-sac's one can end up in should one try to link individual workers with their individual contributions to economic value. Early twentieth-century writer John Spargo, in his *Applied Socialism: A Study of the Application of Socialist Principles to the State*, writes:

Any attempt to trace the share of the individual worker in the sum of associated production would be futile, so thoroughly socialized is the system of production. If we desired to give the individual worker the value of his labor-product, we could not do it. The nearest approximation to that possible under the circumstances would be an equal division among all the workers of the difference between the value of the raw materials used and the value of the finished product, charging the cost of depreciation against each in the same *pro rata* manner.[81]

Spargo wrote in an age in which the factory and its form of production had just achieved dominance in the United States – not without resistance, as we've seen in the previous chapter. It was clear to him that the greater the splintering of work processes within a firm, the more the exact contribution of each worker would be lost in a general wash of value production (the lion's share of it evidently flowing to the factory owner in the form of profit). His understanding, we argue, is even more relevant in our age of complex supply chains, the standardization and compartmentalization of production processes and the prevalence of service work. This global and intricate system of production doesn't lend itself easily to accounting for what each individual worker contributes in terms of value. Knowing how much value is produced by whom is really only possible on an aggregate level in industrial (and post-industrial) economies of our age; hence why labour theories of value have the greatest purchase in the abstract – pointing out the divergences between profit and wages within a firm, a sector or supply chain.[82]

Spargo was part of an early twentieth-century generation – alongside Karl Kautsky and others – debating fundamental questions about what post-capitalist remuneration might look like and how it might be different to wages in capitalist market-driven economies.[83] This can be uncomfortable territory for socialists who, quite rightly, see a money-saturated society – particularly finance capital – as precisely that which needs to be done away with.

Nonetheless, if we follow this line of enquiry, then the inadequacy of the current wages system as an infrastructure for equality and freedom becomes further apparent. Spargo sees the abolition of the wages system (and its various inequalities and abuses of power) as a logical step towards socialism. Crucially, this does not mean the abolition of money payments, however, but rather the abolition of the current *relationships* involved in wage payments.

> By the abolition of wages we mean the abolition of a social relation which is expressed through the form of wages, *the power of the owners of the means of production and exchange to exploit the producers of wealth* ... We are no more concerned to abolish the material *form* – wage payment – than we are

to abolish the material *things* – money, machinery and production goods – called capital.[84]

Spargo thus asks the question: If we agree that capitalism's system of wages has inadequate outcomes and involves undesirable relationships, but we accept that remuneration itself isn't the problem, then what would optimal *outcomes* be in a post-capitalist system of payments? His solution lies somewhere between the wages system and what today we would identify as a basic income for all:

> To secure as close an approximation as possible to an equal distribution of the products of labour among all the members of society is the conscious aim of the [socialist] State. Surely here we have the socialisation of wages, together with the abolition of the wage system as we know it today. Of course, the Socialist State might abolish the name 'wages' if it chose to do so, but it would be little likely to concern itself with such non-essentials.[85]

In this vision, what is important is not a 'fair day's wage for a fair day's work' but a greater equalization and mass distribution of wages, irrespective of individual contribution; post-capitalist incomes, in other words, are designed with societal *outcomes* in mind, rather than perceived rewards for specific work put in.

Gorz writes in a similar vein, but also projecting ahead into a future where our productive output has long outstripped the human hours and days required to carry it out; he sees a guaranteed income explicitly as the logical conclusion of the wage form's decline in relevance – as our more automated production could, in principle, produce all of life's necessities and pleasures for a fraction of the paid hours – meaning that a salary would have to become less attached to time.[86]

> Guaranteed income thus cannot be based on the 'value' of labour (that is, on what the social individual must consume in order to reproduce the labour power which s/he has expended doing waged work), nor seen as a reward for effort. Its essential function is to distribute to everyone the wealth created by society's productive forces *as a whole* and not by the sum of individual labours.[87]

Gorz's vision here clearly presumes a lot about the direction of our economies – and we shall see in the next chapter that we cannot rely on inherent properties of technological development to 'naturally' bring about a post-work world. However, if we *do* achieve shorter and shorter hours across the economy, whether by widespread automation or through the radical redistribution of work, we will need to rethink the distribution of income in a more collective sense, rather than as remuneration for individual hours put in.

Today's theorists of post-capitalist economics are also wrestling with these questions of appropriate post-wage systems.[88] A labour token system – a currency based on how many labour hours you've put in – has been suggested by cybernetic socialist Paul Cockshott amongst others.[89] This evidently won't suffice on its own, however, should we accept an ethic of equality and a distrust of bogus meritocratic principles. Most obviously we must consider the many people who simply don't have the physical ability to work as much as others, or those who have to carry out informal care not currently recognized as 'work'. In the absence of a post-work perspective, the system would be unjustly skewed in favour of those with the physical and time capacity to earn the tokens.[90] Without a baseline of resource allocation, distributed without reference to how much human effort has been put in, we risk simply substituting labour tokens for the wage, and we set ourselves on a maximal-work trajectory (given that more hours would equal more money, and thus greater incentive). Spargo, for his part, dismisses labour time as a new form of currency, criticizing Marx for tarrying with the idea,[91] and goes on to make the case for a post-capitalism wherein incomes become increasingly equalized, separate from productive output.[92] Others, such as Max Grünberg, see the task as one of shifting our accountancy to something that factors in alternative metrics beyond labour time, such as CO_2 emissions. 'Designing such a socialist unit of account', he writes, 'and deciding which qualities are to be represented by it, will be a central task for the society to come'.[93]

The passage from the wages system that is to be abolished to the system of 'from each according to their ability and to each according to their need' is a problem that Marx left us to figure out. The precise role and trajectory of a system of wages, and income in general, in a transition away from capitalist economies is difficult to perceive with clarity: no doubt debates will continue to rage. Perhaps, as we have argued here, we can begin to address this issue by pointing out how anachronistic and arbitrary the individualized wage system is, given the socialized nature of value production and the increasing potential for labour-saving technology to diminish the link between time-production-value. A different system, where wages are not the only means of income, offers itself as a way of recognizing this problem, while also serving to undermine the centrality of the wage as the only resource mechanism available. As a transitional model, then – either towards a civilization with *no* monetary remuneration (with needs met through a new form of exchange or provision) or one of *socialized* monetary distribution – a UBI is a useful and progressive step. It has the potential to act as what Ben Trott calls a *directional demand* pointing to the possibility of a different sort of world, the full realization of which – as part of a package of other demands – might foster a 'break with capitalist social relations'.[94]

It is possible to extend this insight – around the murky (but nonetheless very real) production of economic value – to work which doesn't even factor into accountancy within the formal labour market at all. How exactly does the value of wages feed back to those who work unpaid in the home, for example? Weeks addresses this and more in her arguments for basic income from a post-work perspective. She draws her arguments around value from the 'Wages for Housework' movement of the 1960s and 1970s – a movement which 'expanded not only what counts as the economy but who must be considered as part of the working class'.[95] Like Spargo, Weeks highlights how the wages system falls down as 'a system of both productive reward and income allocation'.[96] The key here is to recognize that

> The wage system, as the main instrument of income distribution, relies on a second institution, the privatised family, which serves as the primary locus for the reproductive labour, performed disproportionally by women, that is necessary to reproduce workers on a daily and generational basis.[97]

What Weeks calls the wage-and-family work system involves hiding this second workplace, which it relies on for its maintenance. The household maintenance and management required to reproduce and cultivate human beings in order that they grow into or can continue to perform their roles as workers – work disproportionately done by women – is the essential, but devalued foundation of the 'independent' world of wage-earners. Contemporary research on *conditional* welfare systems reveals a constant failure to recognize the work of social reproduction.[98] In one recent study, most mothers on conditional benefits 'felt that there was a singular emphasis on paid work and that it was their responsibility to negotiate the work-related requirements.'[99] An *unconditional* basic income is, from this perspective, a more encompassing and radical form of the wage that the Wages for Housework movement were calling for – albeit nominally diluted of the gender analysis facilitated by its focus on social reproduction.

For activist Selma James, it is precisely this dilution – and further disconnection from housework – that reduces the utility of a basic income. Despite agitating for unconditional cash payments in the 1970s ('WE DEMAND A GUARANTEED INCOME FOR WOMEN AND FOR MEN, WORKING OR NOT WORKING, MARRIED OR NOT'),[100] James pivots away from this idea in her later writings, in favour of payments specifically for carers. In 2009, she claims that a guaranteed income 'doesn't address the question of caring and it doesn't address the question of the forced labour and the position of power between women and men or between white people and people of colour or between Third World and industrial people. Wages for housework does. It says: "Pay attention to what people are doing."'[101] Similarly, in 2020, she claims that a care income would be 'light years ahead of a basic income (which hides the unwaged work women are already doing, leaves the market in charge, and may be used to abolish benefits)'.[102]

This change in position represents a move to recognize the work that caregivers do, and an effort to facilitate its ultimate redistribution, but it arguably ends up allowing the work ethic to reassert itself in a different form. A wage once again becomes a reward for labour performed or value created (in whatever form); the radical prospect of not needing to *earn* a living disappears from view, and individual reward continues to be allowed to dominate over equitable societal outcome. It is our view that, by redistributing more income away from profits and to members of the household workplace, basic income could do better than the wages system (including Wages for Housework) at recognizing this labour, without installing a new boss over the shoulder.

A social wage for the social factory

Weeks wants to go further, however, noting the wider, contemporary 'social factory' within which we now operate and arguing that this makes the case for basic income stronger. Her first argument is around the accumulated wealth that is simply a common inheritance that no one alive today is responsible for and yet is not equally distributed:

> As James Boggs argued in 1963, 'society must recognize that the magnificent productive tools of our day are the result of the accumulated labors of all of us and not the exclusive property of any group or class'. Employers make use of social infrastructures produced through collective efforts over generations, commons used and abused in the course of their appropriation as 'natural resources', technologies developed by governments, and capital accumulated through slavery and both settler and international forms of colonialism.[103]

Similar arguments around an expropriated common inheritance (with basic income functioning as a *re*appropriation of this) inform Guy Standing's arguments regarding our accumulated knowledge and technical know-how: the technology and level of development in all areas of life today are all down to the efforts of multiple generations now passed; the massive wealth built today is due to a common inherited thicket of incrementally grown knowledge that is often packaged and sold by private firms but was never entirely generated by them.[104]

> In thinking society afresh, we should reflect that the wealth of all of us is far more to do with the efforts, achievements and luck of those who came before us than what we do ourselves. Morally, we should all have a fair share of the collective wealth, since we cannot know whose ancestors contributed more or less.[105]

Most innovations are derived, with each link in the chain of history building off their sources, by chance or consciously. If we're at the top of the 'Lego castle' of invention, 'there is no justification for giving the person who lays the last brick the whole castle as a reward'.[106] And yet, consider how Big Tech has successfully commodified and ring-fenced the data commons of the web, despite its inventor, Tim Berners-Lee, explicitly not taking out a patent in order that it be a free resource.[107] In some cases, as leading economist Mariana Mazzucato has shown, apparent innovations of private capital are the direct products of public investment – this is the case with Apple's iPhone, with everything from the touch screen to the internet and GPS functions stemming from state-backed research.[108]

We can also think of all of the value we pour into ourselves (generated through 'investment' in skills and education) which is not always accounted for by our employers in the wage that they pay us – despite the fact that these qualifications are often a condition of acquiring the job. According to neoliberal economic theory, money spent on higher education is an investment that will reap higher wages later down the line – hence the justification for vast amounts of student debt. The problem with this is twofold: first, one's earnings prospects are only as good as the jobs available – and in places like the UK and US, things are in a rather sorry state, with precarious work, wage stagnation and a lack of collective voice endemic. Secondly, by this point, after decades of emphasis on employability, there is a market expectation for higher education qualifications – entailing a *saturation* of 'skilled' jobseekers, leading to overqualified applicants for many roles and a devaluation of degrees, starting with bachelors but now also spreading to masters and doctorates. All of the shadow work – or lifework – we discussed in the last chapter, which we often undertake simply to stay afloat: today very little of this 'investment' is captured and remunerated by the wages many of us receive.[109]

Here autonomist and post-autonomist arguments around the wide scale production of wealth in the 'social factory' dovetail with contemporary economic arguments around the providence and exploitation of socially produced wealth. How should the abundant social factory benefit the workers who work in it? Standing proposes a Commons Fund, whereby all rent accrued from our common resources/natural inheritance will be allocated to a central pot owned in common.[110] This Fund 'should invest to generate and preserve ecologically sustainable common wealth, and Commons Dividends should be paid out equally to all commoners'.[111] A basic income, in this way, speaks to this problem of wealth in common, redirecting some of the wealth back into a common form in a way that wages simply cannot.[112] It is in the same spirit that Gorz proposes going beyond the principle of 'to each according to his needs' and instead distributing 'to everyone the wealth created by society's productive forces *as a whole* and not by the sum of individual labours'.[113]

In short, the distribution of value in capitalist economies – through the narrow prism of hourly wages or monthly salaries – is anachronistic and does not accurately represent all of the work carried out – and arguably could never do so. Those who are employed see very little of the value they create – clearly this leads to terrible outcomes in terms of inequality, poverty and social domination: this is in line with standard Marxist accounts of exploitation in the waged workplace. But if we want to grasp all of the activity that goes into producing and reproducing society, then we have to go further and acknowledge that the wages system is nowhere near a suitable system of reward or maintenance. This is a different argument to the ones above around the coercive function of welfare regarding the labour market; this is an argument about distributive justice and wealth capture. This gives us a further reason, to argue, as Spargo did, that we should also be wary of limiting our demands to just 'a fair day's wage for a fair day's work': this risks leaving out huge swathes of the population who can't engage in paid work for whatever reason, or whose work is simply not recognized.

The important point to underline here is precisely *not* that we should find better and more fine-grained forms of accounting, in order for some hypothetical boss (be they capitalist or socialist) to be able to understand what they are 'getting' when we work for them. The point is to change our approach to accountancy altogether, recognizing the futility of accurate value-attribution at scale and for many activities, and to note the pernicious and damaging outcomes that capitalism's focus on employment has delivered. In place of such a myopic channel for resource allocation, post-work theorists argue that a basic income speaks to this more comprehensive view of activity – of *all* of the work and non-work activities carried out that we want to recognize and support (in the moral and material senses of the term).

We don't fit the wage: Dependency and interdependency

There is a broader point to be made here about dependency, independence and interdependency. In the previous chapter we noted the historical shift in the meaning and emphasis on *independence* as a value – driven by wage labourers' newfound rights – and how this came to help guard the wages system from criticisms and revolutionary disruption; to earn a wage was to be understood as to be autonomous. Another profound effect of such a shift was precisely its parallel impact on the meaning of *dependency*. 'As wage labour became increasingly normative – and increasingly definitive of independence – it was precisely those excluded from wage labour who appeared to personify dependency.'[114] These icons of dependency were initially the pauper, the slave, the colonial 'native', the racialized subject, but later came to include the housewife, disabled people and the welfare 'claimant'. Indeed, it should be noted, dependency is particularly stigmatized in certain cases: no one tends to accuse state-funded academic researchers, military defence contractors or companies benefiting from tax breaks of being dependents, even if they all rely on government cash. Instead, groups who require disciplining, excluding and exploiting according to the requirements of industry, profit and dominant material interests more broadly are placed into this category.

This stigmatization of certain categories of people – which is baked into our contemporary welfare systems – hinges on value judgements around independence, which in turn rely on paid work as their moral anchor. In contrast, and rejecting the work ethic's ideological baggage, we should admit that we are all interdependent, and that a public system of support should reflect that.[115] None of us come into this world independently, bring ourselves up, develop a set of characteristics or beliefs without others or come to learn about the world in a vacuum. A great many of us (at least 22 per cent in the UK, around 26 per cent in the US, 1.3 billion people worldwide) have a listed disability of one kind or another, many of which need regular medical and social support but all of which require specific navigation of social and/ or physical environments.[116] And of course, employment is not, in truth, independence at all – as labour movements of the past knew very well, and as our previous chapter showed. To 'earn a living' usually means being dependent on payment from a boss.

We should also take into account the fact that many of us live in steadily ageing societies: in the UK there are over 11 million people over the age of 65 (19 per cent of the population) and this is expected to rise to 22 per cent over the next decade.[117] In mid-2020 there were 1.7 million people aged 85 years and over, making up 2.5 per cent of the UK population; by mid-2045, this is projected to nearly double to 3.1 million, representing 4.3 per cent.[118] As we age, we become less able to carry out previously manageable workloads, our bodies require more care than they might have previously and thus we become more dependent on others to navigate the world.

The absolute independence of labouring for a wage 'is a myth perpetuated by disablism and driven by capitalism', writes Withers:[119] it obscures entire facets of human existence – whether within capitalist societies or beyond them.

> Chances are, disabled or not, you didn't grow all of your food. Chances are, you didn't build the car, bike, wheelchair, subway, shoes or bus that transports you. Chances are you didn't construct your home … The difference between the needs that many disabled people have and the needs of people who are not labelled as disabled is that non-disabled people have had their dependencies normalized.[120]

The simple concept of *interdependency*, when thought through to its conclusion, forces us to radically unravel dogmas and ideals of what we consider to be 'normal' 'independent' life, and thus also, as a subcategory, the standardized, 'independent' labourer too.[121]

Some corners of post-work thinking have begun to theorize what this means for coalition building. Xenomfeminism, for example, makes tentative and imperfect efforts to approach questions of disability and (a)normalcy 'laterally', via demands that can 'slice' through particular identities so as to build a universally enabling future.[122] Notably, it also draws upon broader tendencies within post- and more-than-human feminisms to view humanity as but one element in an ecology of interdependent forces. The xenofeminist manifesto repeatedly points to the entanglement of biotic and abiotic actors, for example, and is influenced by Haraway's propensity to view the world in terms of 'symbiotic assemblages' and 'knots of diverse intra-active relatings in dynamic complex systems'.[123]

Lennard Davis, meanwhile, theorizes the relationship between disability and interdependency via the concept of 'Dismodernism' – a perspective that finds a universalist basis in and through localized bodily identity. While it is too easy to say 'we're all disabled in some way', it is meaningful to expand on this claim by noting 'that we are all disabled by injustice and oppression of various kinds. We are all nonstandard, and it is under that standard that we should be able to found the dismodernist ethic'.[124] With the tools of disability theory, we can understand how useless and pernicious a standardized notion of human ability is – but also recognize how much it is reinforced by our work-welfare systems. 'Impairment is the rule, and normalcy is the fantasy', writes Davis, and yet work-first welfare systems presume normalcy and then ask those who deviate to prove their inadequacy.

These arguments are also pertinent today, post-Covid, for those who are long-term sick – with 'long Covid' or similar/adjacent illnesses.[125] Feminist disability writers such as Sami Schalk and Leah Lakshmi Piepzna-Samarasinha, speaking in the context of the pandemic and its aftermath, note that 'maybe our understanding of disability will change when the majority of people are dealing with PTSD and fatigue & such but the fact remains that the bodyminds of this country are being disabled & debilitated at varying rates & only a disability justice approach will work'.[126] Such a situation raises anew the old question as to what is to be done by, for, and about those who simply cannot work the hours necessary to earn a living, for whatever reason? The widespread mental health problems that symbolize the post-Covid period index a very difficult dilemma for capitalist labour markets and policymakers: that of *invisible* impairments, including things such as trauma that might remain undiagnosed but which are still very much in force in people's lives.[127] A 'right to work' here is clearly an inappropriate solution. Historian of class and poverty Jeremy Seabrook is particularly attentive to these factors:

> What we need is a system that recognises the plight of, for instance, the demotivated, the lost, the bewildered, the unhappy, the bereaved, the luckless and the less intelligent. It's not just 'people with disability'; there is a whole multitude of psychological reasons why people find it hard to interact: the frightened, the agoraphobic, the shut in, the timid [and so on].

There are such a range. Why are all of these [people] treated as if they were a kind of 'labour'?[128]

We've already noted that 'the wage don't fit' for our societies in general,[129] but it is also true that many of us don't fit the limited moulds imposed by the wage. How can a welfare system that is 'work-first' – geared towards moulding human material into labour-market ready tools – possibly deal with the nuances and shocks that set people on paths not amenable to easy adaptation to employment? Such factors are rarely acknowledged in today's welfare systems – and are buried by work ethic dogmas regarding the virtues of 'those that want to work' versus those who 'game the system'. Seabrook's many investigative projects into the lived experiences of working and non-working people in and around the fringes of our system produce the same message:

> Any such deeper interrogation of people's lives would reveal the shallowness of social cant about 'level playing fields', 'equality of access', 'fulfilling their potential', and all the other staples of vacuous political rhetoric.[130]

It is via Davis' suggestion of disablement as central that we can also glean what kind of principles underline a system of social protection that acknowledges this universal condition: 'The idea of a protected class in law [disabled people] now becomes less necessary since the protections offered to that class are offered to all.'[131] Basic income, we proffer, is a policy that could step towards this universalist, difference-accommodating world view. Although surely only part of the solution, UBI usefully dilutes independent/dependent relations by diminishing the uniqueness of waged work's income-generation capacity (hitherto seen as the main source of 'independence'), and with it the 'normal' wage-earning body; it brings into focus the interdependence of society by redistributing from those with 'independent' wealth to not just those labourers who create this wealth but also those who do not or cannot work in the same way at all.

Given the divide between employment-focused and beyond-employment approaches, there have been many debates between disability theorists and campaigners around what kind of proposals mark the best way forward. The positives and drawbacks of demands for cash or for services, for example, or for access to employment options, have provoked fierce argument.[132] While social model theorists and campaigners have claimed that income demands are akin to a 'begging bowl' and that they perpetuate a 'charity' approach to disability,[133] Withers argues forcefully that these criticisms are damaging for the cause as a whole – reinforcing the dominant work ethic's 'scrounger' stigmatization.[134] There is an important difference, they point out 'between private ... charity and the distribution of public resources to disabled people, or to anyone in need, in a community'.[135] In consonance with our arguments above about the needlessly zero-sum UBI versus UBS debate, Withers tries to steer away from income versus employment or services dichotomies:

> It is possible to be anti-capitalist while advocating for social assistance improvements. Many organisations find the room to fight for long-term social change while fighting to deal with the material emergencies in the communities they work in – first and foremost being the desperate need for money to buy food and rent. This struggle can be complementary to the overthrow of capitalism rather than contradictory to it.[136]

Steven Graby further develops the links between basic income and disability struggles. With others, such as Colin Barnes, Graby produces a vision of a future of work that balances the revaluation of certain kinds of activity as well as a rejection of a productivist ethic – leading ultimately to the notion of a basic income.[137] Graby sees the disability case for a basic income as both similar to the Wages for Housework argument (insofar as it is a demand that expands our distributive framework beyond the wage) and also as fundamentally distinct: a basic income here is not recognition of production for society's wealth and labour power (as with domestic work), but would be 'paying people for simply existing';[138] hence it must be given to all. For those who are perennially outside of the labour market, or struggling in the churn between low pay and no pay, such a non-work-first demand would be truly emancipatory.[139] As Trott notes, then, framing UBI as a directional demand 'means recognising its ultimately utopian character. It is a call to undo one of the most basic tenets of capitalist social relations, namely, that the ability to reproduce oneself should be conditional upon the selling of one's labour-power on the market. It is the articulation of a desire to re-appropriate social wealth'.[140]

Eleanor Rathbone, Johnnie Tillmon and the fight for universal welfare

In this section we want to pull out and reactivate two episodes from history that are particularly relevant to the struggle for a universal basic income. Both speak to the above arguments around work, welfare, interdependency and gender – and can teach us valuable lessons about the desirability of something like UBI, as well as the challenges of getting there.

Eleanor Rathbone was an important precursor to the later Wages for Housework movements, post-work thinkers such as Weeks, as well as today's campaigns for basic income.[141] She, like so many others in the late nineteenth century, was voicing discontent at the huge amount of care and charity work that many women were performing unpaid and unrecognized. Coalitions were formed between working-class and middle-class women to drive a more substantial and universal welfare agenda by occupying positions on local government and welfare boards. Around the period of 1908, with falling birth rates worrying government about the labour market's near and long-term future, Rathbone and her fellow activists had a unique opportunity to push through radical and game-changing policies around social reproduction and state support: chief amongst these was the idea of a no-strings-attached income for mothers and family caregivers as support for the work of raising the population.

Rathbone and the movements coalescing around the Women's Cooperative Guild argued that wages – mediated by men of course – were generally inadequate, as both a measure and in terms of payment levels, to capture all of the valuable work women carry out. Even the newly touted 'family wage' that men were earning was imprecise and bound to have gaps through which women were likely to fall. The movement began to campaign for a 'Family Endowment' or 'Mothers' Pension', sensing that just as state pensions for later life after work were being won, cash support could and should also be achieved for mothers: 'What is necessary for others is state aid for every child she gives birth to. If this is necessary for the aged, it is more so for the mother with the children [*sic*].'[142]

Rathbone's argument for substantial and long-standing cash benefits from the state was primarily from the perspective of freedom:

Family Endowment, by relieving women from their present complete dependence on the good will as well as the ability of their husbands to support them, would make them better able to regulate their own destinies in this respect.[143]

With cash 'of one's own', given to all women, a specific, positive form of independence (which is facilitated through public *interdependence*) can emerge. Rathbone's work in this regard formed the first pillar of what became known as the Welfare State in Britain. Beveridge himself wrote of her influence on the post-war settlement:

> The campaign for family allowances … received its greatest impetus in the publication twenty-four years ago of *The Disinherited Family* … In all the legislation of recent years … the greatest break with old tradition under the influence of a new idea is represented by the Family Allowance Act … what [Rathbone] had done was by any standard amazing.[144]

The fruit of Rathbone's campaigning – and her most enduring legacy – has been child benefit policy in the UK: where families are given cash payments for children within their care.[145] But her politics and writing clearly points beyond these outcomes.[146] As with other campaigners of the time, she was purposely vague when it came to what exactly a Mothers' Pension was actually for.[147] In her introductory essay to *The Disinherited Family*, Suzie Fleming writes:[148]

> The main ambiguity centred on whether this was to be a subsistence allowance for children paid to the mother, or a payment for the mother's work, or both … It was of course always easier to argue the case for the children, but women were also referring to their independent needs when they did so. Even when the demand was for a children's allowance only, it was recognised among women that money for the children paid to the mother would in fact mean money for the mother.[149]

Despite her name being attached inextricably to child benefits, and the strategic practicality of arguing the case on the grounds of childcare and health, Rathbone does at points argue for a wage for mothers explicitly.

It is clear that the hardships in the lot of the married mother and her aspirations after a securer and more honourable status … would not be fully met by a form of provision which merely secured to the children the bare minimum necessary for their maintenance and left the mother completely dependent, as she is now, on the will as well as the ability of her husband to support her.[150]

This aperture within the idea, which campaigners were keen to keep open, was astutely recognized by their critics in parliament at the time. They saw the slippery slope that the socializing of income was opening up:

It will be obvious that, despite reassuring assertions to the contrary, Family Endowment, if introduced on any scale that would adequately give effect to its objects, would, for good or evil, involve a violent revolution in the system whereby wages are at present determined. It is doubtless wise policy on the part of the advocates of a fundamental change to represent their panacea as an easily assimilated dose of tonic with which the patient is already familiar; but a wise patient should know what it is that is being prescribed.[151]

Indeed, worries about where such a radical policy could *lead* are instructive for debates around basic income today. In 1914, in the same climate of feminist radicalism, 'the first extensive experiment in a State wage for housework' had in fact already begun: 'separation allowances' were to be paid to wives of servicemen in the war – directly, every week through the Post Office.[152] From the start, there was a campaign for increases in the amounts paid, for the allowances to be paid to war widows too and for them to be paid even after the children of the families were over sixteen (where it initially wasn't). Fears began to mount around what this new financial capacity – and freedom – might mean for labour markets. The editor of *The Nation* wrote at the time:

if [the recipient wife] has enough to live on, she may choose some other mode of life; if she becomes a wage earner, her independence may make her more particular about her terms. A correspondent wrote to *The Times* in alarm the other day to say that if all soldiers' widows were to have pensions that would keep them, the upper classes would soon find themselves short of servants.[153]

Post-work authors would contend that the same worries about shortening the supply – and increasing the options – of human labour would be just as true today, under a basic income scheme. This 'stepping stone' model, where gains from the state are secured and then pressed further, should be kept in mind when weighing up the relative merits of an 'introductory' or 'modest' basic income. This would involve lower payment rates to all (less than enough to live on), but would be more politically feasible in the short term and can be *built* on once in play, just as Rathbone and her affiliates did with their demands. Weeks identifies this potential in the later Wages for Housework campaign too:

> Winning such a wage was not the final goal but only a step in its direction, and demanding that wage was not a simple claim but rather a complex practice. The demand for Wages for Housework was understood as first, a perspective, and second, as an organiser of power ... By their estimation the demand for wages was a way to empower a collective struggle to win the resources that could enable them to make further demands.[154]

Finally, Rathbone and her allies can teach us about the importance of – and necessity to maintain – the 'no strings attached' element to basic income. One of the main fears that critics have around the demand for wages for housework is that, as with other forms of wage labour, such a demand might bring the discipline of the boss down upon the houseworkers – recreating the same structures that exist in waged workplaces. This concern is central to post-work's desire for *unconditional* income streams and again, the case study of wartime separation allowances in 1914 is instructive. The UK government did indeed attempt to impose checks and balances on this cash:

> A circular sent out by the Home Secretary in December 1914, calling for the supervision of women drawing allowances by the charities at the time administering them, and suggesting that the police be called in to investigate any cases of child neglect, drunkness or misuse of the money so that allowances could be stopped for 'unfit' mothers, was met with a barrage of criticism and opposition.[155]

The discipline of work came knocking. The National Union of Women Workers, in response, wrote:

The Government in deciding to stop allowances in certain cases are adopting a principle which must be watched very closely, i.e. that employers of labour have a right to decide how their employees or their dependents shall spend their earnings. It may suit the Government to talk of grants and allowances, but our members, who are ordinary persons, prefer to speak of wages. They maintain that the State has no right to withhold wages when they have been earned, and these so-called allowances have been earned in all conscience.[156]

Future prime minister George Barnes would also raise this state interference in Parliament: 'We have had enough of fussy people pestering the working classes', he protested.[157] Ultimately, the government was forced to climb down and withdraw the circular – a victory brought about through organized pressure and coalition building that Rathbone's inheritors have duly noted and that basic income proponents must heed.[158] As Fleming writes, 'there is no guarantee that the achievement of *any* demand will be an unambiguous victory', but – if people are organized – we can create the conditions wherein it is more likely.[159]

Later in the century, American welfare rights activist Johnnie Tillmon would make similar arguments to Rathbone, bringing the notion of a guaranteed income for recognition of the work of mothers and housewives to the centre stage of public life.[160] Welfare, Tillmon would insist, is a women's issue.[161] She was the first chairperson of the National Welfare Rights Organization (NWRO), a multiracial coalition that came to include 25,000 members. The NWRO was a hub for welfare recipients – many of them mothers – to meet, organize, propose policy and work together to make best use of shared resources.[162] Tillmon had an astute analysis as to the social function of immiserating and stigmatizing welfare within capitalist labour markets:

Society needs women on welfare as 'examples' to let every woman, factory workers and housewife workers alike, know what will happen if she lets up, if she's laid off, if she tries to go it alone without a man.[163]

When the demographic receiving family benefits in the United States began to shift away from predominantly white women towards African American women in the 1960s, stigmatization ramped up, with politicians turning the screws of conditionality – placing greater requirements and rules on receipt of welfare income.[164] This is precisely the historical moment – identified earlier – in which neoconservative and neoliberal fears about the decline of traditional family life began to focus attacks on supposed 'welfare queens' and the push for more universal benefits from Black mothers in particular. Tillmon and the NWRO were, in effect, conservatism's worst nightmare: combining gender, racial and economic justice in a single campaign, right at the heart of the post-war welfare system and directly against the neoliberal-neocon counter-revolution that was gaining ground politically.

Crucial to our story is the way in which Tillmon and the NWRO went beyond the horizons of Rathbone, arguing for cash irrespective of paid *or unpaid* work carried out. The movement's core demand was a Guaranteed Adequate Income (GAI), irrespective of employment situation, gender or marital status – which, although still initially aimed at welfare recipients, pointed far beyond this cohort in its scope.[165] Welfare historian Premilla Nadasen explains the significance of such a move:

> The women in the Welfare Rights Movement had what I would call a radical Black feminist perspective on how to address the question of poverty because what they suggested is, 'We are not poor because we are single mothers [and] we are not poor because we are steeped in a culture of poverty … We are poor because we don't have enough money.' They really divorced that question of economic security from the question of employment.[166]

This captures what post-work theory finds interesting in basic income as an idea: by separating income from employment or from your status as a houseworker, you begin to move the conversation about value, about forms of work and about the distribution of resources away from the trap of a labour market-only focus.

By separating it from gender (giving universally) and giving it individually (independent of 'household' units) you, in Tillmon's words, 'eliminate sexism from welfare': now everyone is technically dependent, so no one is '*a* dependent'. More than this, such a distinction would *materially* open new ways to organize our living and working arrangements, including which work we are forced (or not) to carry out and which kind of household we want to operate. 'Not content to defend the right to stay at home', Sophie Lewis writes, Tillmon 'challenged the notion that staying at home or working are the only options available to women'.[167] Tillmon's tireless work would go on to greatly influence Martin Luther King Jr's welfare position – convincing him that a guaranteed income, or basic income, was necessary for justice and turning him into an advocate from then on.[168] It was also the NWRO's demand that would be mirrored by the programme announced by Nixon – against the advice of his conservative colleagues – in 1969, which we have discussed above.[169]

These case studies from the past century should inform a new politics of welfare today – and we should take note of their resonances for present struggles around income floors, unconditionality and building a coalition of forces to bring about change. Both Rathbone and Tillmon faced huge obstacles and yet maintained a determined – perhaps even utopian – march towards their goals. While some of Rathbone's policy legacy is still with us (in the form of child benefits), Tillmon's vision represents a buried, more radical future so nearly realized, at a high point of radical egalitarian campaigning and hope, where an income could be proposed as detached from marital status, gender or living situation, as well as work. That prospect was shut down and suppressed by the neocon-neoliberal culture that we have been living with since. Today, however, the spirit of the NWRO's work is being reignited with successful guaranteed income campaigns and pilots being run – designed by and involving Black mothers – in Jackson, Mississippi and Stockton, California.[170]

Rathbone and Tillmon's examples also inform us as to the desirable directionality of welfare reform. We can clearly see, from their examples, that the trajectory of their demands – scaling upwards in terms of emancipatory potential – was towards more universal, less conditional cash transfers and away from the punitive grip of both state services and patriarchal family relations. Both of these movements saw cash benefits as essential to women's emancipation, alongside (and not in contrast with or as replacements to) other services, and that this cash should be easily accessible, delivered as a right and to greater and greater constituencies (particularly as the traditional family model breaks apart). They 'cast their relation to the welfare system as active rather than passive, a matter of claiming rights rather than receiving charity'.[171]

Truly universal income allowances today would continue the work of the high point of the post-war welfare system that Rathbone had helped create and that Tillmon and others were trying to burst at the seams: a trajectory of experimentation and financial independence that conservative forces noticed very clearly, and worked diligently to avert.[172] This, we suggest, is a path beyond welfare as we have known it.

Finally, the radical feminist coalitions of both the early 1900s and the 1960s/1970s alike were sensitive to the ambiguities of demanding recognition through cash for women's work: it was both enabling and potentially a cage, if deployed incorrectly and without steering. Federici attempted nuance with regards to the Wages for Housework movement, reminding us that the demand was for wages for *housework* and not for *housewives* – thus usefully separating out the work from the identity of the worker.[173] But, as Weeks notes, 'regardless of the precise slogan many listeners equated them so that the longstanding association of domestic labour with womanhood was often confirmed rather than challenged by the discourse'.[174] This is why post-work thinkers see demands for welfare as best made in the form of a basic income for all: a successor to the family endowment and guaranteed annual income demands, which is justified in large part by the gendered unpaid work of the home but is not given as strict remuneration for it.

> Although the basic income demand does not directly contest the invisibility and gendering of domestic reproductive labour in the way that the slogan of Wages for Housework once could, neither does it invoke the potentially reified vocabularies of a Fordist gender regime.[175]

This is an income that values all work but doesn't prescribe it; it is given to everyone, but will benefit those who have suffered most from our economic system.

Conclusion

Through these historical detours, economic critiques and theoretical arguments, we can now see how some form of basic income might fit the post-work ethos we articulated in the introduction.

Redistribute

Most obviously, a basic income is a redistribution of cash away from the wealthy and towards those in middle and lower income groups. In the most progressive and detailed schemes out there, the substantial cost of a basic income is funded by increased taxation on wealth and on the highest incomes. This would represent a huge equalizing initiative – one that would dwarf the post-war, Keynes-Beveridge economic consensus. As such, and in line with what we know about such precedents, redistributing income on this scale would be a cultural and economic shift of huge significance and power.

As the wage becomes increasingly anachronistic as a way of redistributing value, a basic income or 'social income' as it might become known, would become a better way of sedimenting everyone's claim to some of the wealth socially produced. Crucially, an emancipatory effect of such universalism is to detach income from 'contribution' (in terms of the traditionally recognized form of effort): we could then distribute resources to all because it is the right thing to do and not according to hierarchies of labour undertaken.

Further, drawing on the prior discussion around common wealth, we can note that a basic income – or a Commons Dividend – distributed to all is a strong symbolic recognition, as much as anything, that we are interdependent upon the activities of others (including past generations) in complex and expansive ways. Further – and in a more bluntly pragmatic register – it creates a stable economic floor which can ground our interdependency – a common denominator – given that our 'ableness' for work is precarious and we will *all*, at some point, require resources outside of our ability to work.[176]

Revalue

Basic income would also be a force for the revaluation of forms of work beyond the wage relation – a direction that dovetails with the ambitions of the more radical edges of Marxism and critical thought. Recognizing the other activities that make society function via direct resources decentres the wage relation as the only recognized source of value; this again helps us untether from the cultural urgency of employment and allows for further questioning of the way value is measured and distributed, and which kinds of work are valued or not.

This applies to the unpaid work that is everywhere being carried out but also to paid jobs – which now will be scrutinized and evaluated from more powerful viewpoints than ever before. More radically, an unconditional basic income, not tied to any form of activity as such, would facilitate a revaluation of people simply for being, rather than being productive; it is effectively a commitment to upholding everybody's right to a decent living simply because that is the ethical thing to do and is in the vast majority of people's interest. Of course such a turn away from the work ethic as an organizing principle of society would be a significant gain for those who can never live up to its dictates, and those who justifiably do not *want* to live up to it. In the radical feminist journal *The Power of Women*, one author puts it as follows:

> I need the money – but not on condition I accept one of their definitions of me. I want it whether I define myself as a lesbian, single woman, wife, mother, widow, grandmother, old age pensioner. I don't want money for being old (and useless, according to them), nor do I want money, like the unsupported (we all are) mothers for being a mother (and temporarily useless), nor for being disabled – except that we are all of us all of those things; we are all useless, unsupported and disabled. And for that I want money.[177]

Reduce

Although not as directly related to the reduction of work as the demand for shorter hours, UBI's redistribution of income would also represent a huge redistribution of power in capitalist economies – which has indirect effects on demands around work itself. Our potted history of capitalism through the lens of unemployed life has demonstrated that the 'relations of production', to use Marxist terminology, cannot be properly understood if we don't take into account the threat of unemployment and the measures used to make life outside of waged work intolerable; in short, the relations of production, understood comprehensively, extend outside the office walls.[178] We therefore take our distance from Ciara Cremin's dictum that 'it is the transformation of work not welfare that needs to exercise our imagination;'[179] this chapter has instead been an argument in favour of rethinking both simultaneously. By blunting the threat of destitution, by defanging the coercive, workfare state, universal income schemes also blunt employers' threats of redundancy – one of the key weapons to enforce discipline in the workplace. By giving people a leg to stand on – more cognitive bandwidth – they can have renewed confidence *in the workplace*, including the confidence to demand a reduction in work or higher wages. In this sense, basic income redistributes *power* as well as cash, in order that bargaining for shorter hours can be held on more equal footings.

Just one piece of the puzzle

This chapter's arguments around basic income do not, of course, entail that we should abandon the 'hidden abode of work', that efforts shouldn't be made to change the nature of our paid labour or that workers shouldn't fight for better working conditions. As the previous chapter has shown, workplace struggle can lead to a better future of work for all. In the same vein, it's clear that a basic income would work best in tandem with other progressive policies – things such as rent controls and free public services – and as such we would argue that it is best put forward as part of a programme of change. However, as this chapter has demonstrated, post-work theorizing widens the scope of analysis, and draws on powerful historical precedents, to show the massive potential that a redistribution of income, through channels other than the wage, holds for moving us to a more free and equitable world.

Basic income represents an unavoidable question that post-work poses for progressives, socialists and liberals of all kinds: what vision of welfare is the least coercive, the least stigmatizing and the most enabling, or most facilitating of pathways to systems' change? The welfare state is clearly at a critical juncture: withered since its post-war apex, mangled back into a neo-Poor Law weapon against populations in and outside of work, reinforcing racist and constraining familial structures. The task at hand then is to force a total shift in direction: in Stuart Hall's metaphor of counter-hegemonic struggle, to 'shove it in the direction of a new culture'.[180] Unconditionality is a logical part of this new trajectory – beyond the welfare state as we know it, beyond the Beveridge Plan, the Fordist compromise and the Great Society; the emancipatory direction is to push these reforms above and beyond themselves.[181]

Much post-work politics recognizes the need for a coalition movement to make basic income happen and there is considerable hope in this regard: from activist networks, such as the 'UBI Labs' that have emerged around the UK, to city mayors in the US exploring basic income in their regions;[182] from think tanks modelling how a basic income could impact poverty rates[183] to the charities operating globally to provide direct cash transfers to various groups.[184] Basic income isn't likely to disappear as a policy or demand any time soon, and post-work theorists insist that it be defined (and deployed) in as emancipatory a form as possible.[185]

To this end, we hope that – as in the times of Rathbone and Tillmon – the labour movement and mass campaigning coalitions once again become deeply and actively concerned with welfare provision and expansion. By joining a coalition of workers and non workers, civil society organizations and politicians, key institutions can bring about the logical next step in welfare democratization.

3

Post-work politics with and beyond technologies

This chapter will consider post-work's relationship with technology – perhaps the most controversial area of its remit, as well as arguably the least developed. Looking first at discussions of technological unemployment, we will point to some of the ways in which discourses of 'full automation' have been framed in problematic and ultimately unnecessary ways. We also want to emphasize the role of technology within one gendered (and often forgotten) sphere of labour – that is, social reproduction: What do post-work proposals around automation miss when it comes to things like paid and unpaid care work, for example? What would a sufficient post-work position on this issue look like?

A substantial part of this chapter will thus be critical of existing post-work positions: if it is to be a robust and comprehensive way of approaching the future, post-work needs to acknowledge that there have indeed been lacunas, omissions and failings with regard to its approach to technology – and labour-saving technology in particular. We want to argue, however, that post-work can nevertheless offer useful conceptual and practical resources for the pursuit of more emancipatory societies. Towards this end, this chapter hopes to identify what makes post-work thinking on technology most useful: namely, it's *propositional* rather than *anticipatory* disposition. On our reading – and this is what many critics have missed – post-work techno-politics is at its most powerful when it *demands and struggles for* the technologies that best suit its purposes, rather than simply expecting and waiting for them to emerge. Indeed, there are plenty of good reasons to be sceptical of this latter scenario.

Automation enjoys a particularly high profile when it comes to current understandings of post-work, and it's not hard to see why – it's central to the playful sloganeering that has emerged around the position in the past decade. *Fully Automated Luxury Communism* (or FALC for short) is both the title of Aaron Bastani's first book and a long-standing meme (sometimes taking the modified form of 'fully automated luxury gay space communism'). The front cover of Nick Srnicek and Alex Williams's *Inventing the Future*, meanwhile, features the programmatic slogan 'Demand full automation!' And yet the significance of automation to contemporary post-work goes beyond this quest for maximum slogan density, as we can see if we briefly turn our attention to some of the post- and anti-work manifestos published at the *fin de millénaire* or in the opening years of the twenty-first century.

The paradigmatic post-work demand?

Take 'The Post-Work Manifesto' by Aronowitz et al., for example. First published in 1998, it argues against the work ethic and in favour of a shorter working day. Like Srnicek and Williams (and several others associated with post-work politics), it advocates for a guaranteed basic income as a means by which to support the transition away from dependency on waged employment. Crucially, it also points to the role of automation in reshaping labour practices and declares that 'the bare fact is that technological change can be used to displace all categories of workers, including managers and professionals'.[1] The example they use comes from engineering – particularly, the role of Computer-Aided Design in transforming (and shrinking) the drafting profession.

A year after this comes Krisis Group's 'Manifesto against Labour', which clearly shares many of the same concerns. It declares that, as a result of the development of microelectronics, 'More labour is rationalised away than can be reabsorbed by expansion of markets. As a logical consequence of rationalisation, electronic robotics replaces human energy or new communication technology makes labour superfluous.' This is framed not as something which must at all costs be resisted, but rather as a moment of political opportunity for a new, post-capitalist social order. 'Why', this manifesto asks, 'should we spend long hours in assembly shops or offices when machines of all kinds can do such "work"? Why should hundreds of human bodies get into a sweat when only a few harvesters can achieve the same result? Why should we busy our intellect with dull routine when computers can easily accomplish the objects?' In place of a culture dominated by the work ethic, Krisis Group proposes the automation of unsatisfying drudgery and gives 'priority to the restoration of a culture of leisure'.[2]

The twenty-first century sees the extension and intensification of these currents, with the 2010s in particular witnessing the emergence of a range of agenda-setting post-work texts. Williams and Srnicek's 'Manifesto for an Accelerationist Politics' from 2013 suggests that we should 'accelerate the process of technological evolution', because the existing infrastructure of productive forces can be seen as 'a springboard to launch towards post-capitalism'.[3] This idea is later developed in *Inventing the Future*, which explicitly argues for a fully automated economy. 'Using the latest technological developments', the authors declare,

> such an economy would liberate humanity from the drudgery of necessary labour while *simultaneously* producing increasing amounts of wealth. Without full automation, postcapitalist futures must necessarily choose between abundance at the expense of freedom (e.g. the productivism of Soviet Russia) or freedom at the expense of abundance (e.g. primitivism). With automation, by contrast, machines can increasingly produce the necessary goods and services, while also liberating humanity from the effort of producing them. For this reason, we argue that the tendencies towards automation and the replacement of human labour should be enthusiastically accelerated and targeted as a political project of the left.[4]

Let us point to one final example before we move on: FALC. This idea was articulated by Bastani in 2014, first in an eight-minute video for the leftist platform *Novara Media*,[5] and then in an article for *Vice* magazine.[6] In these short introductory materials, Bastani sets out an emphatically post-work position; he remarks that existing jobs seem increasingly likely to be eradicated through automation, that economic recovery no longer appears reliant upon job creation and that the left needs to develop an appropriate response to this situation. Such a response must not fall back on the unwarranted celebration of work but should instead seize the opportunities presented by technological transformation to ensure a drastically reduced working week, and thus more time for individual flourishing. Bastani fleshes out these ideas in 2019's *Fully Automated Luxury Communism: A Manifesto*, arguing that 'a new machine age […] will herald ever-greater technological unemployment as progressively more physical and cognitive labour is performed by machines, rather than humans'.[7] In his account, the modern transistor and integrated circuit are on course to unleash the same scale of social disruption as did the steam engine.

For the kinds of post-work thinkers mentioned above, automation (be that as a looming encroachment, an emancipatory political ambition or both) takes on particular significance. The kind of technology-centric future-casting in which they engage chimes nicely with that perennial preoccupation of policy makers and journalists alike – the idea of robots stealing 'our' jobs. It is perhaps no surprise, then, that an embrace of automation – whether as a proactive call or as an attempt to make a virtue out of necessity – has come to be viewed as perhaps *the* defining attribute of post-work discourse, more central even than the other two characteristics in our post-work triumvirate (namely, working time reduction and basic income). Given that, for many, the technologization of labour is post-work's flagship idea, it's worth pausing to consider some of the ways in which the analyses offered by such post-work thinkers can themselves fall down.

Automation, when?

In a highly rigorous and carefully evidenced argument about technology and the future of work, Aaron Benanav looks at the claim that, for good or ill, automation is on track to eradicate substantial amounts of human labour. According to his analysis, today's 'automation discourse' – a current that includes tech-centric post-work thinkers, and assorted other futurologists – can be seen as 'a response to a real trend unfolding across the world: there are simply too few jobs for too many people. This chronic labor underdemand is manifest in economic trends such as jobless recoveries, stagnant wages, and rampant job insecurity'.[8] However, he suggests that it would be misguided to chalk this up to the rise of the robots – not least because the countries with the most industrial manufacturing robots are *not* the ones with the fewest humans employed in industrial manufacturing. According to Benanav, 'What automation theorists describe as the result of rising technological dynamism is actually the consequence of worsening economic stagnation, following on decades of manufacturing overcapacity and underinvestment.' In other words, 'As economic growth decelerates, rates of job creation slow, and it is this, not technology-induced job destruction, that has depressed the global demand for labor'.[9]

Along similar lines, but with a broader focus, Jason Smith has identified a particularly stark and puzzling set of phenomena confronting the 'oncoming automation' prognoses. Despite the supposed acceleration of technological development – leading some commentators to declare a Second Machine Age or Fourth Industrial Revolution – we live in an era of vast stagnation, rock bottom productivity rates and flat-lining growth. What can help explain this divergence between rhetoric and reality? Smith argues that part of the answer to this apparent contradiction lies in the makeup of the economic hierarchy that has emerged in recent decades, and the *kinds* of technologies that have come with it.

Emblematic for Smith is the prominence of digital platforms both in terms of market capitalization and profitability. The kinds of 'investments' that platforms such as the FAANG group (Facebook/Meta, Amazon, Apple, Netflix and Google/Alphabet) tend to make do not typically involve new instruments of production, strictly speaking. Instead, huge sums of money go towards the absorption of competitors, in order to ensure increasingly monopolized market shares: 'Rather than incorporate and develop the technologies and innovations [that newly-obtained firms] have begun, all-powerful Silicon Valley megafirms like Apple and Alphabet buy them out in order to relegate them to their margins, preferring they die on the vine'.[10] This trend, as Smith notes, does not produce fertile ground for an industrial revolution – far from it.

This thesis fits neatly with other important literature on 'rentier capitalism'. Economists such as Guy Standing and Brett Christophers have shown in increasing detail that much of the contemporary global economy – but particularly the economies of the UK and United States – is dominated by different forms of rent extraction.[11] Whether it is housing, intellectual property, infrastructure, finance or natural resources – rent is the primary mode of income generation. Nowhere is this more obvious than in the 'Big Tech' sector. The FAANG platforms are built on the extraction of data at one end and the renting out of the use of this data (to advertisers, other companies, business analysts, etc.) at the other. There is, in fact, nothing 'tech' about Big Tech, in the sense of the kinds of productive innovation that capitalism has traditionally known. Instead, the technologies that drive the platform economy are mechanisms for keeping attention, capturing useful information from the user and provoking leisure consumption in other ways. While this rentier, monopolizing operating model remains profitable, there is simply no incentive for large-scale investment in labour-saving, productive technologies. As Smith puts it,

> Where the innovations of the second industrial revolution reshaped the coming [twentieth] century from top to bottom, transforming both the workplace and day-to-day life, the emblematic technologies of the current epoch, like the smartphone, represent little more than a "better" version – more compact and convenient, with more computing power – of already available devices. The primary innovation offered by the Apple iPhone is the layering into a single device of an array of by-now near-ancient technologies: a twenty first century Swiss Army knife, combining the telephone, personal computer, camera and video recorder in a single, pocket-sized, consumer good. As such examples suggest, the technologies characteristic of the past two decades – since the dotcom crash of 2000 – have been concentrated in entertainment and leisure: toys, not tools.[12]

To the extent that post-work politics assumes we're already hurtling towards an automated future, a lack of analysis as to the economic drivers of tech development today, and the actually existing devices being rolled out, can render it fundamentally flawed.

Further objections to the post-work demand for full automation concentrate on things like its focus and its scope. Although arguing forcefully for the importance of freedom from work, for example, and pushing against any idea that people should be compelled to sell their labour at all, the philosopher Martin Hägglund suggests that we must look beyond the reorganization of work, and change our fundamental conception of *value* if want a more just future. As Hägglund notes, capitalism understands wealth in terms of socially necessary labour time – that is, in terms of the total labour-time which is, on average, required to produce an output. If one worker labours for the same amount of time as another but produces fewer outputs during that period, they are seen as producing less social value, because value is the socially necessary abstract labour embodied in a commodity.

When productivity is increased via the introduction of technologies, that productivity can either be used to increase output or to reduce work time. Capitalist logic prefers the former because of the way in which it measures value (and seeks to increase it); the latter route would mean the company risks losing out on potential profits and also competitive position. One need only look at the immense growth in output that capitalism has produced without any significant reduction in labour time over the past century to recognize this. We might also note that the often significant investments required to introduce new technologies mean that capitalists have an incentive to ensure that they are maximally put to use. Rather than let expensive machines sit idle, bosses are driven to create more work to ensure that the technology is kept busy, and that its productive capacity is not allowed to go to waste.[13]

With this in mind, we can see that the overcoming of capitalism hinges on the '*revaluation of value*', which Hägglund views as central to any reorganization – or reduction – of wage work.[14] Crucially, this does leave scope for technologies to be put to emancipatory post-work ends – but only under radically different socioeconomic conditions, in which wealth is measured not in terms of socially necessary labour time but rather in terms of socially available *free time*. In Hägglund's words,

As long as our measure of wealth is socially necessary labour time, machine technologies cannot produce any value for us by virtue of their operations. The technologies that could make us wealthier – that could give us more time to lead our lives – are instead employed to exploit human labour even when such labour is not needed. If we measured our wealth in terms of socially available free time, however, machines *would* produce value for us by virtue of their own operations.[15]

Any post-work position on automation, this reading suggests, will fail to foster genuine transformations if not coupled with a radical rethinking of what constitutes value.

Some of post-work's other critics question the strategic value of focusing on automation, pointing to the fact that a politics of technologically facilitated working time reduction is not (in and of itself) a sufficient basis for a developed emancipatory politics. As Alain Badiou remarks in his response to *Inventing the Future,* while the shortening of the working week is a highly desirable proposal, 'post-capitalism must be defined not by the end of work, but by the end of private property'. He notes that 'Private property can be extended to all forms of automation' and that 'this appropriation of all forms of technology by the system of private property is at the heart of the matter', before going on to argue that any (re)invention of the future must start from this point, rather than from attempts to automate work:

> We can say that it's not a necessity that the key of social organisation lies in private property and monstrous inequalities. […] And we must affirm that we can organise limited experiences (for the moment) which demonstrate that it is not a necessity; that it is not true that forever private property and monstrous inequalities must be the law of the becoming of humanity.[16]

Of course, this can work both ways and we would do well to bear in mind Marx's claim that '"labour" (in today's economic sense) by its very nature is unfree, unhuman, unsocial activity, *determined* by private property and *creating* private property. Hence the abolition of private property will become a reality only when it is conceived as the abolition of "labour"'.[17] Thus, radical approaches to ownership in fact require, in turn, a marked attentiveness to the move beyond work. Nevertheless, Badiou's point is well taken. If post-work draws on the idea that 'capital can become labour',[18] then it would clearly be inadvisable for it to concentrate on labour *to the exclusion* of capital.

What work? Whose work?

It is also important to point out that post-work's treatment of automation has tended to privilege some forms of work over others. One critique levelled at post-work positions is that they rely on a fairly limited conception of what counts as work. Generally, post-work is accused of focusing on 'masculinized' forms of wage labour at the expense of 'feminized' varieties of paid and unpaid work; more specifically, it is accused of failing to account for social reproduction. 'Social reproduction' is the term used to describe the web of processes that together maintain and reproduce biological and social life – things like care work and housework, as well as species reproduction. By regenerating the workforce, both daily and generationally, social reproduction is the often-forgotten foundation of global capitalism – and post-work has been accused of continuing an inauspicious tradition of neglect. Let's pause to consider this claim in relation to the assorted manifestos we considered at the beginning of this chapter.

In 'The Post-Work Manifesto', the prevalent assumption is indeed that 'work' equals financially remunerated activity beyond the domestic sphere and that developments in automation and roboticization will contribute to the end of such activity. Social reproduction is largely sidelined, making a late appearance only in the final two pages of the forty-nine-page text. When it *is* discussed, it is in the context of 'public service' and 'massive care facilities',[19] suggesting that the primary concern here is waged work in the caring professions, rather than the organization of our home lives. This is despite the fact that the distribution of *unwaged* reproductive labour makes a significant contribution to global inequality.[20]

The 'Manifesto against Labour', meanwhile, is quite direct in its attempts to address social reproduction. Its response to the inequitable division of unwaged domestic labour is to propose a redistribution of this work across a wider section of the population – a redistribution facilitated by the emergence of a post-work society: 'When along with the abolition of labour the gender segregation will dissolve, these essential activities can be brought to the light of a conscious social (re)organisation beyond gender stereotypes.'[21] The problem with social reproduction, this analysis suggests, has less to do with the character of the activities involved than it does with their tendency to dominate the lives of particular individuals: 'The repressive character of the "chores" will dissolve as soon as people are no longer subsumed under what essentially constitutes their life.'[22] That this approach is unsatisfactory is, to our minds, reflected in the language used. We are told that 'gender segregation *will dissolve*', that the 'repressive character of the "chores" *will dissolve*'. The manifesto prioritizes the active refusal of that which it considers to be labour; once this terrain has been transformed, gendered forms of oppression will seemingly liquefy and evaporate. There is therefore no attempt to articulate a specifically feminist post-work struggle in the text, and unwaged reproductive labour within the family or the household is condemned to the sidelines.

Fifteen years separate the 'Post-Work' and accelerationist manifestos – a further decade and a half of feminist scholarship querying the exclusion of social reproduction (within and beyond the family) from critiques of work. Still, however, Srnicek and Williams make no reference to reproductive labour. It is left unclear in this text how issues such as unremunerated care and housework factor into their analysis, and whether or not their arguments for repurposing capitalism's technical infrastructure could in any way minimize the burdens of this work. A number of feminist commentators remarked upon this in the wake of the manifesto's publication. Caroline Bassett, Sarah Kember and Kate O'Riordan, for example, link accelerationism with '*automation fever*', with those fevered speculations concerning the putative end of work through automation, the robotization of everyday life, the augmentation and upgrading of humans, and the automation of knowledge and expertise, that are current these days'.[23] In their view, such speculations are 'often striking for the narrowness of their focus, addressing change in highly selective and divided areas', and guilty of uncritically reproducing perceived divisions between 'labour and leisure, production and reproduction'.[24]

For other feminist critics, any consideration of reproductive labour would immediately illuminate left accelerationism's terminal deficiencies. No matter who controls the technology, they argue, and under which conditions, care work cannot be automated away. As such, left accelerationism's fascination with the unleashed powers of technology could only hold emancipatory promise for those willing to forget about an entire domain of work.[25] These are serious and substantial critiques, and to their credit, Srnicek and Williams had already addressed some of them in *Inventing the Future*. They make mention of social reproduction when discussing their demand for full automation, acknowledging that some barriers to a fully automated economy may never be overcome. Aside from technical and economic hurdles, they point to 'the moral status we give to certain jobs, such as care work. These tasks, including the raising of children, are ones that many would argue must be carried out by human beings'.[26] Although it is encouraging to see reproductive labour being taken explicitly into account here, we should also remember that Srnicek and Williams bluntly define work as 'our jobs – or wage labour: the time and effort we sell to someone else in return for an income'.[27]

Fully Automated Luxury Communism runs into similar difficulties. As with the accelerationist manifesto, early efforts at advancing FALC were primarily concerned with transformations resulting from (or occurring within) the realm of wage labour. The activities of unwaged social reproduction are largely skimmed over, and it is clear that they are somewhat less central to the process of communist full automation being envisioned. Although feminists were (again) quick to remark upon this at the time, 2019's book-length extension of the project does little to address the issue. The use of industrial robots in manufacturing is the first piece of evidence Bastani uses to support his claim that we are reaching 'peak human', and he argues that 'it is in this sector where – just as with horses in the opening decades of the twentieth century – the old world will transition to the new more quickly than many imagine'.[28] The author touches briefly on logistics, retail and warehousing in his chapter on full automation, but (as with 'The Post-Work Manifesto') turns to care only in its final pages.

At this point, Bastani gestures to the Da Vinci robot used by surgeons and the role of AI in diagnostics – that is, to trends in the augmentation of highly skilled and highly paid professional labour, rather than to the automation of those low-pay, low-prestige caring tasks that make up the bulk of employment in the sector. Additionally, he doesn't consider the home as either a waged or unwaged workplace in his discussion of full automation – as such, it can hardly be said to be 'full' automation that's really at stake here. In some ways this is disappointing, but perhaps it would be better to understand this form of 'post-work' as being more akin to 'post-jobs' – a partial contribution, to be woven together with other strands of a post-work perspective to give a fuller picture of a more emancipatory future.

So far, we have considered a number of critiques of a certain notion of automation – specifically, a 'technological determinist' position that presupposes a soon-to-be actualized disruptive potential within novel labour-saving devices that are just around the corner, which will lead to a significant drop in demand for human labour. We've also seen how, even if we set aside this question as to the likelihood (or not) of automation, many post-work thinkers continue to prioritize wage work and obscure whole swathes of unwaged work (and workers) in this debate. How can a post-work advocate respond to these not inconsiderable problems and absences? Should, for example, the post-work project ultimately abandon its ambitions for technological augmentation? Is the promise of labour-saving technology, or indeed of progressive uses of tech full-stop, a red herring?

Automation as demand, not destiny

We don't think so. Consider the automation debate, as it is currently framed: it's important to recognize here the slippage, common to criticisms of post-work 'automation theorists', between two quite different positions. Critics such as Benanav and, to a lesser extent, Smith both take aim at what we might call 'the inevitability thesis' – wherein automation is positioned as destiny either in the near, medium- or long-term future. As we've seen, some of Bastani's premises in *Fully Automated Luxury Communism* easily fall into this category – and some of Gorz's texts betray this tendency also.[29] Equally, Srnicek and Williams could be seen as flirting with the inevitability thesis in *Inventing the Future*, especially in their claims that 'the emerging wave of automation will drastically change the composition of the labour market, and potentially lead to a significant reduction in demand for workers'.[30]

It is one thing, however, to suggest that machines and algorithms *are* coming for our jobs and quite another to argue that they *should* be coming for our jobs.

That is to say, the inevitability thesis must be counterposed to the *demand* for full automation in post-work literature. The slippage between inevitability and demand can be found between the lines in Benanav's argument, for instance. His *Automation and the Future of Work* is an argument that both dampens expectations regarding the capacity of capitalism to bring about an automated utopia, *and* recognizes that new utopian visions are necessary in order to resist capitalism's stagnant and malignant forces. Benanav says less, however, about the post-work (utopian) demands for the use of automation themselves – instead ending his text with a set of proposals around ownership and decommodification.

In this vein, it's important to remember that alongside expectations of inevitable automation, post-work authors *do* recognize the need for political struggle.[31] Bastani, for example, asks: 'How can the distance between the future we thought was on offer, and the disappointment of the present, be breached?'[32] In a recognition of capitalism's inability to deliver true abundance, he writes that 'in the absence of an appropriate politics [new technologies] will only lead to novel forms of profiteering'.[33] Equally, the whole thrust of Srnicek and Williams' book is to *invent* the future rather than merely to expect it. They are clear that, left to its own devices, the neoliberal status quo will ensure that '[m]isery remains more likely than luxury'.[34] This points to a tension, both in post-work discourses and also in those of its critics, between assessments of technological *capacity* and the necessity of a collective agential subject that can mobilize and direct this capacity towards emancipatory ends.

From our perspective, it makes little sense to characterize post-work as a mode of thought and action that ebbs and flows with the meagre technological progress that the current form of capitalism allows. Our aspirations for a world of less work should therefore not rest on assumptions of exponential growth and development – as they did for economists such as John Maynard Keynes. Famously, Keynes used historical growth rates for advanced capitalist nations to predict that by the year 2030 technological developments would usher in a fifteen-hour working week and the abolition of scarcity. The conspicuous omission from Keynes' optimism, as we noted in Chapter 1, is that the achievement of shorter working hours in the decades leading up to his prognosis was driven by political struggle, beginning in the workplace. During the inter-war and post-war periods, trade unions in the UK, Australia, the United States and elsewhere were all building on a decades-old movement for shorter working hours that began in the nineteenth century. The lesson for us today is that without significant *political* pressure, workplace technologies will never deliver on any nascent post-work promise. Labour-saving technologies – from the wheel to the printing press to the birth control pill to the microchip – have always held the promise of a life free from monotony and pain; the question is how to realize this potential.

Nevertheless, just because progress is far from inevitable does not mean that we should abandon the question of technology within our political projects. We maintain, in contrast, that it is crucial that the question of labour-saving technology is kept at the forefront of debates around the future of work. This is not to fetishize the corporate-led 'innovation' we see around us but rather to keep the potential for true labour-saving alternatives alive in our political and economic imaginaries. Only by maintaining a nuanced interest in the capacity of technology to further emancipatory ends can we steer a path between a crude anti-technological position (that risks invoking romantic longing for an impossible return to a pre-capitalist past) and a technological determinism bereft of an agential political project.[35] To return to Hägglund,

> Technology should *not* be seen as something that alienates us from a natural form of labor or a primitive communism […] There has never been a natural form or labor for spiritual beings and a primitive communism is neither possible nor desirable. The labor of spiritual beings is from the beginning a matter of technology (some form of tools), and the overcoming of capitalism requires the further development of technology rather than its rejection.[36]

Here, a post-work perspective dovetails with contemporary, materialist philosophies of mind. In this field of research, human beings and their cognitive worlds are not subjective islands amongst – and separated from – an objective world that they perceive around them. Rather, the world we brush up against and particularly the tools we use are part and parcel of our cognitive processes. For philosophers as diverse as Andy Clark and Donna Haraway, the question of technology is not extraneous to concerns about human life itself. We are, in Clark's words, 'natural born cyborgs' – finding ever new ways in which to couple with our environment for purposive ends.[37] This tech-human nexus also chimes with Lennard Davis' Dismodernist approach to subjectivity discussed in the previous chapter – wherein our varying degrees of abled-ness constitute a universal condition that can be augmented and modified by an array of external technological upgrades.[38] Being 'abled' is in this sense also a question of (socially determined) technology in the broadest sense:

> As the quadriplegic is incomplete without the motorized wheelchair and the controls manipulated by the mouth or tongue, so the citizen is incomplete without information technology, protective legislation, and globalized forms of securing order and peace.[39]

The question of technology, then, is not one of 'engaging' (or not) with tech as such but rather one of 'which technologies? Controlled by whom and to what ends?' We are always already technologically augmented, and this ensemble of human and machine is determined by wider socio-economic conditions.

At a gloss, capitalism, as a system of social relations geared towards the production of ever-increasing amounts of value in the form of profit, has facilitated the creation and innovation of a whole range of tools designed to speed up and efficiently trim the mechanisms of production of goods and services. This rapid expansion of productive potential has of course been an ambiguous development. As Moishe Postone notes, under capitalism, 'although the historical *possibility* that the mode of social labour could be enriching for everyone emerges, social labour has *actually* become impoverishing for the many'.[40] That capitalism will not deliver a technologically enhanced future of social emancipation on its own should not therefore dampen our ambitions to achieve it via different political projects and modes of production. The post-work challenge to contemporary readers is not to wait for the wave of robots to come and liberate us but rather to *demand* the repurposing of productive technologies towards the reduction of our necessary labours.

Social reproduction as sacred cow

What, then, of accusations surrounding the exclusion of social reproduction from post-work's technological imaginaries? In order to approach this question, we must first point to what post-work and its critics have in common. After all, if accelerationism, FALC and related twenty-first-century post-work projects exclude gendered reproductive labour from the field of transformation, so too do many of their feminist critics. That is to say, those who so rightly remark upon post-work's frequent failure to provide a robust political response to alleviating the burdens of reproductive labour tend similarly to position this labour as intractable – a problem that cannot be solved. Where does this reluctance to think about the technologized transformation of care work stem from?

The spectre of carebots looms large in anxieties about the automation of reproductive labour, and it's easy to see why. The global personal robotics market reached $21.5 billion in 2019, with one market intelligence firm suggesting that we can expect this to reach $51.5 billion by 2030.[41] Personal robots have a range of uses – security and physical assistance, for example – but the category predicted to witness the fastest growth over the next ten years is companion robots (robots designed to keep the user company, or to evoke a sense of companionship). These technologies have long been heralded for their potential within institutional care settings, with some arguing that they 'can be used as a social tool in the care home, to act as a new medium of communication between residents and staff, and therefore improve the quality of human caring relationships'.[42] Pertinently from our perspective, some of these devices have also been shown to reduce the likelihood of aggressive behaviour and confusion on the part of users – thereby also improving staff experience and reducing stress levels in the workplace.[43]

There has been a marked uptick of interest in these robots over the course of the past couple of years (partly because they are one potential application for Generative AI,[44] and partly because the 'pandemic has provided the ultimate use case for them').[45] Things like the furry robot seal Paro – which responds to stimuli with its own noises and movements – have been viewed as tools to reduce loneliness amongst the elderly during lockdowns, with one article in *Wired* noting that 'in a time when social distancing is exacerbating isolation, devices like Paro can be a psychological salve'.[46]

Where such tools start to generate discomfort, however, is at the point at which their use is imagined as culturally generalized. A world in which companionate care is *primarily* roboticized becomes a kind of nightmare of inauthentic feeling and lack of human connection, prompting activists such as Emily Kenway to ask the question: 'Do you want [your carer] to recognise your expression as sadness because it matches what their internal database says sadness looks like, but have no inner recognition of what that might actually feel like? Do you want to be *serviced*, or *cared for*? They're not the same thing.'[47] For all their affordances, such comments suggest, companion robots on their own can do little to positively reshape the landscape of care. In a similar vein, an early critique of FALC on the *Libcom* blog insists that care robots and other forms of automation 'are ill suited to accommodate the complex needs, requirement for human interaction and demands for dignity and agency which must [...] be a key part of the provision of care in any future communist society'.[48] Indeed, as this post would have it, technology in general can offer only very partial solutions when it comes to emancipatory leftist visions of the future of work, care and care work.

It's worth noting that, while this claim is advanced as part of a wider dismissal of post-work perspectives, such ideas are in fact unlikely to prove controversial in many post-work circles. Most of the thinkers we've been discussing in this chapter would probably agree with it, as reflected in the fact that they either *avoid* talking about automation in relation to social reproduction or explicitly state that the automation of care isn't the intention. The reader of 'Manifesto against Labour', for example, is told that much social reproduction cannot and should not be automated: 'What will not vanish [under a post-work society] are housekeeping and the care for people who became "invisible" under the conditions of the labour society, basically all those activities that were separated from "political economy" and stamped "female".'[49]

Such comments recall a recurring tension within post-work politics. Forms of work that are mainly (and problematically) associated with men are explicitly treated as labour that must be resisted, refused and, through automation, transcended. The responses to forms of work that have conventionally (and, again, problematically) been gendered as feminine, meanwhile, are rather less ambitious. For those currently performing it, it may be somewhat galling to hear that 'all those activities' that have been 'stamped female' will 'not vanish'. In the absence of efforts to articulate a transformative vision of reproductive labour (in terms of either social relations or technological advancement), the implication is that we must reconcile ourselves to work that cannot or should not be minimized. This might prompt us to ask, as Silvia Federici does of the slow-growing economy: Is this 'picture of a life built entirely around reproducing oneself and others not the life that women have always had? And are we not hearing again the same glorification of housework, which has traditionally served to justify its unpaid status [...]?'[50]

Our position is that it's unhelpful for both post-work positions *and* their feminist critiques to start from an assumption about the (normatively or practically) un-automatable character of housework and care work. As Emma Dowling notes, 'technology can assist with caring, giving those in need of support more autonomy, helping with tasks that are part of caring, e.g. lifting, or freeing up capacity and time.'[51] Reproductive labour should not become a sacred cow – a sphere of potential revaluation, and possibly redistribution, but never actual, meaningful *reduction*. And let's be frank: some elements of this labour *deserve* to be resisted and rejected. In the course of a conversation about FALC, James Butler raises a critical point about care and automation. Whereas Bastani largely dismisses the scope for the automation of social reproduction work, Butler – who is otherwise much more critical of the Luxury Communist project – points to the possible benefits of technologies of care: 'automation can do very, very good things like remove the kind of [...] simple basic caring functions that so many carers have to undertake and free them to be in other kinds of emotional relations.'[52] These are, very often, the kinds of relations that carers themselves find particularly rewarding – a source of intrinsic motivation that imbues their activities with a sense of meaning.[53]

Butler's comments point to one area where technologies could provide real social advantages – mitigating some of the more intense demands of 'high touch' care (tasks such as lifting and washing, which can be very hard on carer and cared for alike) to further enable 'high talk' care (the kind of potentially rewarding and stimulating work which, for some, comes closest to an idea of autonomous activity – social, intellectual and creative engagement).[54] This is not the obvious trajectory for care tech as it stands, however; indeed, as the rising popularity of companion robots indicates, many of the devices currently being developed target precisely the 'high talk' activities of communication and recreation. Drawing on his ethnographic research in Japanese care homes and robotics labs, James Wright sounds a note of caution about ongoing efforts to roll out these technologies, remarking that their introduction can in fact 'further reduce time and space for social contact' between care workers and the people they care for.[55] The way in which such devices are currently designed, developed and deployed, he suggests, points towards an 'emerging configuration in which human labour, far from being replaced by machines, instead becomes ever more in demand. Yet the nature of the work itself is increasingly deskilled, devalued, and alienated'.[56]

Rather than taking on the more burdensome elements of care work, then, the rapidly developing field of social robotics concentrates instead on managing the interactive and affective elements of the caring relation. And these developments are not limited to hospitals and care homes, either, given that the ambitions of technologists extend also to the domestic residence; care bots are increasingly being imagined as everyday consumer goods for use by the whole family. Companion robots are particularly interesting in this context because, despite being smart devices now marketed for household use, they are quite unlike domestic labour saving devices in the conventional sense of the term. The activities they perform (or claim to perform) are of a very different character to those we associate with manual housework. Indeed, mirroring their use in institutional settings, one could argue that the tasks they undertake represent that portion of domestic social reproduction which often feels *least* like work, given that they are primarily intended to provide interaction and social engagement. Processes involving emotional connection, thinking, companionship and so on make up that portion of reproductive labour (be it waged or unwaged) which, for many, edges closest to something like quality time – to the idea of autonomous and freely chosen activity.

This is to some extent in keeping with the wider dynamics of domestic technologies; as Leopoldina Fortunati puts it, 'To be able to prepare the food and clean the house, the job of looking after the children has been relegated to the TV set or the computer [...]. It is as if entertaining children by speaking to them and playing with them has been considered less urgent than getting the dinner ready or cleaning the windows.'[57] While that work which is most 'similar to material labor still tends to resist the process of machinization, it is the less tangible part (thinking, learning, communicating, amusing, educating and so on) that has been machinized'.[58] Thinking, learning, communicating, amusing, educating – these are the things that labour saving technologies have been supposed to free us *for,* not *from.* A strange inversion has taken place, then – one exemplified by companion robots, but also evident in better established domestic media technologies.

The TV and the tablet are undoubtedly important tools in terms of facilitating the work of childcare, and it would be unhelpful to dismiss them. However, parents' and carers' attitudes towards them would perhaps be qualitatively different if they weren't forced to rely on such devices to keep the kids occupied while they completed paid work or performed routine domestic tasks (sorting the washing, cleaning the high chair, emptying the nappy bin and so on). If wage labour and intrafamilial reproductive labour didn't occupy so much of people's time, energy and headspace, we argue, their experience and usage of these technologies would likely be very different. As it is, however, we have to reckon with the fact that instead of automating drudgery, we've inadvertently automated quality time; it is the high talk forms of care work that seem to be increasingly delegated to machines.[59]

The way forward is not simply a matter of encouraging the emergence of different and better forms of devices – although that is clearly important – but also of transforming both the tech and the context in which it is shaped, designed and operated (and which it subsequently comes to influence in its turn). We need to heed the guidance of Science and Technology Studies, which has long sought to steer us away from the idea of Technology as a 'metaphysically inflated phantom' and towards approaches that would ground our analysis in specific devices, systems and user behaviours.[60] After all, as Kenway notes in her meticulously even-handed treatment of the topic, 'caretech is wide and varied'.[61] The 'pull cords in disabled toilets that trigger an alarm, the hospital beds that can be raised and lowered, electrified wheelchairs and alarmed pill boxes' are all technologies of social reproduction with profound potential to influence the experiences of everybody involved in the caring process.[62] We must resist the temptation to uncritically extrapolate, grounding our discussions instead in particular examples of caretech before entering into any speculation about generalizable claims that can be advanced on the basis of these specific case studies.

As a society, then, we should not take the un-automatable quality of reproductive labour to be axiomatic, or enshrine it as a welcome inevitability. Its transformation should be as important for high-tech post-work imaginaries as that of any other form of labour. Butler finishes his discussion of care and FALC by adding, crucially, that 'to deal with care requires social change, it requires social revolution'.[63] This is quite true. While we recognize that robotization should not be lauded incautiously, a critical technopolitics of social reproduction, when combined with a commitment to rethinking all aspects of the current arrangement of reproductive labour, could provide real benefits. The idea that an emphasis on emancipatory automation *necessarily* excludes social reproduction should, we argue, be rejected. With Dowling, we would suggest that 'it makes sense to be open to the possibility that technologies can help us to care better, while remaining critical of the ways that technologies are used at the moment'[64] – adding, furthermore, that we should not rule out *reducing* those forms of care work that are not found to function in the best interests of all the people involved.

Conclusion: With and beyond technologies

A more general response to the deficiencies of post-work's technological vision is to note that, despite its high profile, the call for automation is far from the be all and end all of post-work politics. Amongst critics, post-work is often construed as inseparable from (if not identical to) the call for automated production. This characterization, however, can only hold if one is willing to overlook other tendencies and to exclude a number of important thinkers from the post-work canon. Take the work of Kathi Weeks, for example. Published in 2011, *The Problem with Work: Feminism, Marxism, Antiwork Politics and Postwork Imaginaries* popularized the notion of post-work thinking in this century and has had a substantial influence ever since.[65] The impact of Weeks' text would seem to position it at the very heart of contemporary post-work politics. It calls for a shorter working week and a universal basic income – two key elements of the post-work triumvirate – but talk of full automation (and, largely, of technology in general) is absent from the text. One can thus only frame post-work as a perspective wedded to technological acceleration if one wilfully ignores Weeks' influence here.

One could equally point to David Frayne's writings to demonstrate that automation prognostications need not necessarily inform post-work writing. As we have argued throughout this book, while post-work thinkers tend to hold certain key ideas in common, they in no way express a unified perspective or position. We would, for example, tentatively include Benanav's *critique* of automation discourse beneath the banner of post-work, given not only that it argues that the current global under-supply of work demands a proactive response from the left, but also that his final chapter imagines what a world with radically less work could look like, and what we should be collectively striving for.[66] As we've seen, for all their faults, none of the post-work authors mentioned in this chapter would consciously accept that a reduction in waged work or the erosion of the work ethic will come easily, or without labour struggles – even if they might occasionally lapse into talking about the automation of work as if it is a *fait accompli*. Indeed, the very purpose of their texts is often to reignite conversations around working time – and technology – with a view to fostering political mobilization around desirable futures.

Post-work politics has understandably been associated with the widespread expectation of mass, or even full, automation, and with the limitations such a politics involves. While there is undoubtedly some truth to these claims, we have seen that the reality is more complex. Post-work discourse often balances tensions between an attentiveness to the *capacity* to automate away our labours and *demands* for the repurposing of these technologies away from the ends of profit and value extraction. This points to a crucial distinction that we must make between declaring the *inevitability* of an automated future and the *demand for one*. It is in embodying a propositional, rather than reactive, disposition that post-work can remain a useful and relevant vector of thought, distinct from mere techno-futurism and nostalgic anti-modernism.

In their eagerness to bring forth such a future, post-work advocates certainly have resources to draw on from a rich history of progressive engagements with technology. There is much to learn, for example, from the ambitious Cybersyn project, where cybernetic experts worked with the socialist government in Chile in the early 1970s to create an economic planning system that prefigured the internet.[67] Equally, democratic tech innovation in socialist Yugoslavia during the 1980s promised to make computational power available to all through a DIY movement.[68] In the UK, the famous 'Lucas Plan' is perhaps the best known example of democratic tech development: in 1976 workers at Lucas Aerospace went on strike and agreed amongst themselves to start producing socially useful tech and not the weaponry they were used to.[69]

With today's computational power and AI capabilities, such examples of innovation and prototype planning models might be taken up once again (and arguably more easily actualized).[70] Most obviously, we could develop economic systems beyond the chaos of markets – systems robust enough to mitigate some of the worst effects of catastrophic climate change. Theorists such as Max Grünberg are making original theoretical contributions around how to harness the predictive analytics of forecasting systems currently used in firms such as Amazon towards the ends of a socially useful distribution of goods.[71] Others, such as Benanav, are also interested in this kind of tech, but want to flesh out where the democratic, decision-making joints could and should lie once we have neutered the market's 'invisible' choice infrastructure.[72]

Further, today's post-work writers on technology and their fellow travellers, such as Holly Jean Buck and Benjamin Bratton, argue for the *necessity* of leaning into (rather than away from) technological augmentation. Managing the planet's balance of resources, carbon stocks and flows and assessing the complex climate impacts of various policies will likely require extensive sensing, forecasting and correcting infrastructure. These deployments of technology are not just intriguing science-fictional concepts but will likely be necessary tools for our future survival: opting out isn't an option.[73] These case studies are key reference points for post-work thinkers such as Srnicek and Williams as they reactivate alternative pasts and futures of technological innovation – moments where desire for a post-capitalist society (or simply for a liveable planet) fuses with the computational capacity that might help deliver it. What would a Cybersyn-like production system entail if a post-work society was the end goal? What kind of domestic appliances could today's manufacturing workers make, instead of their current output? What does a democratic planning system look like if collectives of different scales could decide on how long they work, how much income they should get and what they should produce? How, in short, can technology help us *reduce, revalue and redistribute* work for all?

This chapter has a number of core messages. We've sought to underline that not everything assumed to be a check on the automation imaginary is actually a hard and fast limit (as we have suggested in our approach to technologies of care). We have also emphasized that not all advocates of post-work concern themselves with automation, and argued that many of those that do may still provide us with useful conceptual resources. It would be an error to reduce post-work to a blunt agitation for automation, or indeed to any single concrete demand; at its heart, post-work is not a self-contained programme of neatly numbered steps but a radical orientation towards freedom. As Srnicek and Williams put it, the ambition here is to build 'an alternative politics – one that seeks to take back control over our future and to foster the ambition for a world more modern than capitalism will allow'.[74] It is with this in mind that we proceed to the second section of this book. If, as we have argued, *freedom* is what is most central to post-work, then we need to give some consideration to what this freedom might consist of. This shall be our aim in the next chapter.

4

Freedom and nothing else

What is freedom? This is the kind of question that could occupy – and has occupied – poets and philosophers for a lifetime, and is surely beyond the scope of a short, non-specialist book such as this. However, if we are to advance the claim (as we did in Chapter 3) that a certain kind of post-work position is best understood as a radical orientation towards freedom – one pursued via a specific engagement with labour – then it is beholden upon us to offer up at least *some* attempt at explanation and qualification. In this chapter, we will seek to do just that, demonstrating that thinkers identified with what is sometimes called a 'Promethean' post-work tendency do indeed address themselves to the issue of freedom, sometimes in a direct and explicit manner.

In the course of our argument, we will explore different ideas of freedom. We start with Marx's notion of the realms of freedom and necessity, which we take to be key to post-work political frameworks, before considering how the meaning of freedom (like that of dependency) has changed over time. We then draw a distinction between two varieties of post-work utopia: one (which we call the 'single-realm utopia') in which all labour is to be transformed into play, and thus all necessity into freedom; and the other (the 'dual-realm utopia') in which labour and play, necessity and freedom, continue to co-exist in a state of ongoing friction. While we ultimately find dual-realm utopias to be more helpful for post-work thinking, we also argue that the persistence of necessity should not limit our capacity to envision a better world. Hence, we argue for a (seemingly oxymoronic) kind of *Promethean necessity* – one grounded in the importance of balancing the inevitability of a realm of necessity with a refusal to dictate in advance what the contents of such a realm might look like.

In short, we make the case for a post-work project that (while acknowledging the intransigence of necessity) insists that nothing in particular be ceded a priori to this realm. Rather than imagining that freedom and necessity can be collapsed, then, with all work transformed into play, we encourage post-work theorists to acknowledge the recalcitrance of work and the obstinacy of necessity *without* mistaking these for the immutability of the world as it stands.

Necessity and freedom

All of us face constraints in our daily lives; such constraints are an inevitable consequence of being alive. As Martin Hägglund notes, 'the need of the living organism to sustain itself […] minimally defines what Marx calls the realm of necessity. Because we are living beings, we must *work* to maintain ourselves.'[1] But the realm of necessity does not occupy our entire existence. As a species, we are capable of more than eating, sleeping and defecating, and we can meaningfully engage in activities that are not immediately implicated in our biological survival. In Marx's words, 'the realm of freedom actually begins only where labour which is determined by necessity and mundane considerations ceases'.[2] While never entirely unfettered, humans have a distinctive capacity to exist beyond our biological needs and to think beyond the immediate data obtained by our sense organs.

As a result, our lives can become something of an open question. What should we do? How should we be? The capacity of individuals to formulate their own answers to these questions will be constrained or enabled by their specific circumstances; the ability to exercise freedom is, as we shall see at various points throughout this chapter, unevenly distributed. It is premised upon a certain degree of physical safety and security; there can be little in the way of human flourishing and freedom when one lives under the shadow of dire necessity. Conditions of famine and genocide will obviously substantially determine what people are able to do with their lives. As Marx's comments make clear, it is only in those activities that go *beyond* bare survival that we find the basis of the realm of freedom. At the most general level, however, and under ideal (or at least, sufficient) conditions, humans *do* have the capacity to act upon ourselves and our worlds, and also to reflect upon our actions both individually and collectively. A project of imagining abundant futures can start from here, even as it acknowledges the practical barriers to freedom marring so many people's lives today.

In the main, Hägglund argues, the less time we must devote to activities that are merely a means to an end, the more time we can devote to activities that we experience as *ends in themselves*. Our aim should be to 'decrease our realm of necessity (the time required to keep ourselves alive) and increase our realm of freedom (the time available for activities that we count as ends in themselves, which includes time for engaging the *question* of what matters to us and which activities *should* count as ends in themselves)'.[3] It is with this in mind that we turn to the issue of work and to the conditions surrounding labour. Have human freedom and human necessity always been understood in broadly the same terms, or have changes in productive technologies and the organization of work had a transformative effect here? Does minimizing our realm of necessity mean the same thing today as it did before the Industrial Revolution, or does it make sense to talk about a specifically capitalist idea of freedom? In order to address these questions, we shall first return to the topic of dependency and briefly consider its changing meanings in relation to wage work.

In Europe in the Middle Ages, many people made ends meet by engaging in subsistence farming – that is, by producing at least some food for their own consumption. In addition to often being allocated a plot of land by their masters in exchange for their labour, the peasantry also had use of the commons. These were spaces of shared resources, owned by no one. In other words, as the name suggests, 'the commons' were resources that – rather than being privately owned – were *held in common*. Examples include meadows, lakes, forests and wild pastures – resources that the whole community had rights of access to.[4] As Simon Fairlie puts it, the 'king, or the Lord of the Manor, might have owned an estate in one sense of the word, but the peasant enjoyed all sorts of […] rights which enabled him or her to graze stock, cut wood or peat, draw water or grow crops, on various plots of land at specified times of year'.[5]

Many people were dependent upon certain shared resources, and upon land over which they did not have exclusive rights or ownership. Indeed, as

Fairlie argues, 'Private ownership of land, and in particular absolute private ownership, is a modern idea, only a few hundred years old: "The idea that one man could possess all rights to one stretch of land to the exclusion of everybody else" was outside the comprehension of most [...] medieval peasants'.[6] Hence, despite the fact that 'serfdom was an enormous burden',[7] in which people were bound to their landlords and dominated by their masters, people could often enjoy a measure of relative autonomy. Before the transition to capitalism, a substantial portion of the population had access to the means of subsistence. They could use their plots of land and the resources of the commons to support themselves and meet many of their own basic needs.

Today, our experience of the material resources of the commons is likely to be much more limited. We still have public access to things like woodland, parkland and so on; we have rights to the air we breathe (although air quality differs substantially depending on where one lives, which is in turn shaped by structural factors such as class and race); and we also have an emerging sense of the *digital* commons, which draws precisely – if imperfectly – on this idea of making resources available and accessible to everyone. But what we certainly do *not* have is a common entitlement to land of the sort that we've been outlining here. We do not have free access to the means of subsistence, and hardly anybody in the core Anglosphere could claim to be self-sufficient in any meaningful sense of the word. (Londoners would be unlikely to get away with cutting down trees for firewood in Hyde Park, for example, or letting flocks graze on Hampstead Heath.)

This brief comparison stresses what will already be fairly obvious to most of us – that there have been substantial changes in the ways in which labour and subsistence have been organized over the preceding centuries. Some of these changes can be traced back to the mid-fifteenth century – the point at which the Middle Ages is seen to shift towards the early modern period, and the beginnings of the transition to capitalism. At this time, people were being increasingly expropriated from the land; rents were increased, tenure contracts were annulled, peasants were evicted and so on.[8] Around the same period, access to the commons was starting to be curtailed. The open field system and communal pastures came under attack from wealthy landowners who wanted to privatize their use, and who earmarked lands for their own sheep to graze on, preventing local residents from farming there. Communally used land was fenced in, rights of access were restricted or eliminated, and greater control was passed to wealthy farmers and landlords. Resources that were once held in common, in other words, were stolen away and newly held in private (a process mirrored and intensified by the operations of colonialism and by the seizure of lands from indigenous peoples across the globe). This continued up until the eighteenth century, and illustrates why, as we've seen, any emancipatory politics must be concerned with issues of property and ownership *as well* as with the organization of labour.[9]

In some ways, these enclosures can be thought to have entailed certain benefits. The changes served to boost productivity, for example, and eased the perpetual anxiety of subsistence farming, in which survival was to some extent tethered to both luck and the land. In this sense, the enclosures could be seen as contributing to the minimization of the collective realm of necessity. Importantly, however, they also stripped the peasantry of access to the means of subsistence, and therefore played a vital role in an extended process of proletarianization. Via this process, a mass of people – no longer able to be self-reliant – became totally dependent upon wage labour for their survival. Without a plot of land or access to the commons, the only resource they had at their disposal was their labour power (increasingly in demand within Europe's burgeoning industrial centres), which they were then forced to sell. As we saw in Chapter 2, this process was twinned with the strategy of state authorities of turning 'unemployed' life into an intolerable, dangerous and punishable existence: a constant coercion for those who previously had access to survival via other means. The emergence of capitalist property and labour relations is not a case of decreasing the realm of necessity and increasing the realm of freedom, then, so much as the exchange of one form of necessity for a different (arguably intensified) form.

What we are (admittedly very loosely) sketching out here is a profound shift in the ways in which many people's daily lives were lived – one which increasingly took hold between the sixteenth and eighteenth centuries. Certainly, people were less immediately at risk in the case of crops failing – but, without access to the means of reproducing themselves, they were totally dependent upon finding and keeping remunerated employment. As William

Clare Roberts puts it, industrialization and the development of the collective forces of production rendered labourers 'ever more dependent upon capital' by eradicating their 'independent capacity to make goods'.[10] This marked a significant change from earlier understandings of the entanglement of individuals and households with the labour required for survival; that is to say, it represented a distinct change in people's experiences of the realm of necessity. While people had been, and would continue to be, dependent on each other in the sense of relying on familial and community support networks, a new, exploitative, vastly asymmetrical dependency had also been installed.

Capitalist 'freedom'

And yet, from some perspectives, the transition to capitalism represented an *extension* of freedom, not just in the sense of decreasing direct reliance on the land but also in the sense of introducing new possibilities for individual agency. Hence, for Moishe Postone, capitalism can be seen as both an enriching and impoverishing historical phenomenon.[11] The forces of urbanization, industrialization and proletarianization led to a partial erosion of patriarchal control and hierarchical authority, for example. As Louise A. Tilly and Joan W. Scott put it, 'parents with no property were unable to prevent a child's marriage, since wage earning gave him or her a certain degree of economic independence. Moreover, for migrants to cities at least, there was greater autonomy in the choice of a spouse than had been possible in village communities'.[12] With the rise of a propertyless waged workforce, inheritance became less powerful as a means via which to solidify bonds or ensure compliance with patriarchal will, and productive property (or the promise of such property) ceased to be as ubiquitous as a tool of enforcement. This might strike us as an extension of personal liberty; individuals were freed somewhat from reliance upon family and state.

As we have seen, however, this freedom within one domain was thoroughly enmeshed with the intensification of necessity in another. With this in mind, it is interesting to note that much of the discourse surrounding wage labour from the time of the Industrial Revolution sought to sideline, downplay, or ignore the different kinds of vulnerability and unfreedom ushered in by proletarianization. As we noted in Chapter 2's engagement with Nancy Fraser, the new industrial socio-economic setup redefined what freedom and 'independence' meant:

> When white workingmen demanded civil and electoral rights, they claimed to be independent. This entailed reinterpreting the meaning of wage labour so as to divest it of its association with dependency. That in turn required a shift in focus – from the experience or means of labour (e.g., ownership of tools or land, control of skills, and the organization of work) to its remuneration and how that was spent.[13]

Importantly, as our discussion articulated, the converse of this independence for some was a recoding of many others as dependent.[14] To work for pay was now to be free, and to be outside of this relationship with capital was to be both unfree and potentially even a burden on others.

Thus, as Livia Gershon notes, 'the pride we take in working for a paycheck is really new. Just 150 years ago, when people talked about the shame of dependency, they were referring to the reality of being forced to hold a job'.[15] Capitalist freedom might therefore be understood as *dependency disavowed*. It is the economic freedom to 'voluntarily' exchange labour, capital and goods, which is in fact something over which one has precious little choice or control. These are the relations which come to masquerade as self-reliance under capitalism – necessity posturing as freedom. Callum Cant expresses this idea particularly forcefully when he restates Marx's position on the matter:

> Yes, workers are 'free' – they are 'free' to sell their labour-power to an employer, and they are 'free' of any ability to survive if they don't get paid. […] In reality workers have no choice: they have to sell their labour-power in order to get a wage and buy the stuff, the commodities, they need to survive. You work and are exploited to make your boss rich, or you starve – some 'freedom'.[16]

As Chapter 1 indicated, time spent in waged work can thus be seen as *unfree* time. This is perhaps most obviously the case because employers control the worker during their time on the job, dictating what they must and must not do, along with the rhythms of their labour. As Roberts remarks, the 'workplace relation between capitalists and wage labourers is one of force because it is one in which the boss directly controls and uses the labourers in order to generate a surplus excessive of the aim of labour itself'.[17] Similarly, for Kathi Weeks, a 'relation of command and obedience, the right of the employer to direct his or her employees that is granted by the contract, is not so much the byproduct of exploitation as its very precondition'.[18] Having a job *means* being under the scrutiny and authority of an employer, and labour under capitalism therefore necessarily represents a realm of hierarchy and domination.

Not all the dominations of work are interpersonal in nature, of course. Wage work is not entangled with the realm of necessity simply as a result of bad bosses or bad managers. Rather, as we have seen in our brief account of capitalist freedom as disavowed dependency, work under capitalism is also a matter of *impersonal* domination: the imperative to exchange our time and energy for money to purchase goods for our survival is experienced as an automatic mechanism – a system without any one particular person pulling the strings. A generalized state of market dependency therefore means that individuals are subject to economic forces on an *extra-human* scale. To the extent that our 'contributions to society are mediated by exchange, we will find ourselves trapped in a giant collective-action-problem-generating machine, a machine that we have inadvertently created and from which it will be extremely difficult to extricate ourselves'.[19] Swapping one boss for another might serve to make our daily lives more bearable, then, but it will ultimately do little to collectively liberate us from the realm of necessity in its current form. With this in mind, one can easily appreciate why Marx might have argued for the 'shortening of the working-day' as the 'basic prerequisite' of the realm of freedom,[20] and also why the relationship between freedom and necessity has proved crucial to so many post-work projects.

Single-realm utopias: Necessity as freedom?

How post-work thinkers conceptualize the freedom/necessity dynamic will fundamentally alter the kinds of proposals they advance and the kinds of visions to which they subscribe. There are two potential understandings of freedom and necessity at issue here – single-realm utopias (in which freedom and necessity become one and the same) and dual-realm utopias (in which the distinction between freedom and necessity is maintained, and it is rather the *balance between them* that is altered). But *which* of these understandings is most useful for post-work politics? Can we plausibly conceive of a post-scarcity future in which labour is dissolved into self-actualization and necessity is absorbed into freedom, or does it make more sense to think in terms of societies which eternally battle necessity in an effort to maximize freedom? In other words, would we do better to strive for futures in which work is eradicated through its *reconceptualization* or through its *reduction*?

Let us begin by outlining the single-realm approach and the imaginaries to which it lends itself. There are a number of thinkers whose utopian visions of the future are underpinned by the reconceptualization of necessity as freedom. In *Automation and the Future of Work*, Aaron Benanav gestures towards people like Charles Fourier and William Morris, 'who essentially suggested that the collapse of spheres could be achieved by turning all work into play'.[21] In 1888's 'Useful Work versus Useless Toil', for example, Morris asks his reader to contemplate, 'what a holiday our whole lives might be, if we were resolute to make all our labour reasonable and pleasant'.[22] In pursuing this project, he acknowledges, work in its most general sense may in fact proliferate in some form:

> if we could be contented in a free community to work in the same hurried, dirty, disorderly, heartless way as we do now, we might shorten our day's labour very much more than I suppose we shall do, taking all kinds of labour into account. But if we did, it would mean that our newfound freedom of condition would leave us listless and wretched, if not anxious, as we are now, which I hold is simply impossible.[23]

Better, then, to insist that 'all labour, even the commonest, must be made attractive' – or, to put it another way, to insist that the distinction between the realm of necessity and the realm of freedom be erased via the seamless synthesis of need and want.[24]

The insistence that work is play (or that it can be made play) may perhaps feel somewhat familiar to us at this point, given that it has come to characterize certain conceptions of work under neoliberal capitalism. As Amelia Horgan notes, this involves 'the merging of work and leisure, with work increasingly resembling play, and leisure treated as something we can and should make profitable; each hobby a potential "side gig".[25] The single-realm utopia is thus arguably prefigured within the contemporary world of work; 'do what you love and you'll never work a day in your life!' Indeed, Heather Berg – writing about the distinctive labour dynamics of pornographic performance – stresses that 'real pleasure can be sustaining. In sex work as elsewhere, it makes work feel less like work'.[26] But as Berg is quick to recognize, this exhortation to have fun (and be fun) at work acts as something of a double-edged sword; it can 'both improve the experience of working [...] and demand more of workers'.[27] In inviting (if not requiring) identification with one's work, the possibility of a life *outside* of work is eroded; 'do what you love, and you'll never *stop* working a day in your life!' Horgan identifies this running together of work and play as the 'jobification of everyday life',[28] while Berg describes it as 'opening up one's whole life to the market to avoid clocking in'.[29] Such fusions of work and play – the monkey's paw version of a single-realm utopia – risk creating the conditions whereby work *which is in fact work* cannot be recognized as such. This limits our possibilities for refusal and restricts efforts to further extend the realm of freedom. After all, as Silvia Federici remarks, making an activity visible as work 'is the most indispensable condition to begin to struggle against it'.[30]

But the tension between self-actualization and self-exploitation in single-realm conceptions of freedom and necessity is hardly the most concerning aspect of contemporary cultures of work. Indeed, we should acknowledge that the putting to work of fun, pleasure and joy is an issue that relates primarily to the most privileged forms of wage labour under capitalism. As Horgan notes, while the 'ludic coworking-space-dwelling start-up-worker might be in some ways paradigmatic of the contemporary economy, they also represent the select few for whom a "fun job" is possible'.[31] Both globally and within the economies of the wealthy nations, a huge amount of work remains in which the leveraging of play is at best a distant concern, and acquiescence and compliance with top-down instructions continue to trump any aspiration towards identifying with one's work or loving what one does.

Of course, necessity (in the form of unpleasant, undesirable and uncelebrated forms of labour) has traditionally been managed via its assignment to specific subsets of the population. This assignment has often taken place in just such a way as to suggest that this work, when performed by particular individuals, is not actually work at all. Women's (particularly racialized women's) perceived responsibility for housework and care work, for example, has frequently been naturalized – waved away as something other than labour – an expression of the gendered self, perhaps, or a personally rewarding pastime. One risk of aspiring to dissolve the realm of necessity into the realm of freedom, then, is that certain groups will continue to be expected to pick up the most burdensome forms of activity without their labour being recognized as such.

It is for this reason that, according to Benanav, 'Single-realm conceptions of a post-scarcity world are [...] both totalitarian and hopelessly utopian (in the bad sense of the term).'[32] Indeed, while actively wishing away exertion and unpleasantness, William Morris struggles even to *imagine* his way out of some undesirable labour, effectively anchoring his single-realm utopia in a dual-realm understanding of necessity. 'Let us grant, first, that the race of man must either labour or perish', he writes. 'Nature does not give us our livelihood gratis; we must win it by toil of some sort or degree.'[33] A character in his utopian fiction *News from Nowhere* similarly describes people as passing their lives in 'reasonable strife with nature'.[34] A sort of disavowed necessity surfaces within these texts, asserting itself within and against freedom at every turn. Morris cannot escape the spectre of the factory system, despite expressing doubts about its potential for generating human flourishing. He also separates out those forms of work which most obviously relate to play (such as artistic creation) from work of the 'more repulsive kind', which he suggests should be managed by 'some arrangement whereby those who did the roughest work should work for the shortest spell'.[35] On some level, these visions imply that *not* all forms of work can readily be transformed into play or autonomously chosen activity; necessity persists.

Single-realm fantasies that see labour absorbed into leisure, necessity dissolved within freedom, are ultimately problematic, then. This is not to disparage somebody like Morris's sweeping ambitions, however; his bracing refusal to allow any element of work's unpleasantness to go unchallenged – his attempt to demand 'compensation for the compulsion of Nature's necessity', as he puts it – is in many ways both refreshing and appealing.[36] We might view it as in keeping with the tone of some of the more effective forms of speculative post-work thinking that have emerged over the course of the past decade – tendencies that have been identified by some as 'Promethean'. Nick Srnicek and Alex Williams's *Inventing the Future*, for example, evinces a somewhat Morris-like energy when it describes post-work as 'an unrelenting project to unbind the necessities of this world and transform them into materials for the further construction of freedom'.[37] This position is premised upon building collective capacities for action. In what follows, we offer a characterization of twenty-first-century Prometheanism, before beginning to explore its relationship with freedom and necessity, as well as with single- or dual-realm utopian frameworks.

Beyond necessity: Post-work Prometheanism

Under what circumstances do we have the greatest capacity to act within and upon our worlds? Where do we have the greatest opportunity to effectuate change, exercise discretion, or understand and act upon our personal and common interests? How can we make ourselves more free (both individually and collectively)? When are we most able to reason through what it is that we want, and reflect upon how best to go about achieving this? It is within these sorts of questions that one finds the basis for extending the realm of freedom. Understanding the issues in these terms makes it clear that freedom is not simply the removal of restrictions or responsibilities. It is not the ability to do things entirely unfettered by either constraints *or* consequences. Rather, freedom as it pertains to politics is inseparable from responsibility – from our ability to think about and to give reasons for our choice of actions, and to be held accountable for those actions. This is what political agency means.[38] Certain approaches to organizing society will maximize or minimize people's capacity to exercise this agency, and will therefore either increase or decrease our access to the realm of freedom.

A truly emancipatory understanding of freedom does not mistake it for what Weeks calls 'an individual possession, something that emanates from the sovereign will'.[39] Rather, it positions freedom as the ability to 'design, within obvious bounds, our own lives'.[40] To the extent that it is a world-building process, freedom is 'a social – and therefore necessarily political – endeavour'.[41] It is inextricable from the processes of collective cultivation, construction and contestation which constitute it and, as such, demands to be understood not as a state but as an action. As per Srnicek and Williams, we should not view the minimization of the realm of necessity as a matter of subtracting synthetic barriers from a pure, organic freedom, because freedom itself is 'a collective historical achievement rather than the result of simply leaving people be'.[42] It is a technology forever in need of assembly. For a number of post-work thinkers, the reduction of work (including, but not limited to, fewer hours spent engaged in wage labour) represents one key means via which to provide the material basis for extending the realm of freedom, offering as it does, in Weeks' words, both 'more time to partake of existing possibilities for meaning and fulfilment, and time to invent new ones'.[43] In this sense, post-work freedom is (as we've seen from the opening pages of this book) the maximization of time for what we will.

Philosophical approaches underpinned by this kind of synthetic perspective – by the idea that freedom is something one *actively builds* rather than simply locates, identifies or accesses – have in recent years attracted the label of 'Prometheanism', and many of its key thinkers have emerged from the fringes of contemporary post-work positions. What is Prometheanism, then, and how does it relate to freedom and necessity? At its most general level, Prometheanism can be characterized as a transformative, world-building and technologically enabled emancipatory endeavour that is oriented towards the future. Peter Wolfendale, for example, describes Prometheanism as a 'politics of intervention' – one that starts from the insistence that nothing be exempted a priori from the enactment of re/visionary processes.[44] Alexander Galloway, meanwhile, suggests that it could be defined as 'technology for humans to overcome natural limit'.[45] It is Ray Brassier's characterization, however, that perhaps brings home the connections between Prometheanism and freedom most forcefully. In his assessment, it is 'simply the claim that there is no reason to assume a predetermined limit to what we can achieve or to the ways in which we can transform ourselves and our world'.[46] Brassier's commitment to freedom exceeds even the commitment to species survival, operating on the assumption that one 'cannot have an emancipatory politics rooted in fear'[47] and that one should denounce an ethos of 'self-preservation at all costs'.[48]

As we have suggested elsewhere,[49] this kind of Promethean perspective may not seem to readily lend itself to feminist frameworks of the type we are committed to developing here. Prometheus himself cuts a decidedly individualist figure, and carries mythical associations with arrogance, machismo and pride – associations that bleed into understandings of the approach that bears his name. Galloway warns of 'bromethanism', for example, while (on a display tag accompanying her art work) Hito Steyerl famously calls accelerationism 'dead white Ferrari envy, dripping from head to toe with stale testosterone'.[50] These are hardly auspicious signals of gender political utility. And yet, Prometheanism, minimally defined, strikes us as a crucial attitude for many feminist projects. That is, the insistence that things might be otherwise, and that we should have the ambition to try to change them for the better, represents the very bedrock of radical politics. After all, only a collective project of Promethean proportions can be fit to dis-embed something as seemingly intractable as the gender division of labour or the need to 'earn a living'; traditionally feminist concerns such as home and family must be viewed, not in opposition to ambitious, emancipatory and highly mediated political endeavour but as a particularly important field of its operations. Prometheanism teaches us not to unthinkingly accept the given – 'to refuse to accede to the world as we find it' – and invites us to collectively engineer emancipatory alternatives.[51] As such, we find it to be a far more hospitable idea – and a far easier feminist tool to wield – than it might initially appear.

A Promethean perspective, then, approaches freedom as an unrelenting project of unbinding what *is* from what *could* (or *ought to*) be, and insists that everything is up for grabs. Because, according to this kind of post-work framework, freedom demands to be seen as an ongoing process rather than a finalized (or finalizable) product, we are able to recognize it as perpetually provisional. How we understand freedom will change in response to the priorities and possibilities of any given era – and this will include specific developments in techno-material conditions. As new pursuits become possible, new desires will emerge, and these desires will in turn foster the development of new pursuits. The possibility space of material reality will be progressively transformed, and with it, the realm of freedom. While what we want and the means via which we can feasibly achieve it will alter, a radical post-work orientation towards freedom has the potential to remain consistent. Indeed, for Srnicek and Williams, the core of post-work is to be found in precisely this orientation. Absolute freedom is never arrived at, and nor does it simply exist to be uncovered, but should instead be considered indistinguishable from its dogged pursuit.

And yet the realm of necessity is *intransigent*. For Marx (as we have seen throughout this chapter), the 'development of human energy which is an end in itself' is the 'true realm of freedom', but this freedom 'can blossom forth only with [the] realm of necessity as its basis'.[52] Basic conditions of survival have to be met before the pursuit of freedom can be entered into. Minimally defined in this way, even the most Promethean post-work thinker must admit the inevitability of necessity and the insufficiency of single-realm utopias. So, there is something of a tension in evidence here. How can one marry an understanding of the obstinacy of necessity with a commitment to the thorough-going and unbounded transformation of the world as it stands? How, in other words, can we square Promethean post-work ambition with a dual-realm conception of a future society?

Dual-realm utopias: Freedom in necessity

Life is materially instantiated and requires some form of interchange between actors and their environments. This is unavoidable. But this is not to suggest that everything we might associate with the realm of necessity is inherently static or immutable. Necessity may be *categorically* necessary, in other words, but its character, contours and contents can be made subject to change. We might be tempted here to draw upon Postone's distinction between two different types of necessity – historical and transhistorical – which are defined by differing degrees of flexibility. Historical necessity 'refers to the sorts of abstract, impersonal compulsions exerted by capitalism's objectified, alienated forms of social relations' – the compulsion to wage labour being the most obvious example.[53] This form of necessity is available for emancipatory change.

To quote Postone, 'the abolition of alienated labour would entail overcoming historical necessity, the historically specific social necessity constituted in the capitalist sphere of production: it would allow for historical freedom.'[54] Liberation from this form of necessity alone, however, 'does not and cannot entail freedom on a total social level from any sort of necessity: society, for Marx, cannot be based on absolute freedom.'[55] The reasons for this lie in the *other* type of necessity Postone identifies: namely, transhistorical necessity.

Transhistorical necessity refers to the idea that some kind of 'concrete labour, however determined, is necessary to mediate the material interactions of humans and nature and, hence, to maintain human social life'.[56] For Postone, this second form of necessity is particularly resistant to attempts at its elimination. There will always be some form of action that we must take in order to ensure our daily and/or intergenerational reproduction. Hence, according to his reading of Marx, 'however playful individual labour may become, labour on a socially general level can never acquire the character of pure play'.[57] This viewpoint shows us that the realm of necessity (when taken as a whole) is not entirely resistant to change, and hints at how a commitment to freedom might operate in relation to dual-realm utopias. As such, it appears to offer a viable and appropriate framework for post-work attempts to navigate the dynamic between freedom and necessity.

We are not completely satisfied with the solution that this offers, however. We are, in fact, somewhat wary of the suggestion that people should subdivide necessity into historical and transhistorical forms, and would question whether such an approach could ever be truly compatible with overarching Promethean ambitions and commitments. Our concerns stem, in part, from questions surrounding which *types* of experience or activity will be seen as historical and which as transhistorical: in other words, which phenomena might people be encouraged to give their all to transforming, and which might they be warned away from and encouraged to endure? Foregrounding any notion of natural necessity risks providing an alibi for forms of politics that overlook, deprioritize or sideline the interests of anyone beyond a relatively privileged minority – a largely white, largely male 'labour aristocracy', for example. What are the risks inherent in rhetorically establishing some areas of unfreedom as more available for or amenable to political intervention than others?

Understanding transhistorical necessity primarily in terms of biological processes – on the basis that humans 'regulate their "metabolism" with their natural environment by means of labour'[58] – does not get us out of this bind either, but rather risks intensifying it. Gestational labour, gendered embodiment, physical suffering and so on (things that humans can and should work to extend their agency to change, mitigate or improve) can all too easily become bound up with ideas of the un-transformable. Separating the realm of necessity into historical and transhistorical forms is no good, then, because drawing up divisions such as these encourages us to relegate huge swathes of human experience to the dustbin of necessity. It is here, we argue, that a key tension animating our discussion of single- and dual-realm utopias lies. If one can recognize the utopian overreach within attempts to fuse the realms of freedom and necessity, and to transform all work into play, but nevertheless remains uncomfortable with the suggestion that particular forms of necessity need to be accepted as un-remakable givens, then whither utopian thinking? What ground does a post-work Promethean have left?

Conclusion: On transformation, intransigence and what one wills

What is demanded here is the seemingly contradictory formation of a *specifically Promethean politics of necessity*. Such a politics would recognize, as we have throughout this chapter, that necessity is an inevitability of a formal, structural or categorical kind. As such, any post-work projects operating within this tendency would need to adopt a dual-realm conception of future societies (one in which some work remains, despite ongoing efforts to minimize it). However, even if one acknowledges that human lives in both the abstract and the concrete will always be defined by needs of one type or another, and that we will necessarily be required to interact with our natural-cultural environments in particular ways in order to stay alive, there is nothing to suggest that the exact *character* of these needs is immutable, or that they cannot be mitigated or managed in more just and equitable ways. We must insist upon an orientation towards freedom – a commitment to pushing back necessity as far as possible on any and all fronts, both within and beyond the idea of 'nature' or indeed of 'work', as we currently understand these terms.[59]

To reiterate: even if a Promethean post-work perspective rejects (as it should) the idea of a single-realm utopia in favour of acknowledging the persistence of necessity, it would nevertheless be well advised to short-circuit debates that seek to chalk up some forms of disadvantage to nature and others to culture.[60] Promethean post-work politics must instead reject any foreclosure of the eradication of necessity (or at least, the eradication of any *specific* necessity) and foreground the maximization of freedom without ascribing predetermined limits to this process. Indeed, we would argue that it is by adopting a Promethean spirit – by behaving *as if* everything is transformable, and refusing to concede in advance that there are things which cannot or should not be made subject to emancipatory change – that we will be best placed to both refuse the world as it stands and discover which changes are actually feasible (or could be made feasible). The ceaseless quest to maximize freedom is in fact the thing that comes closest to being an expression of true freedom itself – and this quest should not be limited in advance by the idea that certain facets of our existence are inherently unchangeable. By saying not only that historical and transhistorical necessity, culture and nature, are inexorably intertwined but also that the emphases or differences one might ascribe to them are irrelevant to whether or not they can be made subject to change facilitates a more thorough-going approach to extending the realm of freedom than that offered by Postone. A truly emancipatory politics should seek to minimize any form of injustice, and this depends upon a fundamental openness to the potential mutability of everything that currently sits within the realm of necessity (be it 'natural' or otherwise), even as we accept the persistence of this realm as such.

If a work process is unjust, or collectively deemed to be undesirable, we should look to find ways to change it, regardless of the cultural category within which it might typically be situated. While the realm of necessity cannot be entirely overcome, we must nevertheless insist on pushing it back as far as possible, wherever we see fit. That is to say, we must focus on cultivating the enabling conditions whereby people are maximally able to exercise meaningful choice over the course taken by their lives. This undertaking may not be limited to wage labour, but it will inevitably involve resistance to work – however one might choose to define it. In the words of one of the most strident twentieth-century post-work thinkers – the second wave feminist Shulamith Firestone – we should organize towards 'the realization of the conceivable in the possible'.[61] And while operating on the assumption that many kinds of changes are realizable, we must develop mechanisms for simultaneously ascertaining which kinds of changes we might collectively deem to be desirable. In the next chapter, we will identify those post-work visions that articulate worlds of greater freedom precisely in terms of the expanded capacity to change our worldly conditions – and the ways in which these visions are articulated as transformative utopias.

5

Post-work's utopianism

The previous chapters of this book have revolved around three political demands that have come to characterize post-work positions, as well as the philosophy of freedom that emerges from post-work politics. Each demand responds to a particular problem regarding the social, economic or technological systems within which we live, but each also points the way towards something more desirable: a radically different future of work. In other words, these demands – a shorter working week, universal basic income and technological labour-saving – are positioned as solutions to the problems of our work-centred society, but *also* as avenues to a new world – a world in which work is not simply better but in which less of it is required for human flourishing. This is symptomatic of post-work as a future-oriented discourse – it is unsatisfied with merely diagnosing the problems of work, but is rather always striving for a world wherein these problems have been rendered as trivial as possible. Indeed, we would argue that despite post-work thus far often being characterized merely as a set of programmatic demands or policy asks, it is in fact at its core a more ambitious philosophical project – one aimed firmly at a future of freedom.

It is arguably this utopianism that distinguishes post-work positions from *anti*-work positions or those that are merely critical of work – be they analyses of present-day labour markets, accounts of automation or critiques of the gendered division of labour. We can find numerous examples of anti-work and critical work sociology across political viewpoints, including heterodox Marxism, anarchist writings on work, and recent, critical texts drawing our attention to labour's complex miseries.[1] Post-work writers see such diagnoses as offering only half the story – useful premises, but certainly not satisfying resolutions or appropriate endpoints for conversations about our shared futures.

By pushing beyond analysis, much post-work theorizing sticks its neck out into arguably more difficult territory – demanding and proposing, making the case for X, Y or Z. These propositions can have short-, medium- or long-term horizons; they can concern a post-work movement's strategy for the years to come, a plan of how to get from here to there; or they can simply point to a destination in the future – a desirable ideal that, when countenanced, clashes creatively with our everyday experiences of the here and now. There exists what Kathi Weeks calls an *impatience* within post-work theorizing: not only is our present, work-centred society inadequate, not only have we taken precious few steps on our way to a new socio-economic arrangement, but we've barely even begun to detail what such a new world might look like! This, then, is the difficult and ambitious task of the more elaborated elements of post-work theory – fraught with the danger of becoming outdated, of seeming too radical or not radical enough, too broad and bland or too niche and particular.

In contrast to the critique-heavy bias of much radical theory, post-work's propositional stance – a spectrum ranging from the possible to the highly speculative – is inherently risky and leaves post-work (and its proponents) vulnerable to attack on the grounds of a lack of realism and pragmatism on the one hand and timidity or a dearth of revolutionary fervour on the other. Such is the nature of dealing with non-existent entities, futures as yet unrealized (which may *never* be realized) and demands that necessarily do not have the details of their implementation fully fleshed out in advance. However, as we will argue, being a utopian discourse is also a great strength of post-work.

Of course, the term 'utopia' means a great many things to different people and we mean it in a specific sense. Utopias in our characterization denote broad, systemic ideals that (while not necessarily unachievable) cannot be realized under existing conditions. Utopia is, after all, a non-place or 'ou-topia' – as much as it is an 'eu-topia', or good place; Thomas More played upon this ambiguity in his coinage of the term.[2] The articulation of a utopian vision calls for the transformation of the world as it stands and in the process highlights the deficiencies of things as they are; it may propose short- and medium-term goals, which can take the form of more or less actionable reforms, but these reforms are conceptualized as steps towards a thorough-going and as-yet-unrealizable shift. While some of the transitional content of specific utopias may be practically achievable, utopia itself retains a structural dimension of unachievability. It is a vector, not a specific endpoint – not something to be arrived at, but the process of striving for something better that will continually evolve in accordance with changing cultural desires, social standards, technical possibilities and political norms.

In this, our characterization of utopia chimes with recent critical thinking around the related practice of demand-making. For example, Katrina Forrester's account of how political demands operate – 'what they are, what they do, and what movements hope to achieve in making them' – reminds us that demands 'have political effects beyond the stipulation of goals and reforms'.[3] In her view, often the most effective kinds of demand-making proffer 'stepping-stone reforms and [a] long-term liberatory horizon', while also offering some 'indication of a process of travelling between the two'.[4] As such, they 'can both reveal hidden dimensions of social reality and build constituencies while also indicating a new world to be built that exceeds agendas for immediate reform'.[5] This broadly corresponds both with our predominant understanding of utopia in the current chapter and with our approach to post-work throughout this book as a whole.[6]

As we shall see in this chapter, utopias as we have defined them above are key ingredients of sociopolitical change. Utopian prospects – dreams of a better world – are often what give energy or force to a political project.

The critics of utopianism

On an everyday level, we often encounter the words 'utopia' and 'utopian' as accusations – a means by which to discredit someone else's argument. If you're calling for something beyond the limitations of the present day, you're being 'dangerously' utopian, denoting a kind of irrationality, or you're being 'naively' utopian, implying signs of immaturity or a lack of strategic intelligence. Given that utopian visions entail radical breaks from the existing order of things, the most vocal critics tend to be conservative: those who, in Corey Robin's succinct phrasing, speak 'on behalf of old regimes – in the family, the factory, the field'.[7] Considering that conservatism as a political force has typically been a defender of the status quo, resistant to everything from gay liberation, trans rights, the civil rights movement, climate action, redistributive economics and much more, this aversion to radical social change should come as no surprise. In her extensive dissection of right-wing anti-utopianism, Weeks specifically identifies Karl Popper and Francis Fukuyama as key figures in the ideological attacks against utopian thought in the twentieth century.[8] As the Cold War developed, utopianism withered within politics in the East and West, and in the post-Soviet world an atmosphere of what Mark Fisher calls 'capitalist realism' saturated left- and right-wing political positions and cultural milieus.[9] This was a general affect, or mood, of inertia: the impossibility of radical political and economic change – and thus the deflation of utopian dreaming of any kind. Our political horizons narrowed.

 It's important to note, however, that this world was itself the product of a utopian thought and practice: reshaping the world in the image of an ideal is by no means the preserve of those on the left wing of the political spectrum.[10] It often goes unacknowledged that conservative projects also tarry with currents that have their own utopian DNA: the close companionship between neoconservative politics and neoliberalism is a case in point.[11] Melinda Cooper has shown that the mid-twentieth-century conservative project of reasserting the primacy of the traditional family as the dominant moral and economic unit in society dovetailed well with the utopia, in neoliberal theory, of the complete integration of aspects of everyday life into economic calculation. Neoliberalism was, at its core, not a project of merely *recovering* the market from illegitimate state involvement but instead involved the active creation of market-worlds, and positioning each individual/family as a rational investor. The neoliberal-neocon pact was a utopia of a family-based market society: a paradoxical utopia of tradition. Regarding the UK's particular brand of this, Stuart Hall identified Thatcherism as a form of 'regressive modernisation': this was a new vision of the future (economically 'dynamic' Britain), albeit with Victorian characteristics of law, order and family.[12] This tension within neoliberal practice is one where traditional forms of power (family, patriarchy, class) are stitched to future states of being; future speculation intermingles with reactionary consolidation. As political economist Martijn Konings puts it, in neoliberalism, 'the future simply imposes itself, albeit in the shape of the past'.[13]

Key neoliberal institutions such as the Mont Pelerin Society were quite literally set up to build the networks and economic theory of a world to come. This thought collective was aimed at 'thinking the unthinkable', to borrow the title of Richard Cockett's history of the movement, and at designing the elements of a new economic arrangement.[14] Most explicitly, neoliberalism's acknowledgement of utopia as a key ingredient of success was noted by one of its influential economic minds, Friedrich Hayek. In 1949, Hayek acknowledged the success of the socialism of his day (i.e. its mainstream acceptance in many countries) and noted its use of utopianism as a source of power:[15]

> In particular, socialist thought owes its appeal to the young largely to its visionary character; the very courage to indulge in Utopian thought is in this respect a source of strength to the socialists.[16]

In response, as a lesson learnt, he calls for a liberal (here in the sense of freedom, but more broadly part of his liberal economic philosophy) strategy that is nothing less than the striving for utopia:

> What we lack is a liberal Utopia, a program which seems neither a mere defense of things as they are nor a diluted kind of socialism, but a truly liberal radicalism which does not spare the susceptibilities of the mighty (including the trade unions), which is not too severely practical, and which does not confine itself to what appears today as politically possible. We need intellectual leaders who are willing to work for an ideal, however small may be the prospects of its early realization. They must be men who are willing to stick to principles and to fight for their full realization, however remote.[17]

Note Hayek's emphasis on the obstinacy, the perseverance and the long-term vision required by political movements in order to bring their radical utopias closer to reality. The gradual construction of neoliberalism's ideological and policy infrastructure – a multi-decade process, involving all sorts of twists and turns – across the globe is testament to the strength of these utopian convictions. Of course, what was once a utopian, radical project has now become the mainstream practice and doctrine of economic life. Idealism has become (capitalist) realism and neoliberal economists and politicians now have the authority to dismiss alternatives as simply 'unrealistic'. Perhaps the lesson we can draw from this case study is that politics is not just 'the art of the possible' but also 'the art of defining the impossible'. The dynamics between existing reality and long-term utopian struggle have not been lost on contemporary post-work authors who – just as Hayek learnt from the successes of Keynesian and socialist forces in his day – have taken their own notes on the uses of utopian thinking.[18]

While Hayek and other conservative forces were well aware that guiding visions are crucial to political success, utopianism today has mixed fortunes. On the political right, we can see efforts to continue to draw from the Thatcherite playbook, wishing to bring about a world where Britain can be further 'unchained' – that is, further deregulated, with reduced workers' rights and increased privatization of public services.[19] Their utopia is one that is desirable for a very small section of society. We can also observe the rise of neofascism, which promises, depending on its national context, utopias of racial 'purity', hierarchical political order or stringent policing of social life.[20] All of this rather stresses the necessity of asking, when confronted with future-oriented political visions, 'utopia for whom?' – after all, no social vision will appeal equally to all.

On the left, anti-utopianism has taken various forms, usually accompanying a period of weakness or defeat. Amongst the movements of the early 2000s, such as the anti-globalization demonstrations or Occupy, there existed the claim that the most radical ethos was to make no demands upon the future whatsoever.[21] In more recent years, the turn to electoralism across many countries has sparked both a resurgence of aspiration (particularly amongst young people) and a necessary pragmatism with regard to parliamentary politics and the various compromises that this entails.[22] Such developments have meant that utopianism remains ambiguous on the left: on the one hand progressive movements have never – in the face of the huge crises of our times – had to dream bigger than they do today (and we will address the existential crises of climate change later in this chapter); on the other, consistent defeat can lead to a bunker mindset, in-fighting and limited horizons. This is a disposition warned against by some post-work authors; as we shall note below, the tension between utopianism and realism within progressive and socialist movements has a long history, upon which post-work draws.

The radical value of utopianism

While capitalist realism and its acolytes embody an inherently conservative cultural mode, utopianism is always oriented towards a future that is yet to be – thereby dislodging and decentring the present.[23] Indeed, both Weeks and Fisher see utopian thinking and practice – whether in the shape of transitional demands such as UBI in Weeks' case, or more provocatively for 'Acid Communism' in Fisher's – as essential ingredients of progressive change. Reclaiming the future as something that can be envisaged, held to as a promise and then ultimately brought into existence helps dissolve the dogma of the eternal present, of 'there is no alternative' and of all of the guises that these positions take. Weeks and Fisher join other post-work authors and Promethean philosophers in seeking to revive utopian thinking as a central part of political strategy – proudly and without excuse. Ray Brassier, for example, ties an orientation towards the future to his understanding of freedom, arguing that the 'you cannot have an emancipatory politics rooted in fear, because freedom from fear is the precondition of emancipation. The politics of fear is ultimately the politics of reaction, of self-preservation at all costs' – and in his view, if 'the best we can hope for is just our own perpetuation then there is no reason to perpetuate ourselves'.[24]

Historically, though, utopianism (as a future-facing politics) has been controversial within radical thought. In Marxism one finds a classic distinction, following Engels, between 'scientific' and 'utopian' socialisms – the former being the more solid and accurate, the latter being a less developed form of thought. It's safe to say that this is an ambiguous history, however. It's simply not true, for example, to say that Marx departed from the utopian tradition once his accounts were settled with the utopian socialists such as Fourier, Saint-Simon and Owen. As Ruth Levitas notes, there is much misrepresentation surrounding Marx and Engels' relationship to future-oriented planning and visionary projection.[25] Their point of contention revolved not around the merits of envisioning socialist society but rather around 'the process of transformation, and particularly about the belief that propaganda alone would result in the realisation of socialism'.[26]

Although often preoccupied with analysis, one can find multiple examples of utopian imagery in Marx's work – not all of them consistent with one another, as his thought developed over time, but all highly relevant to our post-work theme.[27] You have the single-realm utopia of the unalienated life, wherein 'my labour would be the *free expression* and hence the *enjoyment of life*', as opposed to the alienated gulf between work, worker, and the products of work that capitalism imposes.[28] Disalienation, in this utopian image of Marx's, has influenced some post-work authors while being a point of disagreement for others. As we shall see, authors such as Kate Soper use similar heuristics to understand how a more sustainable and connected life requires less work, and David Frayne uses Marx's alienation as a useful way of understanding the source of contemporary disaffection from jobs. Others, however, such as Gorz and Weeks, suggest that the utopia of dismantled alienation can function as something of a false idol – an idea that we will be returning to later in this chapter in our discussion of nostalgic visions of work.

There is also the famous utopian image of a multi-faceted and potentiated humanity in Marx and Engels' *The German Ideology*:

> In communist society, where nobody has one exclusive sphere of activity but each can become accomplished in any branch he wishes, society regulates the general production and thus makes it possible for me to do one thing today and another tomorrow, to hunt in the morning, fish in the afternoon, rear cattle in the evening, criticise after dinner, just as I have a mind, without ever becoming hunter, fisherman, shepherd or critic.[29]

This is a vision of a *plural* and maximally developed humanity, untethered to any particular activity, and with free individual choice as to where one directs one's efforts. It is in the *Grundrisse* and in *Capital vol. III* that we find arguably the peak of Marx's utopian ambition – and it is also at this point that Marx is at his most post-work minded. Here, he drops the pursuit of disalienation – freedom is not to be found in the work process – and sees a positive future in the automation of much labour and the freeing of human activity for other pursuits. In this pathway to the future, to the degree that industries develop new tools – labour-saving technologies – the creation of what Marx calls 'real wealth' starts to depend less on human brains and muscles and more on how advanced our tools can become. 'Labour no longer appears so much to be included within the production process; rather, the human being comes to relate more as a watchman and regulator to the production process itself.'[30]

By the third volume of *Capital*, as we noted in the previous chapter, Marx sketches the logic of an alternative to capitalist labour society and is clear about a separation between the realms of freedom and necessity:

Freedom in this field [of economy] can only consist in socialised man, the associated producers, rationally regulating their interchange with nature, bringing it under their common control, instead of being ruled by it … but it nonetheless remains a realm of necessity. Beyond that there begins the development of human energy which is an end in itself, the true realm of freedom, which, however, can blossom forth only with this realm of necessity as its basis. The shortening of the working day is its basic prerequisite.[31]

It is notable, from a post-work perspective, that in this utopian image Marx clearly considers work in a guise beyond capitalism (even carried out under conditions of shared and rational management) and yet *still* recognizes it as a mere, necessary basis from which true freedom springs and exists separately – a dual-realm utopia. Shifting the economic ownership and control in our economies is clearly necessary, but even in the most utopian, democratic scenario, the problem of work and its reduction persists. The space Marx opens with this brief utopian glimpse of the freedom/necessity partition has been built on extensively by theorists such as Gorz.

Utopian imaginaries have persisted and indeed thrived in Marx's wake, despite Engels' attempts to avert this path. Many have evidently found it powerful to put forward their own specific blueprints for a post-capitalist society, with various degrees of fidelity to Marx's sparse but enticing words on the matter. One such radical is Ernst Bloch – whose *Principle of Hope* has been especially influential on core post-work authors such as Weeks.[32] For Bloch, the value of utopias and utopianism is the cultivation of hope. Everything from daydreaming and fairy tales to film and political manifestos are expressions, in his view, of an in-built cognitive faculty of hope – our orientation towards the 'not-yet' real. This ability to hope, and its cultivation in practice, is a precondition for political change. As we noted above, an anti-utopian (capitalist) realism can deflate and narrow our perspectives, constraining what we think is possible, and the same can be said for the affects of anxiety and fear.

> Whereas the fearful subject contracts around its will to self-preservation, the hopeful subject – the basic contours of which we can glean from Bloch's account – represents a more open and expansive model of subjectivity. Not reduced to defending the self as such, hopefulness enables a more extensive range of connections and purposes.[33]

In her post-work proposals, Weeks attempts to walk the line presented by Bloch insofar as she selects *not yet* fully realized possibilities that are already passing through the present (real-possible) moment in some form: shorter working weeks and basic income. Both of these utopian prospects cultivate hope precisely in the tensions between their very possible *realizability* on the one hand (they are already being piloted, after all) and their existence slightly beyond established historical fact on the other (we cannot yet say they are 'here'). As transitional and/or directional, demands for things like UBI are not utopian in the sense of pointing to *endpoints* but rather in the sense of operating as short- and medium-term goals, crucial steps, towards a thorough-going and as-yet-unrealizable shift.

In stark contrast to a figure such as Bloch, and often seen as a symbol of pragmatic, 'doing what needs to be done' common sense, Lenin also knew very well the important function of utopian dreaming to the communist cause.

> If man were completely deprived of the ability to dream in this way, if he could not from time to time run ahead and mentally conceive, in an entire and completed picture, the product to which his hands are only just beginning to lend shape, then I cannot imagine what stimulus there would be to induce man to undertake and complete extensive and strenuous work in the sphere of art, science and practical endeavour … The rift between dreams and reality causes no harm if only the person dreaming believes seriously in

his dream, if he attentively observes life, compares his observations with his castles in the air and if, generally speaking, he works conscientiously for the achievement of his fantasies. If there is some connection between dreams and life then all is well. Of this kind of dreaming there is unfortunately too little in our movement.[34]

One of the great tensions in Lenin's thought – and indeed Marxism in general – is between the utopian fever for a post-capitalist world and the more immediate analysis of specific conjunctures and the struggles they require.[35] At times these two elements combine and concrete analyses meet concrete utopia. The Marxist writer Rudolf Bahro, for example, saw the very real possibility of an advanced socialism all around him in post-war Europe (specifically the German DDR).[36] Frustrated with the Communist establishment, and the persistence of the core elements of capitalism even in ostensibly socialist states, Bahro began to construct a detailed utopian plan. 'Marxists have a defensive attitude toward utopias', he writes. 'It was so laborious to escape from them in the past. But today utopian thought has a new necessity.'[37] Bahro's 'Alternative' vision to hitherto capitalist and communist societies can be seen as a forerunner of today's degrowth and post-growth economics schools of thought. He was particularly aware of capitalism's unsustainable production-consumption matrix and sought throughout the remainder of his life to articulate a truly post-industrial ecological vision with the potential to win popular support. Crucially, Bahro's 'Alternative' includes a situation in which humankind will be able to exercise its 'surplus consciousness' – that is, a certain quantity of cognitive functioning that is no longer burdened by the labour process. Envisioning work as having been reorganized, reduced and redistributed, he pictures a world in which our species can develop in unforeseen (and unforeseeable) ways.

This, then, is why we view the charge of utopianism sometimes levelled against post-work not as a problem but as a possible strength. The works of Fisher, Weeks, Bahro and Bloch – not to mention Marx himself – teach us the value of a utopian horizon and of striving for a world that is not only different from the one we currently inhabit but meaningfully better. Post-work insists that things can (and must) be otherwise and attempts to thread the needle between navigating the world as it is and working towards a possible world still to come.

The functions of post-work utopias

Having made the case, against common criticisms, for why utopianism should – and perhaps has to – have a place in any project for a better future, we now turn to the various dynamics of utopias and of post-work utopianism in particular. Here we want to unpack the relationship between utopias and our everyday experience. We also want to explore what utopia, and utopianism as a form of writing, *does*: What are the *functions* of being utopian and how does this affect our understanding of post-work? What does post-work thought *do* when it confronts the present state of labour with its ideas and why is it so important that post-work remains 'radically ideal' in the face of an often disappointing reality?

Lodestars

Perhaps the most obvious function of utopias is that of guiding lodestars, or steers, for our actions and experience. The most familiar example of a lodestar is the North Star – an important fixture within the night sky that has guided sailors for centuries. Here we can draw out the theoretical aspects of lodestars by drawing on some of the concepts deployed by Enlightenment philosopher Immanuel Kant, in his philosophy of experience. For Kant, our experience and our practical activity are constituted by an oscillation between sensory data and the transcendental structure of our cognition, or between experience and our 'faculty of understanding'. There are other important ingredients that Kant notes, however – and these he calls 'regulative ideals' (sometimes translated as 'ideas'). Famously these are: the soul, the world and God. These ideals are, according to Kant, built into the structure of our perception, guiding and shaping our activity: we experience ourselves *as if* we had a soul (or self), we act *as if* there is a world outside us, and we are moral *as if* there were a god. Kant argues that these ideals are postulated by our 'faculty of reason' and are without empirical grounding (and are therefore not valid for trustworthy knowledge). Nonetheless, regulative ideals can be treated pragmatically *as if* they existed, or entertained in faith as necessary premises of morality. We never really know the world in-itself, God or the non-empirical self via experience, but we successfully navigate the world by use of these guiding lights.[38]

For Kant, reason always overflows the bounds of what we can know, into the stormy seas of speculation, proposition, thought experiment. This can be dangerous (when our speculation is unmoored from empirical data), but also potentially revelatory. The conservative reading of Kant's conception says that we must limit knowledge to the combination of empirical data and the way we arrange that data with our faculties, that is, in the synthesis of experience. Beyond that, in the realm of 'pure reason', is mere speculation – which is useless and possibly dangerous (a claim reminiscent of the accusation that one can be dangerously utopian). By contrast, the radically *utopian* reading of Kant's theory – from which we argue that we can make sense of transformatory projects such as post-work – lies in the persistence and *power* of this speculative faculty. A utopian theory of knowledge does not, for example, assume such strict boundaries, such non-communication, between the sure footing of experience and the stormy seas of 'pure' thought. Indeed, the introduction of utopian ideas into present-day, empirical realities – an act of comparing, evaluating and contrasting – is, we argue, a process of knowledge production, clarification, and even generation of new questions and avenues of enquiry.

That is all to say that, as with Kant's theory of perception, utopias can provide the steers – the regulative ideals – for our day-to-day practical activity: we act *as if* a radically different and more desirable world were possible. And, just as with Kant's regulative ideals, we never really get to utopia, but it guides us to approximations along its trajectory – we end up in places that are complicated and mixed with non-utopian elements, but are fundamentally shaped by their relationships to their non-realized ideals.

Such dynamics are at play in the writings of post-work theorists and their fellow travellers. We can see them in Pfannebecker and Smith's arguments for cultural change, for example.[39] Bastani's FALC, like *Inventing the Future* and the *Xenofeminist Manifesto*, also takes up the themes of modernity – itself a utopian project, of course – and extends them into the future. Demanding the *full*(er) automation of labour – continuing the mechanization of the nineteenth and twentieth centuries beyond the constraints of profit – is an obvious case in point, and one which we explored in previous chapters.[40] And, as is typical of the lodestar function, such a demand can never truly be fulfilled – what would full automation actually look like anyway? On the way, however, guided by the demands of FALC, undesirable, dangerous or dehumanizing labour is to be replaced by technology wherever possible – activating a cognitive shift away from the proliferation of jobs and towards prosperity beyond them.

Other post-work authors have similarly pointed to a set of lodestars via which we might orient ourselves in the present and target our collective efforts. Peter Frase sets out *Four Futures* in a grid of scarcity versus abundance and equality versus hierarchy.[41] The four possible futures he imagines – rentism, communism, socialism and exterminism – are all images that help us understand our present simply by serving as amplifications of existing socio-economic realities. The message here, of course, is that our actions in the present work to realize certain possibilities while foreclosing others. By parsing the present into four very possible directions, Frase unsticks us from the present; both his utopias and his dystopias provoke us to take positions on how we want to orient our travel.

The sense of directionality that utopian (as well as dystopian) visions can offer is incredibly important for progressive forces, for multiple reasons. Asking for the North Star of a political and philosophical position is particularly useful, for example, in rooting out deeply held ideological beliefs and habits. 'What would your ideal future be?', or 'where do you think we should be heading?' are questions that not only force us to explicitly expand our imaginations beyond the present order of things but also reveal the extent to which our fantasies and ideals are coloured by the society we live in – including the dominant attitudes and practices that we brush up against everyday. Work, as a topic and lived reality, is a particularly good example of this: discussing different futures of our working lives reveals so much about our present attitudes towards work, as well as what we feel is possible at an individual and societal level. Without the breakage that utopian visions offer us, we risk being stuck thinking and living within the confines of the present – too easily seduced by falsely constrained ideas about what is possible.

Such productive tensions, between really existing states of affairs and the ideal potentiality (lodestar) of a better future, flow throughout Western philosophy from Kant to the radical theory of the twentieth century, where critique, or philosophy, is tied closely to utopianism or even 'phantasy'.[42] In a defining essay of the period, Frankfurt School theorist Max Horkheimer sought to distinguish what he called 'critical theory' from 'traditional theory' on the grounds of its relationship to the present. Traditional theory – natural science, for example – is premised upon the mere description of the world, the 'registering and classifying of facts'. This allows for predictions as to the likely outcomes of experiments based on a set of given conditions, identifying causes and relations between things. Critical Theory, on the contrary, approaches the given reality via the acknowledgement of the contradiction between the ideal/goal of a rational state of society and the present, real state that the theorist finds herself in. Horkheimer writes: 'the idea of a future society of free men, which is possible through technical means already at hand, does have a content, and to it there must be fidelity amid all change.'[43]

In essence, while natural science is essentially an accumulation of empirical facts – mere recordings of the world, its causal connections and the predictions that can be based on these findings – *Critical* Theory is predisposed to pushing beyond what merely exists in order to ask whether things *ought* to be thus. Are we a just and equal society? Is our current socio-economic setup one which maximizes freedom? How can we understand our social conditions in relation to the kinds of worlds we aspire to and which we'd wish to inhabit? It is in this way that Critical Theory always keeps the future in frame when it approaches present, modern society. (For Marx, of course, it is imperative that we go further still, moving beyond an understanding of the *ought* to intervene within the *is*; 'Philosophers have hitherto only interpreted the world in various ways; the point is to change it'.)[44]

Horkheimer and his colleague Herbert Marcuse's distinction between natural scientific prediction and Critical Theory's counterposing of ideal states with real conditions helps us think through some of post-work's positions regarding automation, noted in Chapter 3, for example. Post-work doesn't – or shouldn't – make predictions as to the likelihood (or not) of automation within the present system – a task better suited to the specialist disciplines on the matter. Instead, it intends to make – or force – potentials into reality: automation *should* happen, for the 'true labour saving' of humankind.[45] In Critical Theory's language, post-work deploys fidelity to the idea of a certain use of technology, rather than simply awaiting its arrival.

Estrangement and provocation

We can also identify two further functions of utopian ideals, which Weeks sees as essential to understanding the force of post-work visions: estrangement and provocation. 'As a force of negation, utopian forms can promote critical perspectives on and disinvestment in the status quo.'[46] Utopias denaturalize the present situation, render it contingent, perhaps irrational, weird, undesirable. This opens the possibility for a different future (simply by neutralizing the strength of the present).[47] Other utopias, Weeks tells us, provide a vision of a desirable world that *provokes* our sensibilities and imaginations into affirming a position of hope: 'as a mode of affirmation, utopias can function as provocations toward alternatives.'[48] They stimulate us to expand our imaginations. They redraw the lines of what we might think is possible by jumping to a more alien proposition. They might provoke people to act, providing 'something to fight for' (and not just against). Above all, to use E.P. Thompson's eloquent description of William Morris' utopian writings, utopias 'teach desire to desire, to desire better, to desire more, and above all to desire in a different way'.[49]

What is Fully Automated Luxury Communism but a provocative, regulative idea, or, as Bastani calls it, a 'map by which we can escape the labyrinth of scarcity and a society built on jobs'?[50] FALC's title forces us to imagine communism beyond familiar images from actually existing communist states: long queues and supermarket shortages, grey tower blocks, compelled industrial and agricultural labour, and so on. Rather, we are invited to imagine communism as everything for everyone: cutting-edge technologies; opulent, accessible amenities; plenty of leisure time. This counter-intuitive vision establishes a minimal guiding light, leading out of dreary capitalist realism and away from backwards visions of socialism. It estranges us from the bottlenecked luxury of the few that we currently experience, but also provokes us to hope for abundance for all.

Post-work provocations can also be identified in Sophie Lewis' calls for the abolition of the family, in Firestone's demand for cybernetic communism and ectogenesis, and in xenofeminism's call for the superseding of binary gender itself.[51] 'Together', Lewis forces us to countenance, 'we can establish consensus-based modes of transgenerational cohabitation, and large-scale methods for distributing and minimizing the burdens of life's work'.[52] Each of these demands arguably represents a potentially explosive interruption of our usual regimes of socially reproductive labour that outrages and inspires in equal measure. In these cases, there is no detailed plan of policy interventions or programme of incremental reforms, but that is partly the point: their utopianism is a *method* by which to force open our imaginations in those areas of everyday life and work that seem impossibly rigid. For Weeks, indeed, the demand and the manifesto are the most ambitious and impatient forms of engagement with utopia: we want this, now, with no excuses!

Looking backwards: Utopia and work nostalgia

No one has ever substantially changed the world of work for the better by sticking closely to the presently existing *modus operandi*. Everything from the end of slavery and of child labour, the creation of the weekend, statutory sick pay and maternity leave to more modest proposals, such as the minimum wage, have entailed some provocative leap away from the present. Indeed, it goes without saying that an anti-utopian disposition can preclude new visions and practices for our working lives; this is true almost by definition. Nonetheless, a common, often implicit, position claims that we already have the vision of the future of work that we want, and it is usually some ensemble of old demands from a brighter period in history. We do not need to move forwards, such positions suggest, but backwards – to return to the utopia we did not know we had achieved. It is to this, often tempting, tendency that we now turn.

False idols of work

Post-work theory has often lamented the fact that our images of a radically better future of work are largely hand-me-downs from previous eras. Such nostalgia, we argue, highlights the dangers of *not* engaging in utopian thinking: we might continue to unknowingly adopt the visions of the past, wrongly assuming that these utopias are as relevant or desirable today as they were at very different historical moments. As Srnicek and Williams note, the post-war period of social democracy in the Global North is a regular candidate for a historical reality turned into a desirable future. It

> consists of dreams of social democracy and the so-called 'golden age' of capitalism. Yet the very conditions which once made social democracy possible no longer exist. The capitalist 'golden age' was predicated on the production paradigm of the orderly factory environment, where (white, male) workers received security and a basic standard of living in return for a lifetime of stultifying boredom and social repression. Such a system depended on an international hierarchy of empires, colonies and an underdeveloped periphery; a national hierarchy of racism and sexism; and a rigid family hierarchy of female subjugation.[53]

Nostalgia for a pre-neoliberal age gives false hope for a time that is 'both undesirable and impossible to recover'.[54] Srnicek and Williams continue:

> We can do better, and the social democratic adherence to jobs and growth means it will always err on the side of capitalism and at the expense of the people. Rather than modelling our future on a nostalgic past, we should aim to create a future for ourselves. The move beyond the constraints of the present will not be achieved through a return to a more humanised capitalism reconstructed from a misty-eyed recollection of the past.[55]

The same holds for a pre-factory system of labour – of household production. In her treatment of socialist responses to the brutality of modern work, Weeks warns against a humanist response as it can tarry dangerously close to a nostalgia for seemingly more humane, perhaps more humanly attuned, forms of work.[56] Such an attitude represents a nostalgia for a pre-industrial past, where work was apparently less alienating because of the greater control that artisanal modes of working afforded, and because of the relative lack of perceived separation between home and workplace.

However, such boons for certain (largely white) workers should not blind us to the historical situatedness of this trope, nor obscure the dubious features of the moment in history from which its nostalgia draws. The yearning for pre-factory modes of work has been around since precisely the emergence and imposition of the factory system in the second half of the nineteenth century, as we traced in Chapter 1. Daniel Rodgers' critical reconstruction of this period in industrial America reveals the fantasy (utopian ideal) of manual work particularly embodied in the figure of the blacksmith. 'His firmly set jaw revealed the character-building discipline of work, the muscles of his bare arm its usefulness, the tools he held in his hand its skill, and his blacksmith's apron … its sturdy independence.'[57] By the early twentieth century, however, despite the persistent use of the image in popular media, the paper-capped blacksmith was 'simply an unexamined anachronism'.[58]

Weeks points out that romantic (retro)projections of artisanal, pre-capitalist labour are far removed from Marx's own perspective on the issue. He writes in the *Grundrisse,* for example:

In earlier stages of development the single individual seems to be developed more fully, because he has not yet worked out his relationships in their fullness, or erected them as independent social powers and relations opposite himself. It is as ridiculous to yearn for a return to that original fullness as it is to believe that with this complete emptiness history has come to a standstill. The bourgeois viewpoint has never advanced beyond this antithesis between itself and this romantic viewpoint, and therefore the latter will accompany it as legitimate antithesis up to its blessed end.[59]

Marx's point here is simply to say that individual craftsmanship is an objectively less developed, pre-cooperative, mode of producing, which ignores scientific and technical capacities and assumes an originary 'fullness' of individuality that is simply irretrievable today. Indeed, the delicately interconnected and inter-reliant character of the household, and the role of women workers therein, would suggest that this fullness never existed to begin with – or, at least, that it always operated on a level beyond that of the solitary individual. Gorz forcefully picks up on this strand of criticism in his post-work theorizing. In our contemporary world, with advanced, complex and interconnected production processes, complete with vast institutions such as national health services or extensive transport infrastructures, with grand challenges such as climate change and ageing populations, requiring the leveraging of coordinated (state) action as well as highly technical digital tools, returning work to a semblance of artisanal production is (beyond a few occupations) simply not feasible, nor in fact desirable.[60] Nevertheless, in lieu of a modern alternative to destructive capitalist society, such an idea doggedly – but understandably – intrudes upon our imagination as a possible alternative.

No return: Horizontal utopianism

The lesson we can learn from such arguments, and historical realities, is that we need to keep our demands for better worlds – our utopias – updated for our current historical conjuncture. This is what utopia scholar Christopher Yorke calls 'horizontal utopianism': where 'there is no single, ideal blueprint that represents a stable end state for humanity'.[61] In other words, the future we want is always changing – based on the configuration of the present – in a constant feedback loop. We should remember, after all, that a number of the demands included in Marx and Engels' own *Communist Manifesto* have already been achieved in a great many countries: things such as a graduated income tax, the establishment of national banks, state-run transport, free education and the abolition of child labour are all now taken for granted in many places but were radically utopian when Marx and Engels proposed them.[62] Were we to write a 2025 *Manifesto*, it would obviously require a different set of demands.

If there is an enemy of post-work utopianism, then, it is work nostalgia: we should be incredibly suspicious when our images of the future of work resemble conditions of the past so closely. This backwards-looking stance should either underline the unviability of such visions or, perhaps even more importantly, shake our faith in their *desirability* (given the unsavoury nature of much of our industrial past).

The variety of post-work utopias

The content of post-work visions varies remarkably, even if they share the basic premise of a reduction of working time. As a family of resemblances, rather than a single delimited position, post-work texts can often disagree – offering alternative visions of the future of work that might be in tension with one another. It is this variation that simultaneously makes post-work less unified as a world view but also more rich as a resource – a storehouse of ideas capable of speaking to many audiences.[63] To close out this chapter, then, and having already discussed something of the general function of utopia for post-work politics, we want to provide some specific examples. From the lab to the home to the factory and beyond, post-work perspectives offer far-reaching visions of alternative futures – visions which, for all their differences, evince a common commitment to breaking out of the present and upending its ubiquitous dogma of work. We hope that the whistlestop tour below will leave you with a better sense of the breadth and diversity of the utopian approaches that one finds gathered beneath the post-work umbrella.

Autonomous spheres and good work

One region of post-work theorizing sees utopia as constituted by autonomous or self-directed activity. Andre Gorz's vision, for example, is premised on a heuristic division – one we consider useful for a post-work account of freedom – between what he names 'heteronomous' and 'autonomous' spheres. Gorz envisages individual and small-scale autonomy at the level of neighbourhoods or communities.[64] Here he often draws on Ivan Illich's notions of 'convivial tools' – a term denoting commonly used and equality-boosting technologies, as contrasted with the majority of currently existing industrial technologies that sediment hierarchy and facilitate exploitation.[65] Things such as local workshops with a range of commonly held tools, or communal gardens to cultivate shared food, are imagined. This is a vision of post-work that emphasizes the flourishing of *good* work: good for people, community and planet. The aim is

> not to exempt people from doing anything at all, but to open up possibilities for everyone to engage in a whole host of individual or collective, private or public activities – activities which no longer need to be profitable in order to flourish. From childhood onwards, everyone is to be involved in, and feel the attraction of, a general proliferation of groups, teams, workshops, clubs, co-operatives, associations and networks, all seeking to recruit him/ her into their activities and projects. Artistic, political, scientific, ecosophic,

sporting, craft and relational activities; self-providing, work on repairing and restoring the natural and cultural heritage, improving the environment, energy saving; crèches, 'health shops', networks for the exchange of services, for mutual aid and assistance, etc.[66]

The state – part of the heteronomous sphere – provides the necessary means for these autonomous spheres: primarily in the form of a basic income and physical infrastructure.

Under such conditions of socialized income and production, Gorz's vision provides a new taxonomy for what people's new, 'multi-centred' life might be composed of:

1. Heteronomous, macro-social work, organised across society as a whole, enabling it to function and providing for basic needs. [This would be the *heteronomous* work that we all (who can) have to do, but which is to be minimized as much as possible.]

2. Micro-social activity, self-organized on a local level and based on voluntary participation, except where it replaces macro-social work in providing for basic needs. [This would be the work that is more democratically organized and bespoke to local areas.]

3. Autonomous activity which corresponds to the particular desires and projects of individuals, families and small groups. [This would be the fullest expression of human freedom, which would rely on the heteronomous and micro-social activities above.][67]

In certain moments Gorz adopts a fictional, utopian register to give readers a glimpse of what a switch to post-work society might feel like: at the end of *Farewell to the Working Class*, for example, he imagines people waking up to a world that is subtly, but radically different:

When they woke up that morning, citizens asked themselves what new turmoil awaited them … In many places, empty buildings were being transformed into communes, production cooperatives, or 'alternative schools' … At noon, the government announced that it had reached the decision to institute free public transportation throughout the country, and to phase out, over the next 12 months, the use of private automobiles in the most congested urban areas.[68]

Here Gorz's vision chimes with Sylvia Pankhurst's much earlier 1920 vision of neighbourhood and household cooperation – again written as a piece of utopian fiction:[69]

> It is built round a square garden and there is another garden round it. There is also a garden on the roof. The dining-room and kitchen are on the top floor. The school nursery, crèche, and children's garden is at the end of the block of buildings. There are a tennis court, croquet lawn, a hall for meetings, concerts, dances, and so on, a sewing room, workshops for all sorts of crafts, a library and gymnasium, and two big summer houses in the garden, one of which is for the older children.[70]

With strong foreshadowing of Gorz's later work, as well as some of today's post-work design thinking,[71] Pankhurst describes shared facilities for skills cultivation and socializing, as well as communal leisure infrastructure, which is considered to be as important as tools of production.

> That evening, I threw all my reserves away. I went with my children to supper in the Household Common Room, played tennis with some of the other inmates, and finished up, with a dance on the roof.[72]

Many of the components of Gorz's vision also survive in today's post-work theorizing.[73] Kate Soper's intervention into the post-work debate, for example, leans on that part of Gorz's writing that highlights the (apparently) inherent value of certain forms of work and seeks to guard against tech-focused futures. While Soper 'would certainly welcome the role of automation and green technologies in making more free time available', she is critical of a reliance on technology and advocates for a shift in our forms of consumption.[74] She, like Gorz, sees 'domestic and caring tasks – the work of running a house, and especially looking after children' as part of the intrinsically valuable zone of life – one which should not be violated by the mechanisms of automation.[75] We could perhaps say, then, that thinkers such as Gorz and Soper centre demands for *revaluing* certain kinds of work to the extent that we might not want to reduce them.

Complicating autonomy: Post-work visions of the domestic

While many post-work thinkers share the vision of Gorz and Soper of more autonomous spaces and a reduction of the waged working week, they sometimes also problematize the naturalized work of the household or home.[76] As we argued in previous chapters, no post-work vision can be adequate if it fails to address domestic work, the function it plays in the wider economy and the myriad forms it takes.[77] But the glorification of care work can, of course, preclude its redistribution – why should we want to share the load of housework or care work if it is indeed so rewarding and worthwhile? It also runs the risk of preventing the recognition that these activities are indeed *work* – care is a labour of *love*, is it not? These are concerns that, as we have seen, the Wages for Housework movement and others have successfully brought to the attention of many on the feminist left.[78] How, then, can our 'reduce, recognize and redistribute' mantra inform a vision of work that accounts for this gendered, invisibilized and often intimate zone of life?

Fortunately, there is a rich history of such visions, which offer glimpses of a post-work utopia that *redistributes* the work of the home so as to reduce it for all. Take the Soviet house commune, for example, which was for a time widely touted as the most appropriate form of communist housing in Russia. It was intended not only as an efficient use of space but also as a tool for producing new forms of subjectivity and daily life. As part of this vision, communal resources such as laundries, childcare facilities and kitchens were to enable domestic work to be shared and rationalized according to principles of efficiency (although these grand ambitions were unfortunately rarely ever realized).

We could think also of Pankhurst's vision of communist domesticity, in which a team of well-trained professionals uses advanced technologies (vacuum cleaners, 'automatic pan cleansers', collective laundries) and cooperative working practices (high-spec 'domestic workshops') to alleviate many of the burdens of housework.[79] Within these imaginaries, we are confronted by the simple but powerful idea of decomposing domestic work in order to allow for more pleasurable pursuits: 'The introduction of communal housekeeping will open them opportunities for leisure, recreation, and education hitherto unknown.'[80] And of course, there are many other experimental alternatives to single family living that we could and should draw on, from turn-of-the-century co-operative homes and apartment hotels to interwar social housing, all of which include illuminating elements of labour-saving design.[81]

Elsewhere in our own work, we have sought to identify lessons for post-work, post-capitalist thinking from within this history, calling for 'private sufficiency' and 'public luxury'.[82] While 'luxury' is taken, by some theorists of utopia, to signify mainly carbon-intensive, costly lifestyles that are out of the reach of many,[83] we have sought to repurpose this term to mean something closer to an abundance of resources and services of a certain standard: 'luxury is about high-quality regardless of the quantity of supply available, and ... luxury is about things which go beyond mere need.'[84] Rather than seek to render those things that currently only the richest can enjoy as in themselves inherently undesirable, this kind of post-work position wants to broaden access to the joys of life – the roses as well as the bread – to the many. In practice, 'that would mean some space of our own in which personal needs can be met' – the private sufficiency of a room of one's own, for example – but 'massively augmented by a revived commons' which would include things such as public swimming pools and baths, libraries, common workshops, sports facilities, shared vacation accommodation and more.[85]

Here we clearly see resonances with Gorz's utopia of collective, convivial life as a mixture of infrastructural heteronomy and private autonomy. However, there is also room to go further; we would argue that these infrastructures should also accommodate the care requirements that have hitherto been privatized in the family home. Hence, we call for

> the creation of alternative institutions that might better serve the functions that are currently squeezed into the family unit. The point is to create a whole series of new institutions and ways to meet the needs that the family is supposed to handle – to disaggregate the functions that have been combined within the family, often awkwardly even at the best of times. Should a parent really be expected to meet all the caring needs of a child? For education, friendship, guidance, mentorship, and so on?[86]

This step seeks to bring post-work politics into direct conversation with 'family abolitionist' theory – such as that of Sophie Lewis and M.E. O'Brien – in order to stress a particular kind of feminist orientation.[87] Post-work must – if it is to be comprehensive and emancipatory – strive to have socially reproductive work revalued, redistributed and reduced, and those critical of the family's adverse effects as a social form must engage in the politics of (the reduction of) work.[88]

Post-work scientific utopias

In other areas, authors approach post-work themes through scaled-up thinking around future scientific and technological developments. One could mention here the work of Pankhurst's younger contemporary John Desmond Bernal – a world-leading scientist of his age.[89] His *The Social Function of Science* (1939) is in effect a scientific utopia beyond capital, wherein Bernal details the post-capitalist laboratory, articulates a comprehensive strategy for manufacturing, mining and engineering industries, as well as the various ways science could be 'in the service of man'.[90] Key here – presaging twentieth-century post-work themes – are the chapters on work and play. 'Work: The worker, not profit, as a prime consideration; machinery to remove, not create, drudgery' and 'Play: Remaking the world' deserve attention, alongside the chapters on housing, food and health, as part of a modern scientific vision unfettered by the profit motive. Bernal's scientific utopianism, which in other, more extravagant texts extends at times to space travel and the unification of individual brains into a kind of literal hivemind,[91] was written before Big Tech and Big Science drained science of much of its emancipatory purpose. With Bernal, we are given the tantalizing prospect of a post-work science, with the stem of a fairly concrete research programme.

Today, authors such as Leigh Philipps pick up the challenge of a scientific utopia (and generate some often heated debates in the process). Philipps argues against what he perceives as the austere abstention from developing new forms of technology (of the kind that Soper sometimes gestures towards). It is simply too late, he suggests (in the spirit of Bernal), for humanity to 'step back', withdraw from industrial technologies and 'let nature be'.

By turning its back on the possibility of such technologies, on the very idea of progress, green anti-modernism actually commits us to catastrophic climate change.[92]

Not intervening, with the best technologies available for the task, is no longer an option if we are serious about mitigating the damage that we as a species have wrought. As we discussed in our chapter on technology, post-work's Promethean disposition can allow us to ask more nuanced questions about technological development, such as 'who' a particular technology is for; 'where' it might be developed, produced and used; and 'what' function it should ultimately serve – without abandoning tech altogether.[93] In many cases, post-work seeks to retain what is emancipatory and enabling about technoscience while guarding (as far as possible) against its damaging deployments – 'to seize the *technology* without buying the ideology'.[94] The *Xenofeminist Manifesto*, for example, argues for a feminist occupation and repurposing of science – rejecting anti-scientific perspectives that can be a trope of some kinds of progressive movements:

> To claim that reason or rationality is 'by nature' a patriarchal enterprise is to concede defeat. It is true that the canonical 'history of thought' is dominated by men, and it is male hands we see throttling existing institutions of science and technology. But this is precisely why feminism must be a rationalism – because of this miserable imbalance, and not despite it. There is no 'feminine' rationality, nor is there a 'masculine' one. Science is not an expression but a suspension of gender. If today it is dominated by masculine egos, then it is at odds with itself – and this contradiction can be leveraged. Reason, like information, wants to be free, and patriarchy cannot give it freedom. Rationalism must itself be a feminism. XF marks the point where these claims intersect in a two-way dependency. It names reason as an engine of feminist emancipation, and declares the right of everyone to speak as no one in particular.

Such a perspective also famously informs Srnicek and Williams' rejection of 'folk politics', as well as Bastani's insistence on the trajectory of technical innovations in the fields of food, energy and ageing. In these post-work imaginaries, R&D is untethered from the imperative to make profit and put instead towards the re-acceleration of history. We could also mention John Danaher's thought experiments in post-work utopianism ('The Cyborg Utopia' and 'The Virtual Utopia') here, both of which explore new, tech-augmented realities in their ethical and philosophical aspects. In a previous chapter, we have also made various post-work arguments around technology, capitalism and our shared futures which we would suggest fit into this category.

Greening post-work

There is a notable omission from the post-work utopias we have mentioned so far: visions for a green utopia.[95] This is evidently a problem. Climate change and its societal – potentially civilizational – fallout is clearly, in terms of scale and impact, the greatest challenge of our age. No utopian vision can afford to avoid the materiality of this ongoing crisis: it is the reality to which our ideal worlds must respond. Responding to criticisms of their work in the expanded edition of *Inventing the Future*, Srnicek and Williams also pick up on this lack:

> We fully admit that issues of climate change and ecological sustainability are not dealt with in anywhere near enough depth in the text … However, we think a post-work politics has much to offer any attempt to overcome the division between a labour politics premised on growth and jobs, and a green politics premised on reining in pollution and greenhouse gas emissions.[96]

Indeed, this absence within post-work is beginning to be rectified – predominantly because people are beginning to connect the dots between degrowth and post-growth on the one hand and post-work themes on the other, in the manner gestured to in the quotation above.[97] Shorter working weeks, for example, have been part of degrowth literature for decades, as production, consumption and carbon emissions are deeply intertwined, with the intensity and duration of work being a key factor.[98] Simply put, all productive activity is based on material and energy throughputs, which occur in a wider environmental context. Any action on mitigating climate change will have to change the quality and quantity of this activity.[99]

The conversation around shortening the working week is also picking up within 'Green New Deal' literature. Kate Aronoff, Alyssa Battistoni, Daniel Aldana Cohen and Thea Riofrancos, for example, include reduced working time as part of their core set of GND proposals.[100] They point to the burdens and injustices of the contemporary workplace – 'the domination of the workplace still keeps most of us unfree'[101] – and see the obvious benefits of working time reduction being part of green political strategy:

> Under a radical Green New Deal, with efficiency gains and automation controlled by people rather than bosses, we could meet everyone's needs working far less than we currently do – and we should. Study after study shows that shorter workweeks lower carbon footprints – the shorter the better. To cut carbon, we need to work less and share the remaining work more evenly.[102]

This contemporary revival of advocacy for shorter hours chimes with elements of the original New Deal. The Fair Labour Standards Act (1938), for example, included new regulation around working time, establishing a normal working week of forty hours and a minimum wage. These reforms were led by Frances Perkins, the first woman ever appointed to the US Cabinet and an ardent campaigner for workers' rights and gender equality.[103] Prior to this legislation, in the heart of the Great Depression, Roosevelt deployed a 'President's Reemployment Agreement': effectively a seal of approval from the very top that encouraged firms to reduce the average workweek and raise hourly wage rates.[104] These reforms and others like it offered American workers a new collective sense of freedom and prosperity, changing their world of work for the better. Today's demands for a Green New Deal can follow in these footsteps, providing a vision of a future that people can see as immediately desirable *as well as* environmentally necessary.

With the demand for an unconditional basic income, too, there is potential for useful climate action and post-work synergy:

> Postwork undercuts the primary reason to need growth and jobs – namely the attachment of income to work – thereby enabling new connections to be made between the movements.[105]

As basic income campaigns continue to grow alongside the developing climate crisis, useful coalitions could be formed to push economic justice, security and climate goals. Indeed, UBI economists such as Guy Standing advocate for a tax on carbon consumption in order to pay out dividends to populations as part of a 'Commons Fund'.[106]

> Ecological taxes and levies are needed to curb pollution, global warming and the plunder of the commons on which we all depend. But because some of those levies would be regressive, increasing inequalities, they will need to be matched by dividends paid equally to everybody.[107]

The research is also there to support such ambitions – making the utopian vision more concrete. We have been involved in economic modelling – via the Autonomy Institute – that has shown that such a 'carbon UBI' policy would redistribute trillions if enacted globally. As high-carbon consumption tends to be the preserve of those with higher incomes in the Global North, those that are taxed most will tend to be those with the broadest shoulders, who use carbon-intensive goods and services such as air travel. In contrast, middle-class and working-class groups will benefit most from a carbon-tax funded UBI, as well as populations in the Global South, whose consumption tends to be more sustainable.[108]

Other contemporary authors are drawing important connections between post-carbon and post-work futures. Holly Jean Buck, for example, channels post-work theory across her books on climate, citing the *Xenofeminist Manifesto*, Srnicek and Williams and others in the melting pot of her influences. In particular, Buck's perspective chimes with the post-work technological visions articulated above, this time directing them towards the debate around climate technologies. Her work is particularly useful in underlining the fact that *removing* carbon dioxide from our atmosphere is essential to any mission to mitigate or even simply adapt to climate change.[109] We cannot simply revert to some previous state – a 'simpler way of life' – and expect our climate to do likewise. Rather, we will require advanced technologies and applied science in order to combat, and adapt to, our changing climate and all of its effects. We will need to predict, model and act with precision: for this we will need highly advanced sensing apparatuses.[110] The renewable energy infrastructure, too – for tidal power, wind power, and so on – will need continuous innovation and roll-out. 'Having a planetary sensing infrastructure that can recursively act upon ecological events that it models isn't a bad thing … we need to bring [these kinds of infrastructure] under public control and direct them to public aims. Including phaseout.'[111]

An appropriate climate response, in short, will require a Green Prometheanism, of the kind post-work is comfortable with, and on an unprecedented scale. This gives new significance to Shulamith Firestone's comment that 'every fact of nature that is understood can be used to alter it'.[112] Not only should we *not* see nature as an absolute limit to our activity but in fact we *have* to see nature (a category, of course, which includes ourselves) as changeable, workable material if we are to survive this catastrophe. The climate problem thus demands a *recalibration,* rather than a refutation, of Prometheanism's picture of the world, providing a richer sense of our own material conditions of existence in order that we can act upon them. Succeeding in mitigating climate change, and sustaining a liveable planet thereafter, will, after all, be humanity's most Promethean moment yet.

Buck's use of dystopias/utopias – the kind of realistic, complicated and imperfect scenarios that Weeks would describe as 'critical utopias' – is another good example of how post-work imaginaries *estrange* us from present day realities. Here we see the idea of utopia operating in a somewhat different capacity. Each chapter of Buck's *After Geoengineering* comes with a fictional representation of future life alongside carbon capture and storage tech of one kind or another. Climate-mitigated life has its mundane struggles as well as its new opportunities, and such stories are enriched with everyday detail: Buck's text thus performs the utopian function of estrangement – where we are ushered into believing a radically new (post-carbon) world could exist, precisely *by* normalizing it.

Another recent contributor to the field is Cara Daggett, whose research on the energy-work nexus draws important lessons around how to achieve an ecologically sustainable planet *through* a post-work politics. Daggett uses a genealogy of the concept of 'energy' in order to unravel our cultural and economic obsessions with productivity and 'work', both in the thermodynamic sense of energy use and the social effects that this paradigm has had on our societies. By drawing on extensive and diverse research on the nineteenth-century conjunction of Protestantism and physics (around the value of work), as well as the deployment of the work-energy paradigm as part of colonial governance of indigenous peoples, Daggett's work builds out post-work's climate-relevance considerably. In short, considering the human as an organic motor – following the same conservation, waste and 'running down' logics as machines – has infected our understanding of ourselves as living material in all sorts of ways.[113] We have adopted as common sense a 'work-waste' ethos wherein all human resources must be optimized for productivity, all surplus is to be put to work and all waste avoided; the context of slavery and colonial rule brings the effects of such a paradigm into focus, as enslaved and/or indigenous people were routinely stigmatized and violently coerced into line as productive bodies.

Fundamentally, when envisioning our post-carbon world, Daggett argues that we should be wary of using the same paradigms that have dominated our thinking in the West since the industrial era.[114] Reading the implications for today, she warns against climate movements leaning too heavily into a pro-employment, pro-productivity strategy.

> A work-waste ethos stacks the deck in favor of fossil fuels. If environmentalists operate within a work-based argument, positing that alternative energy will support job growth and a healthier economy, they get mired in a back-and-forth over accounting logics that, in the spirit of neoliberalism, sidelines normative and political claims.[115]

Job creation as an end in itself is a good example of the bind in which the work dogma places environmental campaigns. The most common, and currently strongest, argument in favour of maintaining fossil fuel industries is that they are key sources of employment (and therefore livelihoods).[116] 'Jobs, jobs, jobs' is a slogan that will rear its head again and again, and dovetails, as Daggett notes, with a masculine identity tied to 'good jobs' in mining, or heavy industry, which have traditionally come with decent pay. She asks us to imagine, however, an alternative world – one in which carbon-heavy nations had 'instituted the feminist, utopian demands of a basic income and shorter hours, such that full-time, traditional waged work was no longer an economic necessity.[117] In such a situation – where a recognizably post-work vision prevails – the 'jobs, jobs, jobs' argument would be 'toothless'.[118]

Ultimately, Daggett writes 'in the spirit of a new planetary politics', and to this end, she makes the claim that climate-oriented movements and post-work visions actually rely on each other for their realization.

> Without challenging dominant practices of work and leisure, and the high valuation of waged, productive work in a neoliberal economy, it will remain difficult to dislodge fossil fuel cultures … If energy remains tightly bound to productive work, and the work ethic goes unchallenged – a work ethic that applies not only to human labor, but also to the fuels, technologies, and nonhumans put to work for humans – then any threatened decrease in energy consumption becomes automatically tainted as dreary, ascetic, and constrained, even if it espouses vitality and hope.[119]

Post-work critique – unravelling our dominant practices and attitudes to work – might be the necessary route to the modification of our behaviours required for sufficient climate action. In turn, we shouldn't forget, post-work advocacy must reckon with its own carbon implications – and here Daggett is critical of unchecked enthusiasm for automation.[120] She warns that 'full automation, even if harnessed to a postcapitalist economy, will continue to imperil the planet if the underlying spirit of productivism remains'.[121] This is a point we have raised in the context of some of our own attempts to articulate a post-work utopia; a post-scarcity world is nevertheless still a finite world, and will as such demand certain trade-offs, such as 'balancing ecological impacts with post-work ambitions. If a machine made it newly possible to automate away all domestic drudgery, yet its ecological ramifications were significant, a decision would have to be made about whether or not such a technology should be adopted'.[122] Full, luxury communism must be automated within our carbon budgets. What is key, though, is the idea that such trade-offs might become a matter of collective contestation – a utopian notion given that these kinds of decisions are currently 'largely left up to profit-seeking companies and their marketing wings'. Here, deliberation between competing norms and values (of which a drive to minimize the burdens of work is only one) comes to represent a practice of freedom in and of itself.

Daggett's call to 'liberate energy' is a call to recode our relationship to work and life more generally. She calls for a utopia involving 'more ecologically generous ways of life on Earth'.[123] This is close to what philosopher Georges Bataille once named a 'general economy' of energy, in contrast to the 'restricted economy' of accumulation and production.[124] For Bataille – a post-work thinker *avant le lettre*, operating in the Surrealist circles of 1930s Paris – capitalist and communist societies alike had forged their cultures and the everyday lives of populations around the idea of production without end.[125] This, he insisted, was a tragic misunderstanding of the nature of our material lives as living human beings. We are in fact vectors for thermodynamic *expenditure*; we absorb and accumulate energy for our own existence, yes, but it is how we spend that energy that makes us (and all life) unique. Festivals, play, rest, communal endeavour, art of all kinds – these activities, which are ends in themselves and not mere economic inputs, are listed by Bataille as part of a sketch of a rebalanced energy economy.[126]

Daggett and Bataille's insistence on a new relationship with energy, work and production is consonant with the post-work visions of the future that this book has been advancing. For post-work thinkers, as we have seen in previous chapters, the production of goods and services is only reasonable and rational if it minimizes labour in order to make way for more freely chosen activities. While we cannot – and perhaps would not want to – give up much of the complex, technological world in which we now live, we should contain these tools of productivity within a culturally acknowledged zone of necessity or 'heteronomy'. Production and distribution infrastructures are merely the basis for what we might call autonomous explorations of the relations between individuals and of activities without further productive end: new uses of energy.

Conclusion: From utopian vision to post-capitalist realism

This chapter has explored the utopian impulse within post-work theorizing, demonstrating that while the scope and content of specific political visions has varied considerably, an attentiveness to and orientation towards an as-yet-unrealizable future remains consistent. Indeed, we have suggested that this might be a *definitional* element of the post-work project – one of the things which lends this loose constellation of resemblances a recognizable identity, and which elevates it from being simply a set of policy proposals into a wider philosophical project. In order to be considered part of this tradition, texts, authors or positions must contain some (at least minimal) propositional content. Post-work does not simply resist the work ethic or particular forms of labour, then – although of course this is crucial. It also considers a world beyond work and – to a greater or lesser extent – explores how we might strive to bring such a world into being.

This utopian, genuinely creative element of post-work theory has been one of its most enduring strengths. Not only does it insist upon the possibility of systems change but it also helps to guard against the lure of nostalgia – nostalgia for household production, the post-war consensus and cultures of work that are now, thankfully, a thing of the past. While we might be able to turn to history (and to historical utopias) for inspiration, we must ultimately never lose sight of the fact that we cannot return to a previous era – and nor should we want to. Whichever period we might look to, we will find tensions, inequalities and injustices that we would not wish to import wholesale into either present or future worlds of work.

Of course, in seeking to usher in futures that break from both past and present, utopian post-work theorizing can leave itself vulnerable to critical attack. Such theorizing invites scrutiny, and will likely be found lacking, either in detail and pragmatism or in terms of ideological correctness (or both!). Specific utopian visions are also very much a product of and reflection upon their times, and as such are likely to date quickly. As our discussion of climate collapse and green politics has indicated, it is important to keep post-work utopias nimble, responsive and reflective of changing contemporary conditions; as subjectivities and societies evolve, a utopia may lose its relevance and cease to be fit for purpose. Who, then, would risk being a utopian?

As Firestone puts it, the demand that one produce a blueprint for a social alternative is 'the classic trap for any revolutionary', and it is perhaps easier and more comfortable to stick to diagnosis while neglecting prescription. In her view, however, there can be greater political dangers in *refusing* to offer future-oriented concrete proposals, given that such a refusal represents both an abdication of responsibility and a 'failure of imagination concerning alternatives'.[127] The answer to utopia anxiety is not to refuse to stick one's neck out but to understand that any utopia should invite evaluation, and act as a *provisional, perpetually revisable* hypothesis about a better world. In an era in which the necessity of systems change is strikingly apparent (and, it would seem, increasingly accepted), we would do well to foster more such hypotheses.

As a 'non' place, utopia is characterized by its inaccessibility and non-existence – a reaching for the forever-out-of-reach. Structurally, it can never be arrived at, and instead represents difference from the now (or 'progress', to use a deeply unfashionable word). This is something we have negotiated throughout this chapter, as we have explored an assortment of examples of post-work utopianism – some more concerned with long-range speculation, and others more invested in worlds just beyond our fingertips. Even the more ambitious or far-reaching examples go beyond mere empty fantasizing, however. An interest in how alternatives are to be engineered – that is, in how to foster the conditions whereby today's utopias might be brought within tomorrow's field of feasibility – is in all cases retained.

The post-work utopian impulse, then, is in some ways a project of abolishing post-work as a utopia: to move decisively towards the horizon, to the point at which it ceases to be a horizon at all, but becomes rather the very ground beneath our feet. It adopts the perspective of winning, and pushes to ensure that what is impossible in the here and now (in terms of the reduction, revaluation and redistribution of work) becomes in time a new reality and a new form of common sense. At that point, a different version of utopia will emerge, and post-work perspectives as we know them will be transformed into something else – namely, part and parcel of post-capitalist realism.

Conclusion: Post-work's future

In his book on the topic, Lewis Mumford notes that utopias and utopian thought arise in the midst of 'storms' – social, political and economic unrest.[1] Mumford notes that Plato wrote *The Republic* in the wake of the Peloponnesian War, while Thomas More wrote *Utopia* in the transition from the Medieval epoch to the disruptions of the Renaissance. Mumford himself was writing in the 1920s – after the devastation of the First World War and in a time of recovery for Europe and the United States.

His observation regarding crisis and utopia holds true of today's post-work discourse. We are ourselves in the middle of a storm. In the past fifteen years we have witnessed the 2008 financial crisis, the political upheaval of Brexit and Trumpism, the hollowing out of the political centre, the rise of left and right populisms, the Covid pandemic, a global energy and inflation crisis, a genocide in Gaza and ongoing environmental catastrophe.[2] Throughout this period, which has seen a further deterioration of working life across not just the Global South but also more affluent nations, post-work theory has re-emerged with new energy and urgency. Many of the authors we associate with this tendency point to a 'crisis of work' – the precise coordinates of which vary from author to author: it can refer to the huge rise in non-standard, precarious employment; it can refer to the negative – potentially catastrophic – effects of new technologies in the workplace; it might index continued gender inequality or the mental health epidemic that is deeply entwined with overwork; or it can refer to all these things at once.[3]

No matter what version is proffered, however, many post-work authors believe that elements of this crisis will persist and become more acute as the twenty-first century progresses, spurring the need for alternatives. The authors of *Inventing the Future* note correctly that those pushing for post-work utopias missed the opportunity to reconfigure and resignify our working lives after the 2008 crash: that book was in part written in anticipation of the next crisis.[4] It is no surprise, then, that during the Covid crisis, post-work demands – four-day weeks and universal basic income in particular – have become more prominent than they have been for decades: whole swathes of national populations were literally paid to not work, while 'essential workers' – from healthcare professionals to bus drivers, teachers to supermarket employees – were required to put their lives on the line by continuing to do their jobs. In short order the dogmas that informed many of our working lives were thrown into question. We predict that as future crises emerge, we can expect to read more post-work – and post-work adjacent – visions and proposals.

Post-work's longevity

Indeed, the potential longevity of post-work thought and practice is easily grasped if you accept some basic premises about the current historical conjuncture and ongoing material tendencies. Here are four summary arguments in this regard:

- Capitalist economic activity continues to revolve around the (paid and unpaid) working time of the vast majority of the world's population: this time is charged with antagonism and strain, occasionally breaking out into conflict between workers and employers, or else taking its toll on the mental and physical health of workers privately. In this basic sense, just as it has been a feature of struggle throughout the industrial period so far, the reduction of working time will retain its relevance for at least as long as capitalism itself does.
- Secondly, the flipside to the fundamentality of the issue of working time is the equally essential question of welfare – of the treatment

and governance of the unemployed – which is, and has always been, suffused with coercion, violence and discontent. We can expect that calls for universal income floors (basic income) will grow as the crises and tumult of our time become more acute and unemployment (and underemployment) levels fluctuate. Post-work principles can help steer those conversations in more emancipatory directions.

- Thirdly, if we accept that production and workplace technologies will continue to be developed and deployed across industries – or that the very prospect of such technologies is likely to shape debates around futures of work – then we can expect continuing attempts to address this. Demands may work to ensure that the benefits of this tech can be shared between workforce and employers; this is where post-work synchronizes with traditional trade union demands for shorter hours and higher pay as a response.

- Finally, as the climate crisis produces more and more tangible symptoms and effects, the question of production will need to be raised more broadly. This is, at base, a question of how we work, what we produce and what we consume – and it is precisely to this question that post-work politics has responses. Whether this takes the form of degrowth, post-growth or 'green growth' perspectives,[5] the nature of work will be radically different and will require an alternative approach that avoids the drawbacks of hitherto industrial societies.

Whether any, all or just small parts of the various post-work utopian visions come to pass is of course impossible to tell. Indeed, this uncertainty is what drives many post-work authors to adopt demands, write manifestos or push concrete policies: we are not in the business of mere prediction but rather attempt to actively bring about the future we want. We move to collectively invent the future, demand an unconditional income separate from our work, unpick the traditional family model of work or indeed call for Fully Automated Luxury Communism. This is why post-work texts often blur the line between descriptions of the end goal and articulations of the steps to get there.[6]

This is also ultimately another key sense of the label 'post-work', which brings this coterie of authors, collectives and organizations together: its indeterminacy. We cannot know what the future of work looks like for certain – hence the fact that it is not given a specific name ('post-work' as a term is simply a negation – or sublation – of the present, after all). But we *can* envisage all sorts of end goals, non-reformist reforms and alternative living arrangements that act as coordinates for navigating towards (and ultimately shaping) that future. Post-work can be filled with content of many different varieties – and we have been showcasing something of that variety throughout this book.

Of course, providing the lodestar of a world where work is drastically reduced, revalued and redistributed is not enough: as we saw in Chapters 1 and 2, a world of shorter hours and freedom beyond labour-or-starve societies has to be fought for collectively.

Post-work's coalition

Towards this end, we must consider who will make up the allies within post-work's coalition for change. For whose material interests does post-work advocate, and who might actually fight for a world that approximates a post-work vision? More specifically, what role do our three post-work proposals – working time reduction, unconditional income and automation – play in bringing different people together as a post-work 'shared front'?

These questions are essential, given that a push for universal basic income, mass shorter working weeks or the progressive steering of labour-saving tech will require a social base or coalition from which to build. Such a movement focus was central to past campaigns for the five-day week, the struggle for child benefits and the Wages for Housework movements. In a sense, there was a productive reciprocity at play: demands gave shape and desire to movements, and an expanded social mass in turn gave more power to the demands. Of course, we think that post-work's thematics can gain traction over a very wide, even universal, social landscape; the organization of work is, after all, relevant to all (whether you 'have' it, or not). However, we will here concentrate on just three key groups of potential beneficiaries, identifying how their broad interests dovetail with the arguments in this book.

Labour movements

In contrast to the position of post-work's critics, we argue that there isn't a zero-sum game between workplace organizing to build labour's power, on the one hand, and wanting to reduce the dominance of work in our lives, on the other. While this might be obvious in the case of the demand for shorter work weeks – given the rich labour movement history around this issue – there is also a clear case for pushing for strong, universal income schemes above and beyond workplace reform.[7] Even a cursory look at high points of labour militancy – particularly the 1960s and 1970s – reveals that strong and widespread trade unionism and substantial welfare policies make for a potent foundational cocktail. This correlation makes sense when put in context of the threat of unemployment that is always lurking in the background of capitalist labour markets.[8]

The question for labour movement actors – both leaders and rank and file – is exactly what kind of unemployment system would improve their situation with respect to their position *vis-à-vis* employers? Is it one where you need to 'sign on' and be threatened with sanctions should you not comply with intrusive behaviour tests, or is it one upon which you can rely for support as a matter of right? It is a question, as we have argued above, that cannot be ignored or deflected by arguing for public services over, or instead of, cash benefits. With millions of people relying on this income in some form week to week, and with conservative cultural attacks and material cuts ongoing, the question of cash benefits for workers – both inside and outside the formal labour market – cannot be ignored.[9]

As Keir Milburn remarks: a strike is effectively a race to see who runs out of resources first – you or your employer;[10] this is why unions build strike funds. Having an extraneous source of income, a resource beyond that which your employer can control, is a source of power – a basic capacity that can support action and ultimately lead to positive changes in the workplace. For those in and around the Wages For Housework movement (which was not strictly speaking part of the 'Labour Movement' but which was nevertheless a movement of labourers) getting paid for socially reproductive work unlocks a radical potentiality beyond mere recognition. For Federici, the recognition of the value of the unpaid work of the home is merely a stepping stone to reducing it. She declares, 'we want money for each moment of it, so that we can refuse some of it and eventually all of it'.[11] Unconditional cash is thus in service of what is sometimes called 'anti-productivist' tendencies – or it at least facilitates a revaluation of work according to our own ends.[12]

Rathbone too saw the usefulness of her proposed family allowances (a proto-universal cash payment) in light of greater leverage at work:

> There is another advantage to the wage-earners which might follow from direct provision, though whether it did so or not would depend on the form adopted. If family allowances were paid by the State out of taxation, they would naturally continue throughout periods of unemployment and strikes.[13]

Once again, Rathbone's point underlines the porous nature of the 'relations of production', into which direct (non-wage) cash benefits intervene and upon which they can have significant impact. This view was in fact shared in 1930 by the Labour Party and the Trades Union Congress, whose Majority Report stated:

> We agree with those … Trade Union leaders who have told us that they are very firm in their view that a system of [State] Family Allowances would not hamper the Unions at all in their negotiations. Indeed, we believe that during industrial conflicts the Unions will be very considerably helped by the existence of such a scheme, since the workers' children will be removed from the 'firing line' and a great factor of weakness will thus be removed.[14]

The same argument follows for a basic income: it would be another pipeline of support to those in the middle and working classes, whether they are working or on strike, giving them an extra crutch with which to face the labour market on terms more favourable to them. Continuing the logic, let's take adults 'out of the firing line' too. Decoupling income and work – and giving more leverage to working people – would in this way bolster worker confidence and therefore likely diminish the supply of workers for the worst paid work and for work that is experienced as meaningless.[15]

Finally, as Weeks argues, augmenting trade union activity with coalitions that do not fall within its usual remit is in fact absolutely crucial for achieving a more emancipatory future of work:

> Traditional union-based politics, with its continued tendency to focus on some employment sectors over others, waged workers more than unemployed workers, and waged rather than unwaged workers means that it is a necessary but certainly insufficient approach to the struggle over work.[16]

The question then becomes how these non-traditional cohorts can be empowered and brought into solidarity with one another. If the trade union movement can become an advocate for better life outside of employment, as well as for shorter hours within it, it will be all the more powerful as a result.

Unemployed movements

As we noted in Chapter 2, capitalism as an economic system always maintains a 'surplus' or 'reserve army' of unemployed people desperate for work; it does this by making employment the only means via which to access the goods we need to survive and by making life outside of work essentially intolerable – a constant, disciplining threat to those working in the labour market. With Weeks, we argue that there is huge potential – though of course many challenges – to be found in engaging the masses of people that pass through unemployment, and underemployment, on a daily basis.[17] As a toolkit to push back against this pernicious state of affairs, post-work's demands for less work for all and unconditional cash support offer a pincer movement of non-reformist reforms.

As Gorz argues at various points in his work, shortening the working week – by *reducing and* redistributing work – would mean that everyone works, so everyone *works less*. This would greatly reduce the headcount in the unemployed reserve army and take the pressure off those in work too. Add in unconditional cash floors and some of the sharp edges of capitalism have been decisively blunted: life outside of the labour market has become less precarious and more normalized. As we saw with Rathbone and Tillmon's pioneering precedents, guaranteed income floors – some form of basic income – would be transformatory for de-stigmatizing welfare and activating a constituency that has been suppressed through poverty, non-participation and often outright shaming. A basic income would therefore obviously be a demand in the interests of the unemployed, but could also, as with the precedent of separation allowances in the First World War, facilitate the confidence and material basis for *further* demands of the state. One successful demand begets others.

Crucially, a basic income's universality and material support would help dilute the artificial divisions between the unemployed and the employed.

> When workers are completely market-dependent, they are difficult to mobilise for solidaristic action. Since their resources mirror market inequalities, divisions emerge between the 'ins' and the 'outs', making labour movement formation difficult.[18]

Overcoming such distinctions in practice is particularly relevant in today's labour market, which is beset by the 'low pay, no pay' cycle in which workers often find themselves unemployed and precariously employed in quick succession; some post-work thinkers have developed new categories such as 'malemployment' to describe this phenomenon.[19] During the Covid pandemic, as many people faced the prospect of unemployment, or fire and rehire practices deployed by opportunistic firms,[20] we witnessed the pressing need for a strong unemployed workers' movement that could make demands on the government for resources, support and industrial strategy. Instead, while trade unions understandably fought to keep jobs and get adequate protection equipment into workplaces, the unemployed remained largely unrepresented. As the history of such movements has taught us, they can be a powerful social and political force for better and more equally distributed work as well as liveable welfare incomes.[21]

Equally, we shouldn't forget the social consequences of those unique moments in the twentieth century where welfare payment levels competed with and sometimes outstripped the going wage rates – producing rare glimpses of joyous free time. This was the case in many areas of the UK at points in the 1920s and 1930s. One survey in Cardiff showed that 45 per cent of married men had received less cash in wages from their previous employment than they were receiving in unemployment allowances.[22] Mowat alerts us to this counterintuitive history that often goes forgotten:

> Many people, particularly the young married men, were better off on the dole than on the low wages which they could earn if employed – especially if work was intermittent ... Many men out of work accepted their fate ... To such men a spell of employment was a holiday ... Some might join a WEA [Workers' Educational Association] class, like the Durham miner who took a five-year course in English literature; others found a use for their leisure in reading, or in taking part in plays or joining in the other activities of a community house or unemployed men's club. Some went for long walks – a week's walking holiday on 3s 5d was the recollection of one; others played football ... Some worked on an allotment, others kept poultry ... The young men had never known steady work and did not fret at the lack of it ... In Cardiff, 52 per cent of the unemployed youths interviewed visited the cinema once a week and almost half of these twice a week ... Others, resorted to the many licensed clubs which existed in the cities, where billiards, gambling and raffles flourished.[23]

The point is not that a low-wage economy is something to aim for; rather, it is that, should sufficient means be available, and time outside of employment be facilitated even just a little, a culture of leisure and experimentation can be expected to flourish; self-formation beyond the workplace and its impositions can emerge. Achieving such moments of welfare-enabled freedom – as was experienced occasionally in the 1930s and then again in the 1960s – will require a critical attitude towards work, an ambitious attitude towards making resource demands of the state and a coalition of forces assembled to be the vehicle of these things.[24] But such a movement needs demands that can speak to their congregated interests, which would materially improve their situation; a critical push to shorten the working week (potentially, but not necessarily, supported by automation and the judicious deployment of labour-saving technologies), and some form of universal basic income, could be good candidates for such demands.

Disability movements

It is well evidenced that the current system of welfare conditionality – in the UK but elsewhere too – has been catastrophic for disabled people[25] – from invasive, sometimes humiliating assessments as to whether they can work or not to systemic oversight when it comes to less visible impairments, and from years of cuts to an inhospitable labour market. Today's injuries and insults follow a long line of systematic attacks on disabled people since the onset of industrialism and the creation of the labour market.[26] Arguably it is this constituency that has most to gain from shorter, more sustainable working hours and extensive redistributions of unconditional cash.

Mainstream ideology – the kind of thinking that informs news coverage, everyday interactions and political discourse – positions disability as an individual's personal, medical tragedy. The solutions to this 'problem' – if there are any – are therefore also taken to require an individualistic focus.[27] The common rebuttal to such an ignorant, dangerous and segregating perspective is what is known as the 'social model' of understanding disability. This distinguishes between, on the one hand, people's various *impairments* and, on the other, the ways in which their social, physical and economic environments (all of which are determined by social relations) *disable* them from equal participation alongside those without these impairments.[28]

Emerging from this model, the predominant strategy for overcoming the barriers to including disabled people within broader, societal day-to-day life has been to facilitate routes into employment – the idea being that those with disabilities are best served by being *enabled* into more productive functions. Employment is indeed, for better or for worse, a very real facilitator of social recognition and this should not be underestimated.[29] As social model advocate Vic Finkelstein articulates it, 'the predominant factor contributing to the disablement of different groups is the way in which people can participate in the creation of social wealth' – that is, through paid work.[30] This makes sense in a society in which the wage is the primary route to resources (but not, as we have noted, necessarily the route to prosperity), as well as one in which the work ethic deems hard work to be one of the highest virtues. Those left segregated from employment

– and the moral achievement that it facilitates – simply due to a certain impairment are thereby structurally disabled.

There are pronounced limits to employment-focused strategies for disabled people, however, and radical disability theorists argue against work-accommodation along strategic lines, and occasionally more explicitly post-work ones. Despite the huge pressures on disabled people to enter the labour market, in whatever impoverished state they find it, employment rates for this cohort remain much lower than for non-disabled people. In 2021, 53 per cent of disabled people were in employment in the UK, compared to 81 per cent of non-disabled people.[31] In the United States, only around 20 per cent of disabled people are in employment.[32] In the UK, disabled workers move out of work at nearly twice the rate of non-disabled workers and workless disabled people move into work at nearly one-third of the rate (11 per cent) of workless non-disabled people (26.9 per cent).[33] These outcomes are certainly in part due to persistent employer bias – something that social model theorists identify as disabling; workplaces, cultures and practices are not set up in an inclusive manner.

But labour market non-participation is also due to the nature of people's impairments *themselves* – and here we start to see the limits of adaptation as a strategy. Disability theorists have always pointed out how persistently unaccommodating modern labour markets are to those who don't fit a certain physical and cognitive mould. Sunny Taylor articulates this with a class inflection:

> Many, though by no means all, disabled people will never be good workers in the capitalist sense: if you cannot move or speak, it is hard to succeed in a mainstream career. There is a small but significant percentage of the disabled population that has 'made it' and has achieved economic equality working as professionals, lawyers, artists, professors, and writers. They are a fortunate minority and the work they do is important. These opportunities have everything to do with class and are not open to all impaired individuals. I, like many people, will never make a good waitress, secretary, factory worker, or bus driver (unless there were massive and expensive adaptations to the bus I was driving).[34]

Paul Abberley also follows this line of thinking, writing that 'even in a society which DID [*sic*] make profound and genuine attempts, well supported by financial provision, to integrate impaired people into the world of work, some would be excluded'.[35] He continues:

> a society may be willing and in certain circumstances become eager to absorb a portion of its impaired population into the workforce, yet this can have the effect of maintaining and perhaps intensifying its exclusion of the remainder.[36]

As we argued in Chapter 2, 'the wage don't fit' our societies in general, and many of *us* don't fit the limited moulds imposed by the wage. Abberley also states:

> Jobs designed around the capacity, stamina and resources of the average worker, nine-to-five, five day a week employment, what we might call 'job shaped jobs' are inimical to the needs of a wide variety of citizens.[37]

Abberley and others here clearly adopt the social model theory of dis-ablement, but extend and dissent from it through a radical critique of work. They specifically reject the premise that an employment-focused strategy is itself emancipatory – both insofar as it might only cater to a certain set of people with disabilities (those more easily accommodated by employers and certain professions) but also because it is too in tune with the problematic work ethic that disabled people (like all of us) are being asked to internalize.[38] 'Rather than arguing that disabled people can be productive in a capitalist paradigm', writes A.J. Withers, 'the radical model of disability sees capitalist values as problematic'.[39]

These thinkers do not 'deny that the origins of our oppression, even for those with jobs, lie in our historical exclusion, as a group, from access to work, nor ….. oppose campaigns for increasing access to employment'.[40] However, they argue that the aspirations of the wider disabled movement should not be tied to full integration into the system of wage labour, nor the work ethic that legitimates it. Thus, some theorists add a 'right not to work' as an alternative to the usual 'right to work' slogan.[41] Shouldn't disabled people, of all groups, writes Sunny Taylor, recognize that it is not work that would liberate us (especially not menial labor made accessible or greeting customers at Wal-Marts across America), but the right to not work and be proud of it? How would this shift in thinking affect the goals and attitude of those concerned with the rights of impaired people or the self-image of those who are impaired themselves?[42]

In contrast, 'the right not to work', Taylor writes, 'is the right not to have your value determined by your productivity as a worker, by your employability or salary'.[43] Of course, there should be as much support as possible for facilitating the return to income-generating work for those who want it, but 'we should simultaneously think beyond the system in place'.[44]

Abberley, Withers, Taylor and others thus provide rich resources by which to bring radical disability movements and post-work politics together. In both discourses we find the diagnosis that there needs to be material and symbolic forms of recognition, beyond the system of wages – which currently merely recognizes work performed: here a 'social wage' or, better, an unconditional income paid to all make the most sense. Equally, the five-day, full-time working week clearly only suits the cognitive and physical abilities of certain people (and even then, these 'normal' individuals face burnout on a very large scale).[45] Reducing the working week will allow more people to participate in paid work should they wish – thus speaking to the need for social inclusion – but on healthier and more feasible hours.

Moving towards a new economics and culture of work

For all of the above reasons – coalition building, material power within workplace relations, facilitating capacity for the unemployed to be able to live more dignified lives and for building a culture of solidarity for those who, for one reason or another, are unable to participate in labour markets – we think post-work demands have huge potential to be part of the system change we require; at their most potent, they would help shift our societies to a new culture of work. The key here is the *transitional* nature of things like shorter hours, basic income and increased automation – something that is often lost in more policy-oriented readings.[46] Weeks gives a succinct clarification of the position, specifically on basic income, in her paper:

> A demand for a universal, liveable, basic income is not a proposal to replace the capitalist wage system, but only to loosen its grip on us somewhat by providing income to those of us now shut out of or rendered precarious in relation to waged work and to those of us whose contributions to social (re)production are not now remunerated with wages. It would also give individuals a stronger position from which to negotiate more favourable employment contracts, some leverage to demand better jobs, and better enable them to make choices about what kinds of households and intimate relationships they might want to exit from or to form.[47]

This understanding fits with sociologist Erik Olin Wright's thesis around 'eroding capitalism' – a strategy for systems change that relies on utilizing multiple leverage points and cracks within capitalism's edifice as well as surges of activity on the part of coalitions of those who have a stake in change.[48] Wright advocates for a more gradualist post-capitalist approach, as opposed to a crisis and catastrophe-informed, revolutionary communism which sees the welfare state simply as a means of pacification of the working class.[49] As Stuart Hall often emphasized, we should acknowledge the new opportunities and challenges that the post-war welfare state afforded us. It was

> a contradictory structure, a 'historic compromise', which both achieved something in a reformist direction for the working class and became an instrument in disciplining it. Why else should anyone on the left be now campaigning for the restoration of the cuts in the welfare state if it did nothing for the working class?[50]

In the same vein of working within and against capitalism, Wright's scheme allows us to see how post-work demands would not only tame some of the worst elements of capitalism, but also help people escape coercive relations within the system and work to dismantle key capitalist infrastructure (punitive welfare, unequal and gruelling labour markets, etc.).[51]

Having a four-day week, basic income or socially managed automation in place will not, in themselves, mean that we are beyond capitalism of course. But it would mean, initially, that we exist in a variety of capitalism that is not only better for whole swathes of people but in which the foundations have shifted to become more conducive to its eventual overcoming.[52] Again, this chimes with how those involved in Wages for Housework saw the significance of their struggle: 'Wages for Housework', Federici writes, 'is a revolutionary demand not because by itself it destroys capital, but because it attacks capital and forces it to restructure social relations in terms more favourable to us'.[53] As an organizing focal point, the demands for – and ultimate achievement of – unconditional cash for all or a reduction of people's work week, or a managed automation of drudgery would, we argue, generate a new 'political perspective which opens a new ground of struggle'.[54]

This is a kind of cultural and philosophical shift around work that will take years, decades even. But, as Weeks reminds us, it all starts with a demand:

> A demand is not just a goal but a process; as such, it must be explained, justified, argued for, and debated; the ambitions of the demands for Wages for Housework and basic income are not just policy-oriented but are also epistemological and ontological. That is, they are also opportunities for articulating a critical vocabulary through which we can interrogate the present, and for cultivating desires for new ways of living.[55]

Thus, although this book has not focused on delivering a strategy,[56] it has presented the theoretical and historical raw materials that can – we hope – inform one. Ultimately, it will be up to a great many of us to combine vision with strategy, purpose with tactics to bring about a world of less and better work. Only then can the prehistory of humankind be truly put behind us, and only then will we discover the true extent of our collective possibilities.

Notes

Introduction

1   Seccombe, Wally 1995 *Weathering the Storm: Working-Class Families from the Industrial Revolution to the Fertility Decline*. London: Verso, p. 49.

2   Weber, M. (1958) [1904–5], trans. by Talcott Parsons. *The Protestant Ethic and the Spirit of Capitalism*. New York: Charles Scribner's Sons.

3   Weeks, K. (2011) *The Problem with Work: Feminism, Marxism, Anti-Work Politics and Post-Work Imaginaries*. Durham: Duke University Press, p. 39.

4   Weber (1958), p. 51.

5   Ibid., p. 83; Weeks (2011), p. 45.

6   Weber (1958), p. 182.

7   Weber, M. (1946) 'Science as Vocation', in Weber, M., *From Weber: Essays in Sociology*, trans. and edited by H. H. Gerth and C. Wright Mills. New York: Oxford University Press, pp. 129–56, p. 149.

8   Weeks (2011), p. 46.

9   Ibid., p. 70.

10   Boltanski, L. and Chiapello, E. (2018) *The New Spirit of Capitalism*. Verso: London.

11   Hochschild, A. (1983) *The Managed Heart: The Commercialization of Human Feeling*. Berkeley: University of California Press, p. 6.

12   Frayne, D. (2015) *The Refusal of Work*. London: Zed Books.

13   De Grazia, v. (1981) *The Culture of Consent: Mass Organisation of Leisure in Fascist Italy*. Cambridge: Cambridge University Press, p. 239.

14   Ibid., p. 18.

15   De Grazia notes that 'by the late thirties, however reprehensible the authoritarian organization of leisure in fascist countries may have appeared, nowhere in the international conferences or in the reports and studies on workers' spare time [in non-fascist states] was their leadership in the field seriously disputed.' De Grazia, p. 240.

16 World Committee of the YMCA, 1924 report, quoted in De Grazia, *The Culture of Consent*, p. 239.

17 Amira, D. (2010) '"Jobs, Jobs, Jobs": The Allure, and Danger, of a Favorite Political Mantra'. *New York Mag.* Available at: https://nymag.com/intelligencer/2010/02/jobs_jobs_jobs_the_allure_and.html

18 Johnson (2019) 'We Can Improve Mental Health, Save Money and Boost the Economy All in One Go'. *The Telegraph.* July 2019. Available at: https://www.telegraph.co.uk/news/2019/07/14/can-improve-mental-health-save-money-boost-economy-one-go/

19 Withers, A. J. (2012) *Disability, Politics & Theory.* Winnipeg: Fernwood Publishing, p. 108.

20 Gorz (1989) *The Critique of Economic Reason.* London: Verso Books, p. 101.

21 E.g. ONS (2016) 'Women Shoulder the Responsibility of 'Unpaid Work'. Available at: https://www.ons.gov.uk/employmentandlabourmarket/peopleinwork/earningsandworkinghours/articles/womenshouldertheresponsibilityofunpaidwork/2016-11-10#

22 Graeber, D. and Frank, T. (2014) 'The More Your Job Helps Others, The Less You Get Paid'. *Z Network.* Available here: https://znetwork.org/znetarticle/the-more-your-job-helps-others-the-less-you-get-paid/

23 This touches on the 'socially useful production debate', which thrived particularly in the 1960s and 1970s. See Design Collective (1985) *Very Nice Work If You Can Get It: The Socially Useful Production Debate.* Nottingham: Spokesman Books.

24 It should go without saying, in this regard, that the question of the redistribution of work is of course also inherently political; that is, it is decidable consciously and in view of wider outcomes and consequences.

25 Bowring, F. (1999) 'Job Scarcity: The Perverted Form of a Potential Blessing', *Sociology*, 33 (1): 69–84. https://doi.org/10.1177/S0038038599000048, p. 81.

26 Critics such as Paul Thompson, for example, diagnose post-work advocates as positing 'an embrace of automation to finally kill off work that everyone hates in order to embrace a universal basic income (UBI) that will abolish (most) wage labour and liberate individuals to do something fulfilling'. Ana Dinerstein and Frederick Pitts, meanwhile, similarly equate post-work positions with a specific set of proposed reforms. Discussing one influential post-work text, which they take as exemplary of a wider trend, they argue that UBI 'works in tandem with foregoing technological trends to accomplish the outcome of a postcapitalist society of automated worklessness'. Thompson, Paul, 2018. 'The Refusal of Work: Past, Present and Future'. https://futuresofwork.co.uk/2018/09/05/the-refusal-of-work-past-present-and-future/; Dinerstain, A. and Pitts, F. H. 'From Post-Work to Post-Capitalism? Discussing the Basic Income and Struggles for Alternative forms of Social Reproduction', *Journal of Labour and Society*, 21: 471–91, p. 475. https://researchportal.bath.ac.uk/en/publications/from-post-work-to-post-capitalism-discussing-the-basic-income-and

Chapter 1

1 Sanchis, J. (2021) *Quatre Dias*. Valencia: Sembra Libres. See also Miliband E. (2021) *Go Big: How to Fix Our World*. London: Penguin.

2 See Autonomy, the research organization that we are both involved. E.g. https://autonomy.work/portfolio/uk4dwpilotresults/

3 Frayne, D. (2015) *The Refusal of Work*. London: Zed.

4 Mau, Søren (2023) *Mute Compulsion: A Marxist Theory of the Economic Power of Capital*. London: Verso Books.

5 Of course, the question as to whether there really is a free choice involved in these decisions to sacrifice free time for labour (i.e. if a choice between a wage and destitution really is a meaningful choice at all) is skirted over in most mainstream accounts.

6 Marx, Karl (1973) *Grundrisse*. New York: Penguin, p. 173.

7 YouGov (2017) '45% of Working Brits Would Retire on the Spot for £1m'. Available at: https://yougov.co.uk/topics/politics/articles-reports/2017/10/16/how-much-money-would-you-want-to-retire

8 See also the 'FIRE' (Financial Independence Retire Early) movement, in part inspired by Robin and Dominguez (2008) *Your Money or Your Life*. London: Penguin

9 Eberstadt, N. (2022) *Men without Work*. West Conshohocken, PA, US: Templeton Foundation Press.

10 The contract is theorized in more depth in Read, J. (2003) *The Micro-Politics of Capital*. New York: State University of New York Press.

11 Marx, Karl (1976) *Capital vol. 1*. London: Penguin, p. 279.

12 Anderson, E. (2017) *Private Government*. Princeton: Princeton University Press, p. 37.

13 We would question Anderson's definition of workplaces as 'communist', however. Just because work equipment, the physical space and other production materials are owned by a particular subset of people does not make such a state of affairs communist (even if this is what occurred in countries that called themselves communist). Communism, under most definitions, would be a situation where everything is owned and governed by all – including the workers.

14 In his schema of post-work argumentation, philosopher John Danaher names this argument the 'problem of dominating influence'. Danaher, J. *Automation and Utopia*. London: Harvard University Press. 2019.

15 Delfanti, A. (2021) *The Warehouse: Workers and Robots at Amazon*. London: Pluto Books.

16 Ibid., p. 32.

17 For a fascinating study on the use of fear as a workplace technique in haute cuisine restaurants see Gill, M. and Burrow, R. (2018) 'Fear in Haute Cuisine: The Interplay of Emotions and Institutions'. *Organization Studies*, 39 (4): 445–65.

18 Frayne, D. (2017) 'Is Work in Crisis?' *Autonomy*. Available at: https://autonomy.work/portfolio/david-frayne-response/

19 Horgan, A. (2021) *Lost in Work*. London: Pluto Books.

20 These rare opportunities are normally 'perks' – gifts to employees who are recognized as valuable to the firm and are seen to require conditions such as these so as to retain them.

21 See, for example, Bivens, J. and Kandra, J. (2021) 'CEO Pay Has Skyrocketed 1,460% since 1978'. *Economic Policy Institute*. Available at: https://www.epi.org/publication/ceo-pay-in-2021/; Neville, Rosie, Andrew Speke and Luke Hildyard (2023) 'Analysis of UK CEO Pay in 2022: High Pay Centre'. *High Pay Centre*. Available at: https://highpaycentre.org/ftse-100-ceos-get-half-a-million-pound-pay-rise/.

22 Cholbi, M. (2018) 'The Duty to Work'. *Ethic Theory Moral Prac*, 21: 1119–33. https://doi.org/10.1007/s10677-018-9942-2. The flip side of this is also true, of course – our jobs may be socially valuable while being personally insufferable. This is the experience of some people in socially reproductive work such as nursing and teaching, for example, who find themselves driven from their professions by work-related stress and anxiety.

23 TUC (2023) 'New TUC poll: 2 in 3 Young Women Have Experienced Sexual Harassment, Bullying or Verbal Abuse at Work'. *TUC*. Available at: https://www.tuc.org.uk/news/new-tuc-poll-2-3-young-women-have-experienced-sexual-harassment-bullying-or-verbal-abuse-work#:~:text=The%20TUC%20poll%20found%20that,three%20incidents%20of%20sexual%20harassment; TUC (2019) 'Sexual Harassment of LGBT People in the Workplace'. Available at: https://www.tuc.org.uk/research-analysis/reports/sexual-harassment-lgbt-people-workplace#:~:text=Main%20findings,report%20it%20to%20their%20employer;The ILO (2022) reports that one in five people globally have experienced violence or harassment at work. 'Violence and Harassment at Work Has Affected More than One in Five People'. *The ILO*. Available at: https://www.ilo.org/global/about-the-ilo/newsroom/news/WCMS_863177/lang–en/index.htm.

24 Kamerade, D., Wang, S., Brendan, B., Balderson, U., and Coutts, A. (2019) 'A Shorter Working Week for Everyone: How Much Paid Work Is Needed for Mental Health and Well-Being?', *Social, Science & Medicine*, 241, p. 6. doi: 10.1016/j.socscimed.2019.06.006.

25 For a thorough deconstruction of the well-being argument for employment, see Frayne, D. and Maher, M. (2021) 'Jobs and Wellbeing: Re-opening the Debate'. *Autonomy*. Available at: https://autonomy.work/portfolio/jobswellbeing/.

26 This form of paid work, as some have noted, can also be compared critically to earlier forms of 'piece work'. See Cant, C. (2019) *Riding for Deliveroo*. Cambridge: Polity

Press; see also: Snyder, B. (2016) *The Disrupted Workplace*. Oxford: Oxford University Press, p. 131; Whiteside, N. (1991) *Bad Times: Unemployment in British Social and Political History*. London: Penguin, p. 31; Andre Gorz discussed the 'neo-proletariat' and its difference from the traditionally conceived working class in (1982) *Farewell to the Working Class*. London: Pluto Books. Bloomsbury. Standing's term 'precariat' is preceded conceptually (and historically) by Andre Gorz's notion.

27 Aronowitz, S. et al (1998) 'The Post-Work Manifesto', in Aronowitz, S. and Cutler, J. (eds) *Post-Work*. London: Routledge, p. 45. See also Gorz, A. (1982) *Farewell to the Working Class*. London: Pluto.

28 Standing, G. (2011) *The Precariat*. London: Bloomsbury. Standing, G. (2014) *The Precariat Charter*. London: Bloomsbury.

29 Standing, G. (2011) *The Precariat*. London: Bloomsbury.

30 Snyder, B. (2016), p. 163.

31 Ibid.

32 Wood, A. (2022) *Despotism on Demand: How Power Operates in the Flexible Workplace*. New York: Cornell University Press, p. 78.

33 Apostolidis, P. (2019) *The Fight for Time: Migrant Day Labourers and the Politics of Precarity*. Oxford: Oxford University Press, p. 6.

34 Ibid., p. 8.

35 Illich, I. (1981) *Shadow Work*. London: Marion Boyars.

36 Lambert, C. (2015) *Shadow Work*. Berkeley: Counterpoint.

37 Cowan, Ruth Schwartz (1979) 'From Virginia Dare to Virginia Slims: Women and Technology in American Life'. *Technology and Culture* 20 (1): 51–63, p. 59.

38 Cowan, Ruth Schwartz (1989) *More Work for Mother: The Ironies of Household Technology from the Open Hearth to the Microwave*. London: Free Association Books. For a recent revisitation and updating of Cowan's thesis, see Hester and Srnicek (2023) *After Work: A History of the Home and the Fight for Free Time*. London: Verso.

39 For more on the Cowan Paradox, see Hester and Srnicek, *After Work*, pp. 22–28.

40 Charmes, Jacques (2019). 'The Unpaid Care Work and the Labour Market: An Analysis of Time Use Data Based on the Latest World Compilation of Time-Use Surveys'. Working paper. Geneva: International Labour Organization. http://www.ilo.org/gender/Informationresources/Publications/WCMS_732791/lang–en/index.htm.

41 Charmes, Jacques (2022). 'Variety and Change of Patterns in the Gender Balance between Unpaid Care-Work, Paid Work and Free Time across the World and over Time: A Measure of Wellbeing?' *Wellbeing, Space and Society* 3, 100081.

42 Pew Research Centre. (2015). 'Raising Kids and Running a Household: How Working Parents Share the Load'. Available at: http://www.pewsocialtrends.org/2015/11/04/raising-kids-and-running-a-household-how-working-parents-share-the-load/.

43 See Sayer, Liana (2005). 'Gender, Time and Inequality: Trends in Women's and Men's Paid Work, Unpaid Work and Free Time', *Social Forces* 84 (1): 285–303, p. 296; Goodin, Robert E., et al (2008) *Discretionary Time: A New Measure of Freedom*. Cambridge: Cambridge University Press, pp. 89–90.

44 Bianchi, Suzanne (2011). 'Family Change and Time Allocation in American Families', *The ANNALS of the American Academy of Political and Social Science* 638 (1): 21–44, pp. 27–9.

45 Goodin, Robert E., et al (2008), p. 91.

46 Helen Hester (2020) 'Why Women Deserve a Four-Day Week'. *International Politics and Society*. Available at: https://www.ips-journal.eu/regions/europe/why-women-deserve-a-four-day-week-4610/

47 Roediger and Foner (1987) *Our Own Time: A History of American Labor and the Working Day*. London: Verso, p. 276.

48 Although some might work on the train into their workplace, of course.

49 See Stronge and Murray (2021) 'Claim the Commute'. *Autonomy*. Available at: https://autonomy.work/portfolio/claimthecommute/

50 TUC (2017) 'Average Worker Now Spends 27 Working Days a Year Commuting, Finds TUC'. https://www.tuc.org.uk/news/average-worker-now-spends-27-working-days-year-commuting-finds-tuc#

51 Institute for Fiscal Studies (2023) 'Remote working is probably here to stay, and these are the reasons why'. Available at: https://ifs.org.uk/articles/remote-working-probably-here-stay-and-these-are-reasons-why

52 Quoted from Lambert (2015), p. 7. Illich (1981). Stiglitz, J. (2018) 'From Manufacturing Led Export Growth to a 21st Century Inclusive Growth Strategy: Explaining the Demise of a Successful Growth Model and What to Do about It'. United Nations 'Think development – Think WIDER' conference paper. Available at: https://www.wider.unu.edu/sites/default/files/Events/PDF/Papers/Draft-paper-Juseph-Stiglitz-Sept2018.pdf

53 We refer the reader to our definition of work, above.

54 See Foucault, M. (2008) *Birth of Biopolitics*, trans. by Graham Burchell, Basingstoke: Palgrave Macmillan. Ch. 9.

55 For more on the relationship between New Labour and/or neoliberalism and employability, see Moore, P. (2010) *The International Political Economy of Work and Employability*. Basingstoke: Palgrave Macmillan. Peck, J. (2001) *Workfare States*. New York: Guildford Press.

56 Moore (2010).

57 New Labour's emphasis on employability as a way of 'advertising' yourself to employers, is concurrent with self-branding literature from the period. See Phil Jones (2019) for a review of this literature. Jones, P. 'Employability in the New Economy', Autonomy. Available at: https://autonomy.work/portfolio/employability-in-the-new-economy-brand-you/

58 Moore (2010), pp. 39–40.

59 Cremin, C. (2011) *Capitalism's New Clothes: Enterprise, Ethics and Enjoyment in Times of Crisis*. London: Pluto Books, pp. 45–6.

60 Pfannebecker, M. and Smith, J. A. (2018) *Work Want Work: Labour and Desire at the End of Capitalism*. London: Zed.

61 E.g. Jon. Cruddas (2021) *Dignity of Labour*. Polity, Cambridge. We should also note that 'Jobs, jobs, jobs' is a preferred slogan of UK Labour Party (and various others).

62 Danaher (2019), p. 56.

63 Marx (1990) *Capital Volume One*. Penguin: London, p. 644.

64 Aristotle *De Anima. Politics.*

65 Komlosy, A. (2018) Work: The Last 1,000 Years. London: Verso, p. 39.

66 Arendt, H. (1998) *The Human Condition*. London: University of Chicago Press.

67 Thompson, E. P. (1967) 'Time, Work-Discipline, and Industrial Capitalism', *Past & Present*, 38 (1), December 1967, pp. 56–97; https://doi.org/10.1093/past/38.1.56; Hunnicutt, B. (1988) *Work without End*. Philadelphia: Temple University Press.

68 Roediger and Foner (1987), p. vii.

69 Ibid.

70 Braverman, H. (1974) *Labour and Monopoly Capital. The Degradation of Work in the Twentieth Century*. New York: Monthly Review Press.

71 E. P. Thompson (1967), p. 86.

72 Quoted in Roediger and Foner (1989), p. 20.

73 Ibid., pp. 20–1.

74 Pettit, P. (1997) *Republicanism: A Theory of Freedom and Government*. Oxford: Oxford University Press.

75 Gourevitch, A. (2013) 'Labor Republicanism and the Transformation of Work', Political Theory, 41 (4): 591–617. See also Jones (2020) 'Campaigns around working time have always been about freedom'.

76 Rodgers, D. (2014) *The Work Ethic in Industrial America, 1850–1920*. Chicago: University of Chicago Press, p. 35. Lincoln's sentiment was widely shared in the

US: David Roediger notes that 'the followers of Tom Paine and Thomas Jefferson held that a free government required "independent" small producers who owned productive property and therefore were neither cowed nor mercenary, as lifelong "hirelings" would inevitably be'. Roediger, D. (2007) *The Wages of Whiteness*. London: Verso Books, p. 45. The 1829 Webster dictionary even gives 'prostitute' as a synonym for hireling. Ibid.

77 According to Rodgers, 'the Knights of Labour, the chief recipient of this influx, ballooned from 104,066 members in July 1885 to 702,924 members a year later'. Rodgers, D. (2014), p. 158.

78 Roediger and Foner, chap. 5.

79 Marcel Van Der Linden gives an excellent survey of the historical admixture of unfree and free labour within capitalism, as well as the proximity between slave labour and early wage labour – in their shared struggles as well as their working conditions. Van der Linden, M. (2008) *Workers of the World: Essays toward a Global Labor History*. Leiden: Brill.

80 Van Der Linden (2008), p. 32. Emphasis in the original.

81 Roediger (2007), p. 49. 'In looking at US working class history, it is clear that the existence of slavery, not just of antislavery, stalled the development of a telling critique of hireling labor – a critique that might have built on and transcended the republican heritage' (2007), p. 87.

82 The abolitionist debate is well-covered in Mandel, B. (2007) *Labor, Free and Slave*. Chicago: University of Illinois Press.

83 See James Hammond's risible defence of slavery as a favourable life in contrast with the impoverishment of wage labour, for example in Mandel (2007), p. 96. Arguments such as these were lambasted and ridiculed by emancipated slaves and abolitionists, for good reason: as Roediger's history details, 'Black abolitionists recounted telling stories about informing "white slaves" that their former position on the plantation was open after their escape but never finding anyone eager to take the job' (2007), p. 82.

84 Rodgers (2014), p. 32.

85 Ibid.

86 Address of Hon. Fred. Douglass, delivered before the National Convention of Colored Men, at Louisville, Ky., 24 September 1883. Available at: https://omeka. coloredconventions.org/items/show/554

87 Roediger (2007), p. 176.

88 Ibid.; Fones-Wolf, Kenneth (1981) 'Boston Eight Hour Men, New York Marxists and the Emergence of the International Labor Union', *Historical Journal of Massachusetts*, 9: 48.

89 Hence why it was common for employment to be referred to, dramatically to our contemporary ears, as 'wage slavery'.

90   Reform Committee of the South Wales Miners, (1970) 'The Miners' Next Step', in
     K. Coates and T. Topham (eds) *Workers' Control*. London: Panther Books, pp. 23–4.
     Special mention should be given here to the school children in Llanelli, Wales,
     who in 1911 went on strike from their school work in order to win the demands
     of shorter hours and pay for their toil. 'We want 30s a week and less hours per day
     … and free pencils and rubbers', they were quoted in *The Weekly Express*. Marson,
     Dave *Children's Strikes in 1911*, History pamphlet no. 9 Oxford, 1973. From Fleming,
     S. (1986) 'Eleanor Rathbone: Spokeswoman for a Movement', in Rathbone, E. *The
     Disinherited Family*. Bristol: Falling Wall Press, p. 25, footnote 51.

91   Fraser, N. and Gordan, L. 'Dependency: a Genealogy', in Fraser (2020) *Fortunes of
     Feminism*. London: Verso, p. 122.

92   Ibid. p. 123.

93   Roediger and Foner, pp. 266–7.

94   John F. Kennedy. 'Speech of Senator John F. Kennedy, United Steelworkers of
     America Convention, Convention Hall, Atlantic City, NJ' Available at: https://
     www.presidency.ucsb.edu/documents/speech-senator-john-f-kennedy-united-
     steelworkers-america-convention-convention-hall

95   Roediger and Foner, p. 269.

96   Ibid., p. 267.

97   Leading figures such as Walther Reuther were calling for four-day, or thirty-two-
     hour weeks in the late 1950s and early 1960s. Equally, more radical groups such
     as the League of Revolutionary Black Workers and the Progressive Labor Party, it
     should be noted, continued to fight for shorter hours for many years afterwards –
     often directly against trade unions such as UAW's attempts to quell this radicalism.
     Roediger and Foner

98   Quoted in Mann (1987) *Taking on General Motors*. Los Angeles: Institute of Labor
     Relations, p. 56; See also, Dyer-Witheford. (2015) *Cyber-Proletariat*. London: Pluto
     Books, p. 41.

99   Rodgers (2014), p. 181.

100 For example it can be found in ILO (2022) 'Working Time and Work-Life Balance
     around the World'. Available at: https://www.ilo.org/wcmsp5/groups/public/—
     dgreports/—dcomm/documents/publication/wcms_864222.pdf; Source is
     Huberman and Minns (2007), 'The Times They Are Not Changin': Days and Hours
     of Work in Old and New Worlds, 1870–2000'. *Explorations in Economic History*,
     44 (4), October 2007: 538–67.

101 NEF (2019) 'Average Weekly Hours Fell Faster Between 1946 and 1979 Than Post-
     1980'. Available at: https://neweconomics.org/2019/03/average-weekly-hours-fell-
     faster-between-1946-and-1979-than-post-1980

102 ONS. (2019) 'Long-term trends in UK Employment: 1861 to 2018'. Available at:
     https://www.ons.gov.uk/economy/nationalaccounts/uksectoraccounts/compendium/

economicreview/april2019/longtermtrendsinukemployment1861to2018#womens-labour-market-participation

103 Walsh, Margaret and Wrigley, Chris (2001) 'Womanpower: The Transformation of the Labour Force in the UK and the USA since 1945', *Recent Findings of Research in Economic and Social History* (30). Available at: https://ehs.org.uk/womanpower-the-transformation-of-the-labour-force-in-the-uk-and-usa-since-1945/; OECD, Manpower Statistics, 1950–62, Paris, 1963: OECD, Labour Force Statistics, 1959–70, Paris, 1972: OECD, Labour Force Statistics, 1965–85, Paris, 1987: OECD, Labour Force Statistics, 1969–80, Paris, 1982: OECD, Labour Force Statistics, 1978–98, Paris, 2000.

104 The biggest leap in work time reduction happened instead, for many countries, between the world wars. Michael Huberman, Chris Minns (2007) 'The Times They Are Not Changin': Days and Hours of Work in Old and New Worlds, 1870–2000', *Explorations in Economic History,* 44 (4): 538–67.

105 Marx, K. (1996) *Wages, Price and Profit*, 1st edition, 1975. Peking: Foreign Languages Press, p. 111.

106 Russell, B. (2004) *In Praise of Idleness*. London: Routledge, p. 14.

107 Frayne (2015), p. 220.

108 Pfannebecker, M. and Smith, J. A. (2018) *Work Want Work: Labour and Desire at the End of Capitalism*. London: Zed.

109 Weeks (2011), pp. 168–9.

110 Ibid., p. 169.

111 Keynes, J. M. (2013) *The Collected Writings of John Maynard Keynes*. Volume X: Essays in Biography (first published 1933), ed. by Robinson, A. and Moggridge, D. Cambridge: Cambridge University Press.

112 Apostolidis (2019).

113 Ibid. p. 242.

114 Hester and Stronge (2020).

115 We have addressed these misconceptions previously here: Hester and Stronge (2021) https://autonomy.work/portfolio/post-workmisconceptions2/

116 Frayne (2015), p. 37; Gorz (1989), p. 93.

117 Danaher (2019), p. 83.

118 Gorz (1989) *The Critique of Economic Reason*. London: Verso Books, p. 191.

119 Ibid.

120 Gorz (1989), p. 206. See also Cubioniks, Laboria (2018) *The Xenofeminist Manifesto: A Politics for Alienation*. London: Verso Books.

121 Gorz (1989), p. 206.

122 Ibid.

123 See also Hester and Srnicek (2023) *After Work*. London: Verso.

124 Autonomy. (2020) 'Long Term Care Centres'. Available at: https://autonomy.work/wp-content/uploads/2020/11/LTCCv7.pdf

Chapter 2

1 The 'universality' of UBI tends to mean residency in a specific country – for pragmatic reasons – although global basic income schemes have been proposed. Van Parijs and Vanderborght (2017) *Basic Income: A Radical Proposal for a Free and Sane Society*. London: Harvard University Press.

2 Exactly which other benefits would remain or be replaced, and over what timescale, varies according to different models of basic income. The most progressive versions maintain things such as disability payments, bereavement allowances and other elements on top of the basic income, which would only replace job-related benefits, child benefit and state pensions.

3 E.g. Gorz, A. (1999) *Reclaiming Work*. Cambridge: Polity Press, p. 99; Parijs and Vanderborght (2017).

4 Srnicek and Williams (2016).

5 Frase, P. (2015) 'Ours to Master'. *Jacobin*. Available at: https://jacobin.com/2015/03/automation-frase-robots/

6 Bregman, R. (2016) *Utopia for Realists*. Amsterdam: De Correspondent.

7 Gorz (1999), p. 80; Gorz, A. (1985) *Paths to Paradise*. London: Pluto Press, p. 40.

8 Hägglund, Martin. (2020) *This Life: Secular Faith and Spiritual Freedom*. New York: Profile Books; Bastani, A. (2019) *Fully Automated Luxury Communism*. London: Verso. Ciara Cremin (2018) is also critical of basic income, yet writes within what we would count as a post-work frame.

9 Paine, T. (1974) *Agrarian Justice*. In Foner, Philip S., (ed) (1993) *The Life and Major Writings of Thomas Paine*. New York: Citadel Press, 605–23; Russell, B. (1966) *Roads to Freedom*. London: Unwin; King, M. L. (2010) *Where Do We Go from Here: Chaos or Community?* Boston: Beacon Press; Black Panther Party (1966) 'Ten-Point Program'. Available at: https://www.marxists.org/history/usa/workers/black-panthers/1966/10/15.htm. Other supporters include influential Post-Keynesian economists John Kenneth Galbraith and James Tobin.

10 Sheffey (2021) 'Elon Musk says we need Universal Basic Income because 'in the Future, Physical Work will be a Choice'. Available at: https://www.businessinsider.com/elon-musk-universal-basic-income-physical-work-choice-2021-8?r=US&IR=T

11　Though Hayek did indeed support some form of 'minimum income' in the name of liberty (1986), he didn't flesh out the idea in concrete policy terms and consistently wrote against unconditionality, redistribution and what he called 'social justice' – all of which are integral to the basic income here defended. If the welfare state were to try and impose a more just and even distribution of resources, Hayek writes, then 'this is the kind of welfare state that aims at 'social justice' and becomes 'primarily a redistributor of income. It is bound to lead back to socialism and its coercive and essentially arbitrary methods'. Hayek 'The Meaning of the Welfare State', in Pierson, C. and Castles, F., (eds) (2006) *The Welfare State Reader*. Cambridge: Polity Press. Friedman, for his part, never advocated for a basic income strictly speaking, but preferred a 'negative income tax', which is a similar but crucially different policy. See Van Parijs and Vanderborght (2017) for a longer discussion. Melinda Cooper makes the convincing argument that any enthusiasm for such schemes on the part of neoliberal intellectuals fell away during the 1970s, as discussed below. Generally speaking, neoliberal policy prefers cash *loans*, or cash with strings, to unconditional cash payments. For Hayek's minimum income idea see Hayek (1986) *The Road to Serfdom*. London: Routledge.

12　For one expression of this claim, see Kleiner, D. (2016). 'Universal Basic Income is a neoliberal plot to make you poorer'. *openDemocracy*. Available at: https://neweconomics.opendemocracy.net/universal-basic-income-is-a-neoliberal-plot-to-make-you-poore/; see Peck, J. (2001) for neoliberal welfare policy in practice: *Workfare States*. Guildford: Guildford Press.

13　As Srnicek and Williams warn: 'The demand for a UBI … is subject to competing hegemonic forces. It is just as open to being mobilised for a libertarian dystopia as for a post-work society – an ambiguity that has led many to mistakenly conflate the two poles' (2016), p. 119. See also Gorz (1985), p. 40 on this point.

14　Mary Lawhon & Tyler McCreary (2023) 'Making UBI Radical: On the Potential for a Universal Basic Income to Underwrite Transformative and Anti-Kyriarchal Change', *Economy and Society*, 52 (2): 349–72.

15　This nuance might seem obvious, but it has unfortunately been a real sticking point for critics. See Gourevitch, Alex and Stanczk, Lucas (2018). 'The Basic Income Illusion'. *Catalyst*, 1 (4): 151–77. Weeks' response is: Weeks, K. (2020) 'Anti/Postwork Feminist Politics and a Case for Basic Income'. *tripleC*, 18 (2): 575–94. See also our notes on this debate: Hester, H. and Stronge, W. (2020) 'Towards Post-Work Studies: Identifying Misconceptions in an Emerging Field'. Available at: https://autonomy.work/portfolio/post-workmisconceptions2/.

16　Chandler, D. (2023) *Free and Equal*. London: Penguin.

17　Piketty, T. (2021) 'From Basic Income to Inheritance for All'. *Le Monde*. Available at: https://www.lemonde.fr/blog/piketty/2021/05/18/from-basic-income-to-inheritance-for-all/

18　Standing's eight giants are: inequality, insecurity, debt, stress, precarity, automation, populism and extinction. Standing, G. (2020) *Battling Eight Giants: Basic Income Now*. London: Bloomsbury.

19   Pickett, K. and Wilkinson, R. (2009) *The Spirit Level: Why More Equal Societies Almost Always Do Better*. London: Allen Lane; Pickett, K. and Wilkinson, R. (2019) *The Inner Level: How More Equal Societies Reduce Stress, Restore Sanity and Improve Everyone's Well-Being*. London: Penguin.

20   This would take the level of child poverty from 27.3 per cent to 12.5 per cent – below the level of 14.0 per cent that existed in 1977. The paper also proposes a level of £190 per week for over 65s, which would reduce pensioner poverty by over half. Reed, H. et al (2022) *Tackling Poverty: The Power of a Universal Basic Income*. London: Compass. See also Stronge, W. et al (2021) *A Future Fit for Wales: A Basic Income for All*. Autonomy. Available at: https://autonomy.work/portfolio/walesubi/

21   UN (2018) 'Home, the Most Dangerous Place for Women, with Majority of Female Homicide Victims Worldwide Killed by Partners or Family, UNODC Study Says'. Available at: https://www.unodc.org/unodc/en/press/releases/2018/November/home–the-most-dangerous-place-for-women–with-majority-of-female-homicide-victims-worldwide-killed-by-partners-or-family–unodc-study-says.html. Quoted in Weeks (2020).

22   Federici, Silvia and Arlen Austin (eds) (2017) *Wages for Housework, The New York Commit-tee 1972–1977: History, Theory, Documents*. New York: Autonomedia, p. 154.

23   Womak, A. (2018) 'How a Universal Basic Income Could Help Women in Abusive Relationships'. Available at: https://www.independent.co.uk/voices/domestic-violence-abuse-bill-theresa-may-financial-independence-a8260736.html

24   Standing (2020), p. 21.

25   Ibid., p. 22.

26   This last point refers to one finding from the Finnish basic income experiment where the randomly selected participants reported feeling greater trust in government. See Finland Toolbook: https://toolbox.finland.fi/life-society/finlands-basic-income-experiment-2017-2018/

27   Forget, E. (2011) 'The Town with No Poverty: The Health Effects of a Canadian Guaranteed Annual Income Field Experiment'. *Canadian Public Policy*, 37 (3).

28   'Higher spend' states taken from Nanda, S. and Parkers, H. (2019) 'Just Tax'. IPPR. Available at: https://www.ippr.org/files/2019-09/just-tax-sept19.pdf

29   Mullainathan, S. and Shafir, E. (2013) *Scarcity: Why Having Too Little Means So Much*. New York: Times Books.

30   Coote, A., Percy, P. (2020) *The Case for Universal Basic Services*. London: Polity. See also the UCL report 'Social Prosperity for the Future: A Proposal for Universal Basic Services' (2017). Available at: https://www.ucl.ac.uk/bartlett/igp/news/2017/oct/igps-social-prosperity-network-publishes-uks-first-report-universal-basic-services. Recall that Bastani (2019) makes this zero-sum argumentative move.

31 This is either implicitly or explicitly the argument of those who see Universal Basic Services as a replacement for a universal basic income. This is historically not how welfare and public service provision has been considered by progressives.

32 This is a shorter version of an argument made earlier via Autonomy. Stronge, W. (2020) 'What Counts as Basic?'. Available at: https://autonomy.work/portfolio/incomenotservices/

33 A longer discussion of this issue can be found in Lansley, Stewart and Mack, Joanna (2015) *Breadline Britain: the Rise of Mass Poverty*. London, Oneworld Publications.

34 Stronge (2020).

35 For the most recent of these kinds of survey, see JRF (2020) 'A Minimum Income Standard for the UK in 2022'. Available at: https://www.jrf.org.uk/report/minimum-income-standard-uk-2022; for the 2012 'Poverty and Social Exclusion' survey, see here: https://www.poverty.ac.uk/system/files/WP_Analysis_No3_Focus-groups_Fahmy-Pemberton-Sutton.pdf

36 Lansley and Mack (2015); Stronge (2020) See Chapter 4 for further discussion of the changeable character of the realm of necessity.

37 Calnitsky, D. (2017) 'Debating Basic Income', *Catalyst*, 1 (3) FALL 2017. Available at: https://catalyst-journal.com/2017/12/debating-basic-income#ch-0; See also Offe, Claus and Wiesenthal, Helmet (1980) 'Two Logics of Collective Action: Theoretical Notes on Social Class and Organizational Form', *Political Power and Social Theory*, 1 (1): 67–115.

38 Fraser, N. (2022) *Cannibal Capitalism*. London: Verso, pp. 156–7.

39 Ibid.

40 Ibid.

41 In other texts Fraser acknowledges that within less neoliberal regimes, basic income would act as a non-reformist reform, since despite 'leaving intact the deep structure of capitalist property rights', it could 'set in motion a trajectory of change in which more radical reforms become practicable over time'. Fraser, N. 'Social Justice in the Age of Identity Politics: Redistribution, Recognition, and Participation', in Redistribution or Recognition? A Political-Philosophical Exchange, by Nancy Fraser and Axel Honneth (2003). London: Verso. pp. 78, 79. Discussed in Chamberlain, J. (2017) *Undoing Work*. New York: Cornell Press.

42 Others, such as Frederic Jameson, have suggested this approach with regard to Marx's *Capital*. Jameson, F. (2014) *Representing 'Capital': A Reading of Volume One*. London: Verso.

43 Note that 'unemployed' and 'unemployment' are terms that were invented really only after 1910 and the deployment of labour exchanges to distinguish strictly between 'employed' and 'unemployed' workers.

44 Quoted in Seabrook, J. (2013) *Pauperland: A Short History of Poverty in Britain*. London: C Hurst and Co, p. 45; Lansley and Mack (2015), p. 122.

45 Hartlib, S. (1646) 'The Parliament Reformation', quoted in J. C. Davis (1983) *Utopia & Ideal Society*. London: Cambridge University Press, p. 318.

46 Anderson, Elizabeth (2023) *Hijacked: How Neoliberalism Turned the Work Ethic against Workers and How Workers Can Take It Back,* Cambridge: Cambridge University Press, p. 80.

47 Ibid., p. 83.

48 Chadwick quote in Dean, M. (1991) *The Constitution of Poverty: Toward a Genealogy of Liberal Governance*. London: Routledge. Chadwick, E. (1837) *An Article on the Principles and Progress of the Poor Law Amendment Act*, reprinted from *Edinburgh Review*, London: C. Knight.

49 Shilliam, R. (2018) *Race and the Undeserving Poor*. Newcastle Upon Tyne: agenda publishing, p. 31.

50 Jaffe, S. (2021) *Work Won't Love You Back: How Devotion to Our Jobs Keeps Us Exploited, Exhausted and Alone*. London: Hurst, p. 26.

51 Cooper, M. (2017) *Family Values*. New York: Zone Books.

52 Englander (2013), p. 31; See also Longmate, N. (2003) The Workhouse: a Social History. London: Pimlico. This is explicit in the official documents of the Poor Laws themselves: 'The first and essential of all conditions, a principle which we find universally admitted … is that [the pauper's] situation on the whole shall not be made really or apparently so eligible as the situation of the independent labourer of the lowest class' (Report on the Royal Commission on the Poor Laws, 1834, pp. 127, 146–7).

53 Anderson (2023), p. 78.

54 Churchill, W. (1909) *Parliamentary Debates,* House of Commons, 5th series, 19 May 1909, vol. 5, col. 503.

55 King, D. (1995) *Actively Seeking Work? The Politics of Unemployment and Welfare Policy in the United States and Great Britain*. Chicago: Chicago University Press. Cootes, R. J. (1966) *The Making of the Welfare State*. London: Longmans, Green and Co.

56 Gough, I. (1979) *The Political Economy of the Welfare State*. London: Macmillan Press, p. 14; Rose, N. (1989) *Governing the Soul: The Shaping of the Private Self,* London: Routledge.

57 Pfannebecker, M. and Smith, J. A. (2018) *Work Want Work: Labour and Desire at the End of Capitalism*. London: Zed, p. 14.

58 For example: Jones, K. and Kumar, A. (2022) *Idleness*. Newcastle: Agenda Publishing.

59 Cooper (2017), pp. 43–5.

60 It should be noted, as Cooper does, that many liberals and leftists (including civil rights groups) also attacked the AFDC for the same reasons as conservative voices – i.e. its perceived anti-familial bent; this history is useful for today's debates, where very different attitudes towards the family on the centre and left might deliver different levels of support for things such as an *individual*, basic income.

61 Quoted in Cooper (2017), p. 52.

62 'In text after text, neoconservative critique of the counterculture somehow transmutes into a critique of AFDC, the welfare program that they perceived, no doubt correctly, as the linchpin of the Fordist social order, and a virulent attack on the activists whom they saw as most responsible for disestablishing this order', Cooper (2017), p. 53.

63 See Cooper (2017), p. 54.

64 It is also useful for dispelling lazy and obfuscatory accounts that draw false equivalences between basic income schemes and neoliberal ideology. Arguably, as Cooper has pointed out, Friedman always caveated his support for things such as redistributive welfare (p. 48).

65 Cooper goes into great detail as to this period.

66 Cooper (2017), p. 48.

67 Quoted in Cooper, ibid.

68 Friedman's distinct lean against universal, high spend and redistributive welfare, and the neoliberal paternalism that was to follow this historical conjuncture, should give pause for thought to those who want to portray our world as one wherein basic income is somehow victorious. E.g. Jäger, A. and Zamora, D. (2023) *Welfare Against Markets*. Chicago: Chicago University Press.

69 Hall (1988) 'The Great Moving Right Show', in *The Hard Road to Renewal*. London: Verso Books, p. 26.

70 Jones and Kumar (2022), p. 54.

71 Cooper (2017).

72 Mandelson, P. and Liddle R. (1996) *The Blair Revolution: Can New Labour Deliver?* London: Faber & Faber, p. 102. Italics added.

73 Peck, J. (2001) *Workfare States*. New York: Guildford Press, p. 280.

74 Dwyer, et al (2023) *The Impacts of Welfare Conditionality*. Bristol: Policy Press, p. 160.

75 Wright, S. and Dwyer, P. (2022) 'In-Work Universal Credit: Claimant Experiences of Conditionality Mismatches and Counterproductive Benefit Sanctions', *Journal of Social Policy*, 51 (1): 20–38. Neoliberal paternalism, when it comes to welfare, is best symbolized in the figure of Lawrence Mead – an organic intellectual of the Third Way era. Dwyer et al (2023), pp. 139–40. See also Boland and Griffin (2023) *The Reformation of Welfare*. Bristol: Bristol Policy Press.

76 Meiksins Wood, E. (2017) *The Origins of Capitalism: A Longer View*. London: Verso.

77 Polanyi, K. (2002) *The Great Transformation*. Boston: Beacon Press; Marx, K. (1990) *Capital Volume One*. Penguin: London; Cleaver, H. (2000) *Reading Capital Politically*. California: AK Press; Postone, M. (1993) *Time, Labor, and Social Domination*. Cambridge: Cambridge University Press.

78 Mary Murphy also uses this as the premise of her 'ecosocial welfare' futures. Murphy, M. (2023) *Creating an Ecosocial Welfare Future*. Bristol: Policy Press.

79 Esping-Anderson's classic text on welfare understands the decommodifying form welfare state as the most radical iteration – even if it has yet to be achieved in actuality. Esping-Anderson (1990) *The Three Worlds of Welfare Capitalism*. Cambridge: Polity Press. This is also why Stuart Hall understands the 'Keynesian Welfare State' as ambiguous (Hall, 1988).

80 Esping-Anderson (1990), pp. 35–54. Gorz discusses the benefits and drawbacks of even such 'low conditional' systems in *Reclaiming Work* (1999), pp. 96–8.

81 Spargo, John (1912) *Applied Socialism: A Study of the Application of Socialist Principles to the State*. New York: B.W. Huebsch, p. 82.

82 Some of the best examples of the general deployment of the labour theory of value today are John Smith *Imperialism* (2017); see also Intan Suwandi (2019) *Value Chains: The New Economic Imperialism*.

83 Kautsky, K. (1903), trans. by Algie Martin Simons and May Wood Simons. *The Social Revolution*. Chicago: Charles Kerr & Co.

84 Spargo (1912), p. 192.

85 Ibid., p. 194.

86 Gorz (1985), p. 42.

87 Ibid.

88 For example, this talk by Zachariah, David and Härdin, Tomas. 'Cybernetic Planning and Climate Change Reversal'. Available at: https://www.youtube.com/watch?v=65LjjI QdNw8&list=LL&index=2

89 Cockshott, P. and Cottrell, A. (1993) *Towards a New Socialism*. Nottingham: Spokesman Books.

90 The labour tokens concept also must answer questions around the variability and elasticity that exists in many jobs between quality/quantity output and hours. Education, for example, doesn't necessarily improve if teachers and students put in longer hours each day – in fact the opposite can easily happen; this equally applies to all occupations with elements of creativity involved, but also jobs in social care, for instance, where longer hours result in a depleted workforce – thus risking diminishing the quality of care.

91   Spargo (1912), p. 189. Marx, K. (1971) *Critique of the Gotha Programme*. Moscow: Progress Publishers, pp. 16–17. Marx sees this 'labour exchange' model of work as the 'first phase' of communist society, as it emerges from capitalism: in 'higher phases', labouring will not be a burden but 'life's prime want' (p. 18). For post-work theory, such a proclamation is ambiguous: on the one hand, we should be sceptical of any visions of work as fully internalized with life (given the current toxic blurring of work and life as well the disciplinary work ethic that is frequently wielded against workers); on the other hand, post-work seeks the abolition of work as we know it – and in Marx's brief sketch the activity of 'labour' has indeed changed imaginably, so as to no longer be experienced in the same burdensome way as before. For our perspective on this, see the discussion of dual and single realm utopias in Chapter 4.

92   Spargo does note that while what he defines as 'socialism' involves differences in wages in many cases, what he calls 'communism' would likely involve equalized incomes.

93   Grünberg, M. (2023). 'The Planning Daemon: Future Desire and Communal Production', *Historical Materialism* (published online ahead of print 2023). doi: https://doi.org/10.1163/1569206x-bja10001

94   Trott, B. (2007) 'Walking in the Right Direction?' *Turbulence*, 1: 14–15. http://www.turbulence.org.uk/turbulence-1/walking-in-the-right-direction/index.html

95   Weeks, K. (2020) 'Anti/Postwork Feminist Politics and a Case for Basic Income', *tripleC*, 18 (2): 575–94, 2020. See, for example: Cox, Nicole and Federici, Silvia (1976) *Counter-Planning from the Kitchen: Wages for House-work, A Perspective on Capital and the Left*. Brooklyn: New York Wages for Housework Committee.

96   Ibid., p. 576.

97   Ibid.

98   Out of the plethora of studies, we can pick Wright, S. (2011) 'Relinquishing Rights? The Impact of Activation on Citizenship for Single Parents in the UK', in S. Betzelt and S. Bothfeld (eds) *Activation and Labour Market Reform in Europe: Challenges to Social Citizenship*. Basingstoke: Palgrave Macmillan, pp. 59–78; Wright, S. and Patrick, R. (2019) 'Welfare Conditionality in Lived Experience: Aggregating Qualitative Longitudinal Research', *Social Policy and Society*, 18 (4): 597–613.

99   Andersen, K. (2023) *Welfare that Works for Women?* Bristol: Policy Press, p. 56. See also: Wright, S. (2023) *Women and Welfare Conditionality: Lived Experiences of Benefit Sanctions, Work and Welfare*. Bristol: Policy Press.

100   James, Selma (2012) 'Women, the Unions, and Work, or What Is Not to Be Done (1972)', in *Sex, Race, and Class: The Perspective of Winning: A Selection of Writings, 1952–2011*. Oakland: PM Press, pp. 60–75, p. 72.

101   James, Selma (2012) 'Interview Excerpts (2009)', in *Sex, Race, and Class: The Perspective of Winning: A Selection of Writings, 1952–2011*. Oakland: PM Press, pp. 250–3, p. 253.

102 James, Selma (2020) 'I founded the Wages for Housework Campaign in 1972 – and Women Are Still Working for Free'. *Independent*. Available at: https://www.independent.co.uk/voices/international-womens-day-wages-housework-care-selma-james-a9385351.html

103 Weeks (2020), p. 577; The quotation comes from Boggs, J. (2009), *The American Revolution: Pages from a Negro Worker's Note-book*, New Edition. New York: Monthly Review Press, p. 47; Robeyns, Ingrid (2001) 'An Income of One's Own: A Radical Vision of Welfare Policies in Europe and Beyond', *Gender & Development*, 9 (1): 82–9, p. 84.

104 Standing, G. (2019) *The Plunder of the Commons: A Manifesto for Sharing Public Wealth*. London: Penguin.

105 Ibid., p. 310.

106 Ibid., p. 276.

107 Ibid., p. 275.

108 Maccucato, M. (2011) *The Entrepreneurial State Debunking Public vs. Private Sector Myths*. London: Penguin.

109 Pfannebecker and Smith (2018).

110 The concept of a commons fund is in effect a more ambitious version of sovereign, or social, wealth funds. See: Angela Cummine (2016) *Citizen's Wealth: Why (and How) Sovereign Funds Should Be Managed by the People for the People*. Llandysul: Gomer Press.

111 Ibid., pp. 310–11.

112 Other authors have made similar commons-based arguments for basic income. See Barnes, P. (2021) *Ours: The Case for Universal Property*. London: Polity.

113 Gorz (1985), p. 42.

114 Fraser, N. and Gordan, L. (2020) 'Dependency: A Genealogy', in Fraser *Fortunes of Feminism*. London: Verso, p. 123.

115 Of course, it follows that what matters is the *character* and dynamics of that interdependency.

116 UK Parliament (2022) 'UK Disability Statistics: Prevalence and Life Experiences'. Available at: https://commonslibrary.parliament.uk/research-briefings/cbp-9602/#:~:text=How%20many%20people%20have%20a,22%25%20of%20the%20total%20population. Centers for Disease Control and Prevention 'Disability Impacts All of Us'. Accessed at: https://www.cdc.gov/ncbddd/disabilityandhealth/infographic-disability-impacts-all.html#:~:text=26%20percent%20; WHO, 'Disability'. Available at: https://www.who.int/news-room/fact-sheets/detail/disability-and-health

117 ONS (2022) 'National Population Projections 2020-based Interim'. Available at: https://www.ons.gov.uk/peoplepopulationandcommunity/populationandmigration/

populationprojections/bulletins/nationalpopulationprojections/2020basedinterim#c
hanging-age-structure

118 Ibid.

119 Withers, A. J. (2012) *Disability, Politics & Theory*. Winnipeg: Fernwood Publishing,
p. 109.

120 Withers (2012), p. 109. Withers continues: 'Each of us relies on others every day.
We all rely on one another for support, resources and to meet our needs. We are
all interdependent. This interdependence is not weakness; rather, it is part of our
humanity' (ibid.).

121 See Chapter 4 for further discussion of- freedom and dependency and see the
Conclusion for a further discussion of the intersection between post-work thinking,
the social model of disability and the potential for a political coalition.

122 Xenofeminism. https://laboriacuboniks.net/manifesto/xenofeminism-a-politics-
for-alienation/ The manifesto makes only fleeting reference to disability, and
uses patronizing and euphemistic language in order to do so – namely, the term
'differently-abled'. It has so far largely fallen to thinkers such as Emma Sheppard to
tease out the ways in which xenofeminism offers a framework via which to 'embrace
the pleasures of misfitting' and via which to explore how disability can 'be made
desirable'. This generous and comradely critique has been well-taken. See Sheppard,
Emma, 'Cripping Queer Futurities', 2021. Available at: https://www.youtube.com/
watch?v=uzfnkAKIuiE

123 Haraway, Donna (2016) *Staying with the Trouble: Making Kin in the Chthulucene*.
Durham, NC: Duke University Press, p. 60. See also Hester, Helen (2018).
Xenofeminism. Cambridge: Polity.

124 Davis (2002), pp. 31–2.

125 ONS (2022) 'Economic inactivity by reason (seasonally adjusted)'. Available
here: https://www.ons.gov.uk/employmentandlabourmarket/peoplenotinwork/
economicinactivity/datasets/economicinactivitybyreasonseasonallyadjustedinac01sa;
Strauss, D. (2022) 'Rise in long-term sickness poses threat to UK economic growth'.
Financial Times. Available here: https://www.ft.com/content/8eb63de7-6b08-4714-
9435-d3c42d2e4ba2

126 Schalk, S. quoted in Lakshmi Piepzna-Samarasinha (2022) The Future Is Disabled.
Vancouver: Arsenal Pulp Press, pp. 23–4. Prompted by this, Lakshmi Piepzna-
Samarasinha speculates: 'What would a future look like where the vast majority of
people were disabled, neurodivergent, Deaf, Mad? What would a world radically
shaped by disabled knowledge, culture, love, and connection be like? Have we
ever imagined this, not just as a cautionary tale or a scary story, but as a dream?'
(ibid., p. 22).

127 Note also that according to official stats (ONS, 2022), 'the increasing number of
people reporting a disability is being largely driven by an increase in mental health

conditions'. This is most pronounced amongst young women. Available here: https://www.gov.uk/government/statistics/the-employment-of-disabled-people-2021/the-employment-of-disabled-people-2021

128 Seabrook J. and Stronge, W. (2018) 'In and Out of Work: an Interview with Jeremy Seabrook'. *Autonomy*. Available at: https://autonomy.work/wp-content/uploads/2018/08/Jeremy-Seabrook-interview-V3.pdf

129 One of Srnicek and Williams' section titles (2016) taken from the Sleaford Mods song of the same name.

130 Seabrook, J. (2016) *Cut Out: Living without Welfare*. London: Pluto Books, pp. 45–6.

131 Leonard Davis (2002) *Bending Over Backwards: Disability, Dismodernism and Other Difficult Positions*. New York: NYU Press, p. 30.

132 Oliver (1990) *The Politics of Disablement*. London: Springer, p. 107. The Disablement Income Group supported a 'national disability income' for instance, whereas the Union of the Physically Impaired against Segregation were highly critical of such an approach (Withers (2012), p. 89).

133 E.g. in Oliver (1996) *Understanding Disability: From Theory to Practice*. New York: St. Martin's Press, p. 25.

134 Withers (2012), p. 89.

135 Ibid., p. 90.

136 Ibid. There is no doubt a useful combination of social model theory and the more anti-productivist disability theory. As Clifford notes, social model writers such as Finkelstein do see a profit-driven labour market as a fundamental limit to full inclusion of disabled people. Clifford, 2020, p. 321.

137 Barnes, C. (2012) 'Re-Thinking Disability, Work and Welfare: Disability at Work', *Sociology Compass*, 6 (6): 472–84.

138 Graby, S. (2015) 'Access to Work or Liberation from Work? Disabled People, Autonomy, and Post-Work Politics', *Canadian Journal of Disability Studies*, 4 (2): 149.

139 This universal (therefore non-subject specific) nature of UBI is also what distinguishes it from the contested 'disability income' noted above.

140 Trott (2007).

141 James, S. (2016) 'Child Benefit Has Been Changing Lives for 70 Years. Let's Not Forget the Woman Behind It'. *The Guardian*. Available at: https://www.theguardian.com/commentisfree/2016/aug/06/child-benefit-70-years-eleanor-rathbone

142 Women's Cooperative Guild, *Maternity*, quoted in Fleming, S. (1986) 'Eleanor Rathbone: Spokewoman for a Movement', in E. Rathbone (ed.), *The Disinherited Family*. Bristol: Falling Wall Press.

143 Rathbone, E., 'Family Endowment in its Bearing on the Question of Population', paper read before the Eugenics Society on 12 November 1924, p. 4.

144 Beveridge, W. (1949) 'Epilogue', in E. Rathbone (ed.), *Family Allowances: A New Edition of The Disinherited Family*. London: Allen & Unwin, p. 269.

145 This policy is genuinely progressive and has largely withstood decades of neoliberal economic policy making and cultural assault from the news media: only in 2017 did a cap on the amount of children that would be covered come into force. Reeves, R. (2019) 'Eleanor Rathbone, the Forgotten MP who Changed Women's Lives by Pioneering Child Benefits'. Available at: https://inews.co.uk/opinion/comment/eleanor-rathbone-mp-family-allowances-international-womens-day-266610

146 Ultimately, Rathbone would see the Family Allowances Bill as a 'compromise': 'This Bill gives the mother through her children her share, although it is only a very little share so far'. Hansard, Family Allowances Bill Volume 411: debated on Monday 11 June 1945. Available here: https://hansard.parliament.uk/Commons/1945-06-11/debates/117f1481-7ae3-4f85-834c-065d1b9b7529/FamilyAllowancesBill

147 See, for example: Gollancz, V., (ed) (1917) *The Making of Women: Oxford Essays in Feminism*. London: Allen and Unwin; Davies, M. L. (1918) 'The Claims of Mothers and Children' in Marion Phillips (ed.), *Women and the Labour Party*. London: Headley Bros.

148 Fleming, S. 'Eleanor Rathbone: Spokewoman for a movement'; see also Selma James on Rathbone's legacy: James, S. (2016) 'Child Benefit Has Been Changing Lives for 70 Years. Let's Not Forget the Woman Behind It'. *The Guardian*. Available at: https://www.theguardian.com/commentisfree/2016/aug/06/child-benefit-70-years-eleanor-rathbone

149 Fleming, S. (1986) 'Eleanor Rathbone: Spokewoman for a Movement', in Rathbone, E. (ed.), *The Disinherited Family*. Bristol: Falling Wall Press, p. 39.

150 Rathbone (1986), p. 362.

151 Alexander Gray, 1927, quoted in Fleming, S. (1986) 'Eleanor Rathbone: Spokewoman for a Movement', in Rathbone, E. (ed.), *The Disinherited Family*. Bristol: Falling Wall Press, p. 44.

152 Fleming (1986), p. 45.

153 *The Nation*, 21 November 1914. Fleming, S. 'Eleanor Rathbone: Spokewoman for a movement', p. 46.

154 Weeks (2020), p. 581.

155 Fleming (1986), p. 47.

156 Quoted in Ibid., p. 47.

157 Quoted in *Daily News and Leader*, 19 November 1914, in Fleming (1986), p. 47.

158 Fleming (1986), p. 47, footnote 143.

159 Ibid., p. 66.

160 Germain, J. (2021) 'The National Welfare Rights Organization Wanted Economic Justice for Black Americans'. *Teen Vogue*. Available at: https://www.teenvogue.com/story/national-welfare-rights-organization-black-women

161 Tillmon, J. (2010) 'From the Vault: "Welfare Is a Women's Issue" (Spring 1972)'. Republished in *Ms*. Available at: https://msmagazine.com/2021/03/25/welfare-is-a-womens-issue-ms-magazine-spring-1972/

162 Germain, J. (2021) 'The National Welfare Rights Organization Wanted Economic Justice for Black Americans'. See also the discussion in Bhargava, D. and Luce, S. (2023) *Practical Radicals: Seven Strategies to Change the World*. New York: The New Press, p. 23.

163 Tillmon, J. (2010) 'From the Vault: "Welfare Is a Women's Issue" (Spring 1972)'

164 Cooper (2017), pp. 89–98.

165 See also the hugely influential Cloward-Piven strategy, which advocated an overloading of the welfare system in order to bring about a guaranteed income scheme; however, their perspective is threaded with a distinctly pro-family focus, which Cooper notes chimed very well with conservative opposition to welfare at the time. Cloward and Piven (2010) 'The Weight of the Poor: A Strategy to End Poverty'. Republished in *The Nation*. Available at: https://www.thenation.com/article/archive/weight-poor-strategy-end-poverty/

166 Quote in Germain, J. (2021) 'The National Welfare Rights Organization Wanted Economic Justice for Black Americans'.

167 Lewis, S. (2022) *Abolish the Family*. London: Verso, p. 70.

168 Nadasen, P. (2012) *Rethinking the Welfare Rights Movement*. London: Routledge.

169 Cooper (2017), p. 43.

170 Abello, O. P. (2021) 'Guaranteed Income in Jackson Designed by Black Moms for Black Moms, Showing Results for Black Moms'. *Next City*. Available at: https://nextcity.org/urbanist-news/guaranteed-income-in-jackson-designed-by-black-moms-for-black-moms; see other similar movements in this legacy, e.g. Mothers Uncovered's campaigning for basic income: https://mothersuncovered.com/2020/05/17/mothers-and-basic-income/

171 Fraser and Gordan (2020), p. 144.

172 Cooper (2017).

173 Federici, Silvia. 2012. Revolution at Point Zero: Housework, Reproduction, and Feminist Struggle. Oakland, CA: PM Press, p. 9.

174 Weeks (2020), p. 587.

175 Ibid.

176 The phrase used by disability activists is 'we are all only temporally able', referred to in Sunny Taylor's (2004) piece 'The Right Not to Work: Power and

Disability': https://monthlyreview.org/2004/03/01/the-right-not-to-work-power-and-disability; it is also in line with Leonard Davis' Dismodernist ethics.

177   Farrar, E. (1974) 'The Invisible Woman', in 'The Power of Women', vol. 1, No. 1 (March/April), 1974, p. 8.

178   This, we argue, is where Hägglund's dismissal of basic income falls down: unconditional cash outside of the wage relationship *does* affect the relations of production within that relationship. As has been documented in this chapter, the history of the encroaching market is the history of funnelling the means of subsistence through the wages system – causing asymmetries of power, domination and familial forms that would be significantly shifted if new resource channels were guaranteed for all.

179   Cremin (2018), p. 166.

180   Hall (1988), 'Gramsci and Us', in *Hard Road to Renewal*, p. 173. The full quote refers to countering Thatcherism as a whole: 'Is it possible that the immense new material, cultural and technological capacities, which far outstrip Marx's wildest dreams, which are now actually in our hands, are going to be politically hegemonised for the reactionary modernisation of Thatcherism? Or can we seize on those means of history-making, of making new human subjects, and shove it in the direction of a new culture? That's the choice before the Left.'

181   Perhaps, as Boland and Griffin argue, 'welfare is a salve to moderate rather than address inequality', and therefore something truly transformative will need to go beyond prior framings and deployments of these salves. A good test of such a thing would be to see how hostile the establishment has been to a concept – the above histories of Rathbone and Tillmon speak for themselves. Boland and Griffin (2023). p. 56.

182   UBI labs: https://www.ubilabnetwork.org/about; US city mayors: https://www.mayorsforagi.org/

183   For think tanks researching basic income see Autonomy, https://autonomy.work/; Compass, https://www.compassonline.org.uk/; and the Jain Family Institute, https://www.jainfamilyinstitute.org/our-work/guaranteed-income/

184   See GiveDirectly: https://www.givedirectly.org/about/

185   See our discussion of what a post-work coalition could look like in the conclusion.

Chapter 3

1   Aronowitz, Stanley, Esposito, Dawn, DiFazio, William, and Yard, Margaret (1998) 'The Post-Work Manifesto', in Stanley Aronowitz and Jonathan Cutler (eds) *Post-Work: The Wages of Cybernation*. New York: Routledge, 31–80, p. 35.

2	Krisis Group (1999) 'Manifesto against Labour'. http://www.krisis.org/1999/manifesto-against-labour, n.p.

3	Williams, Alex and Srnicek, Nick (2013) '#Accelerate: Manifesto for an Accelerationist Politics'. https://criticallegalthinking.com/2013/05/14/accelerate-manifesto-for-an-accelerationist-politics/, n.p.

4	Srnicek, Nick and Williams, Alex (2015) *Inventing the Future: Postcapitalism and a World without Work*. London: Verso, p. 70.

5	Bastani, Aaron (2014) 'Fully Automated Luxury Communism'. https://novaramedia.com/2014/11/10/imo-w-aaron-bastani-e003/, n.p.

6	Bastani, Aaron (2015) 'Britain Doesn't Need More Austerity, It Needs Luxury Communism'. https://www.vice.com/en/article/ppxpdm/luxury-communism-933, n.p.

7	Bastani, Aaron (2019) *Full Automated Luxury Communism*. London: Verso, p. 23.

8	Benanav, Aaron (2020) *Automation and the Future of Work*. London: Verso, p. x.

9	Ibid., p. 39.

10	Smith, Jason (2020) *Smart Machine and Service Work: Automation in an Age of Stagnation*. London: Reaktion Books, p. 48.

11	Christophers, B. (2021) *Rentier Capitalism: Who Owns the Economy, and Who Pays for It?* London: Verso Books; Standing, G. (2017) *The Corruption of Capitalism: Why Rentiers Thrive and Work Does Not Pay*. London: Biteback Books.

12	Jason E. Smith (2021) *Smart Machines and Service Work: Automation in an Age of Stagnation*. Chicago: University of Chicago Press, p. 43.

13	All of which, we should note, would seem to suggest the need for an emancipatory post-work politics that encompasses the human-machine assemblage.

14	Hägglund, Martin (2019) *This Life: Secular Faith and Spiritual Freedom*. New York: Pantheon Books, p. 259.

15	Ibid., p. 60.

16	Badiou, Alain. 'Nick Srnicek and Alex Williams in Conversation with Alain Badiou', Miguel Abreu Gallery. https://vimeo.com/193993130, n.p.

17	Marx, Karl (1975) 'Draft of an Article on Friedrich List's Book Das nationale System der politischen Oekonomie', in *Marx/Engels, Collected Works, Vol. 4*. New York: International Publishers, pp. 278–9.

18	Bastani (2014), p. 70.

19	Aronowitz et al (1998), p. 79.

20	Samman, Emma, Presler-Marshall, Elizabeth and Jones, Nicola (2016) '*Women's Work: Mothers, Children and the Global Childcare Crisis*'. London: Overseas

Development Institute. https://odi.org/en/publications/womens-work-mothers-children-and-the-global-childcare-crisis/, n.p.

21 Krisis Group (1999) 'Manifesto against Labour'. http://www.krisis.org/1999/manifesto-against-labour, n.p.

22 Ibid.

23 Bassett, Caroline, Kember, Sarah and O'Riordan, Kate (2020) Furious: Technological Feminism and Digital Futures, London: Pluto Press, p. 43.

24 Ibid. It is worth noting that a number of critiques in this vein concentrate primarily on the manifesto, and tend not to engage with Srnicek and Williams's later works (which largely avoid these perceived missteps).

25 Kate Soper also makes similar criticisms, to which we turn in the final chapter on post-work utopianism. Soper, Kate (2020) *Post-Growth Living: Towards an Alternative Hedonism*. London: Verso.

26 Srnicek and Williams (2015), p. 113.

27 Ibid., p. 85. In Srnicek's later work, co-authored with Helen Hester, the post-work agenda is definitively extended beyond a post-jobs horizon. Hester and Srnicek (2023) *After Work: A History of the Home and the Fight for Free Time*. London: Verso.

28 Bastani (2014), p. 77.

29 See, for example, Gorz, A. (1985) *Paths to Paradise: On the Liberation from Work*. London: Pluto Press.

30 Srnicek and Williams (2015), p. 111.

31 Others have argued a defence of Bastani along similar lines. Fishwick and Kiersey (2021) *Post-capitalist Futures: Political Economy Beyond Crisis and Hope*. London: Pluto Books. Chap 2.

32 Bastani (2014), p. 185.

33 Ibid., p. 186.

34 Srnicek and Williams (2015), p. 129.

35 See the final chapter on utopianism for a more in-depth discussion of nostalgia.

36 Hägglund (2019), p. 399.

37 Clark, A. (2003) *Natural-Born Cyborgs: Minds, Technologies, and the Future of Human Intelligence*. Oxford: Oxford University Press; Clark, A. (2011) *Supersizing the Mind*. Oxford: Oxford University Press; Haraway, D. (1985) 'A Manifesto for Cyborgs: Science, Technology, and Socialist Feminism in the 1980's', *Socialist Review*, 80: 65–108.

38 This also dovetails well with the concept of 'synthetic freedom' in Srnicek and Williams (2016), which we refer to later in our discussion.

39 Leonard Davis (2002) *Bending Over Backwards: Disability, Dismodernism and Other Difficult Positions.* New York: NYU Press, p. 30. It goes without saying that (unlike the wheelchair) the literal and figurative technologies of citizenship can frequently be oppressive and, to varying degrees, undesirable – as can the category of the 'the citizen' itself.

40 Postone, M. (1993) *Time, Labor, and Social Domination.* Cambridge: Cambridge University Press, pp. 35–6.

41 Prescient and Strategic Intelligence, 2020. 'Personal Robots Market Research Report: By Offering (Hardware, Software), Type (Cleaning Robots, Entertainment & Toy Robots, Educational Robots, Handicap Assistance Robots, Companion Robots, Personal Transportation Robots, Security Robots) – Global Industry Analysis and Growth Forecast to 2030'. https://www.psmarketresearch.com/market-analysis/personal-robot-market

42 James Wright (2023), *Robots Won't Save Japan: An Ethnography of Eldercare Automation.* Ithaca: Cornell University Press, 100.

43 Angela Johnston (2015) 'Robotic Seals Comfort Dementia Patients but Raise Ethical Concerns'. KALW. Available at: https://www.kalw.org/show/crosscurrents/2015-08-17/robotic-seals-comfort-dementia-patients-but-raise-ethical-concernsSee also: Hung, L., Liu, C., Woldum, E. et al (2019) 'The Benefits of and Barriers to Using a Social Robot PARO in Care Settings: A Scoping Review', *BMC Geriatr*, 19 (232). https://doi.org/10.1186/s12877-019-1244-6

44 As Seth Lazar (2024) would have it, Generative Agents 'will power companions that introduce new categories of social relationship, and change old ones'. 'Frontier AI Ethics: Anticipating and Evaluating the Societal Impacts of Generative Agents'. https://arxiv.org/abs/2404.06750

45 Samuel, Sigal (2020) 'You Can Buy a Robot to Keep Your Lonely Grandparents Company. Should You?' Vox. https://www.vox.com/future-perfect/2020/9/9/21418390/robots-pandemic-loneliness-isolation-elderly-seniors

46 Knibbs, Kate (2020) 'There's No Cure for Covid-19 Loneliness, but Robots Can Help'. Wired. https://www.wired.com/story/covid-19-robot-companions/

47 Kenway, Emily (2023) Who Cares: The Hidden Crisis of Caregiving, and How We Solve It. London: Wildfire, p. 108.

48 Libcom (2015) 'Fully automated luxury communism: a utopian critique'. https://libcom.org/article/fully-automated-luxury-communism-utopian-critique, n.p.

49 Krisis Group (1999) 'Manifesto against Labour'. http://www.krisis.org/1999/manifesto-against-labour, n.p.

50 Federici, Silvia (2012) 'The Restructuring of Housework and Reproduction in the United States in the 1970s', in *Revolution at Point Zero: Housework, Reproduction, and Feminist Struggle.* Oakland: PM Press, pp. 41–53, p. 53.

51 Dowling, E. and Hester, H. (2021). 'The Future of Care: Helen Hester in Conversation with Emma Dowling'. *Autonomy*. Available at: https://autonomy.work/portfolio/ffp-hester-dowlingconvo/

52 Bastani, Aaron, Ash Sarkar and James Butler. 'Fully Automated Luxury Communism'. NovaraFM. Accessed 22 August 2022. https://novaramedia.com/2015/06/19/fully-automated-luxury-communism/.

53 See Wright (2023), p. 72.

54 See Hester (2024) for more on the distinctions between and relationships amongst high-tech, high touch, and high-talk forms of care work. Parts of the argument developed here draw upon this analysis. Hester, Helen (2024). 'The Automated Heart: Digital Domesticity and Emotional Labour Saving', New Vistas 10(2).

55 Wright (2023), p. 141.

56 Ibid., p. 20.

57 Fortunati, Leopoldina (2007) 'Immaterial Labor and Its Machinization', *ephemera*, 7 (1): 139–57, p. 141.

58 Ibid., p. 140.

59 Of course, not all care workers (paid or unpaid) are attracted to the high-talk components of the work, and not everybody in receipt of care will particularly desire the emotional and relational element of caring interactions – some people will find these uncomfortable, unwanted, intrusive or unnecessary; nevertheless, it strikes us as a rather painful irony that the elements of care and of our collective social lives most commonly associated with the potential for human freedom and self-determination are the ones being most effectively outsourced to machines. See also the increasing use of artificial intelligence to produce imagery or copy; art and writing – two spheres historically associated with human self-realization, not to mention 'good' (or at least, less shit) work – have become the routine domain of the machine. The fact that both paid care work and corporate creativity often treat human beings like tools, and that (under current conditions) neither form of work represents autonomously chosen activity or necessarily functions as an end in itself, can sometimes be downplayed in these discussions – but the fact remains that such technical developments are perceived as a threat by some because they seem to push us further away from a world in which work is more bearable.

60 Rowan, Rory (2015), e-flux journal 56th Venice Biennale – SUPERCOMMUNITY – Rory Rowan.

61 Kenway, Emily (2023) Who Cares: The Hidden Crisis of Caregiving, and How We Solve It. London: Wildfire, p. 97.

62 Ibid., p. 96.

63 Bastani, Aaron, Sarkar, Ash and Butler, James 'Fully Automated Luxury Communism'. NovaraFM. Accessed 22 August 2022. https://novaramedia.com/2015/06/19/fully-automated-luxury-communism/.

64 https://autonomy.work/portfolio/ffp-hester-dowlingconvo/

65 Weeks, Kathi, *The Problem with Work: Feminism, Marxism, Antiwork Politics, and Postwork Imaginaries*. Durham, NC: Duke University Press, 2011. This text is cited approvingly by Srnicek and Williams, as well as in related texts, such as David Frayne's *The Refusal of Work* and Sophie Lewis' *Full Surrogacy Now*.

66 Benanav himself disavows the post-work label, as he implicitly takes it to mean a situation where literally no work is carried out. See the final chapter of *Automation and the Future of Work* (2020).

67 Medina, E. (2014) *Cybernetic Revolutionaries*. Cambridge MA: MIT Press.

68 Jakic, B. (2014) Galaxy and the New Wave: Yugoslav Computer Culture in the 1980s. 10.1007/978-1-4471-5493-8_5.; See also Eby, M. (2020) 'The Lost History of Socialism's DIY Computer'. *Jacobin. Available at: https://jacobin.com/2020/08/ computer-yugoslavia-galaksija-voja-antonic*

69 Smith, A. (2014) 'The Lucas Plan: What Can It Tell Us about Democratising Technology Today?'. Available at: https://www.theguardian.com/science/political-science/2014/jan/22/remembering-the-lucas-plan-what-can-it-tell-us-about-democratising-technology-today

70 As has been argued by many, including for example: Phillips and Rozworski (2019) *The People's Republic of Walmart*. London: Verso.

71 Grünberg, M. (2023) 'The Planning Daemon: Future Desire and Communal Production, Historical Materialism (published online ahead of print 2023)'. doi: https://doi.org/10.1163/1569206x-bja10001

72 Benanav, A. (2020) 'How to Make a Pencil'. *Logic Magazine*. Available at: https:// logicmag.io/commons/how-to-make-a-pencil/

73 Buck, H. (2019) *After Geoengineering: Climate Tragedy, Repair and Restoration*. London: Verso; Bratton, B. (2021) *The Revenge of the Real*. London: Verso. More on the confluence of climate mitigation and tech in the final chapter on utopianism.

74 Srnicek and Williams (2015), p. 3.

Chapter 4

1 Hägglund, Martin (2019) *This Life: Secular Faith and Spiritual Freedom*. New York: Pantheon Books, p. 22.

2 Marx, Karl (1971) *Capital vol. III*. Moscow: Progress Publishers, p. 820.

3 Hägglund (2019), pp. 22–3.

4   Standing, Guy. (2019) *The Plunder of the Commons: A Manifesto for Sharing Public Wealth*. London: Penguin.

5   Fairlie, Simon. 'A Short History of Enclosure in Britain'. *The Land* 7, 2009. Available at: https://www.thelandmagazine.org.uk/articles/short-history-enclosure-britain

6   Fairlie (2009).

7   Ibid.

8   Perelman, M. (2000) *The Invention of Capitalism: Classical Political Economy and the Secret History of Primitive Accumulation*. Durham: Duke University Press; Mingay, G. (1997) *Parliamentary Enclosure in England: An Introduction to Its Causes, Incidence and Impact, 1750–1850*. London: Routledge.

9   Standing, G. (2019) *The Plunder of the Commons: A Manifesto for Sharing Public Wealth*. London: Penguin.

10   Roberts, William Clare (2016) *Marx's Inferno: The Political Theory of Capital*. Princeton: Princeton University Press, p. 18.

11   Postone, Moishe 1993 *Time, Labor, and Social Domination: A Reinterpretation of Marx's Critical Theory*. Cambridge: Cambridge University Press, p. 35.

12   Tilly, Louise A. and Scott, Joan W. (1989) *Women, Work, and Family*. New York: Routledge 1989, p. 96.

13   Fraser, Nancy and Gordon, Linda (1994) 'A Genealogy of 'Dependency': Tracing a Keyword of the U.S. Welfare State', *Signs* 19 (2): 309–36, 315.

14   Fraser and Gordon (2020), p. 316.

15   Gershon, Livia. 'Why Do We Take Pride in Working for a Paycheck?' *JSTOR Daily*, 2017. Available at: https://daily.jstor.org/why-do-we-take-pride-in-working-for-a-paycheck/

16   Cant, Callum. *Riding for Deliveroo: Resistance in the New Economy*. Cambridge: Polity, 2020, pp. 5–6.

17   Roberts (2016), p. 18.

18   Weeks, Kathi (2011) *The Problem with Work: Feminism, Marxism, Antiwork Politics, and Postwork Imaginaries*. Durham: Duke University Press, p. 21.

19   Roberts (2016), p. 102.

20   Marx (1971), p. 820.

21   Benanav, Aaron (2022) *Automation and the Future of Work*. London: Verso, p. 132.

22   Morris, William (2008) *Useful Work vs. Useless Toil*. London: Penguin, p. 14.

23   Ibid., p. 24.

24   Ibid., p. 18.

25 Horgan, Amelia (2021) *Lost in Work: Escaping Capitalism*. London: Pluto Press, p. 52.

26 Berg, Heather (2022) *Porn Work: Sex, Labor, and Late Capitalism*. Chapel Hill: University of North Carolina Press, p. 73.

27 Ibid., p. 75.

28 Horgan, p. 89.

29 Berg, p. 7.

30 Federici, Silvia (2012) *Revolution at Point Zero: Housework, Reproduction, and Feminist Struggle*. Oakland: PM Press, p. 19.

31 Horgan, p. 53.

32 Benanav (2022), pp. 132–3, n. 7.

33 Morris (2008), p. 1.

34 Morris, William (1993) *News From Nowhere and Other Writings*. London: Penguin, p. 92.

35 Morris (2008), p. 27.

36 Ibid., p. 12.

37 Srnicek, Nick and Williams, Alex (2015) *Inventing the Future: Postcapitalism and a World without Work*. London: Verso, p. 82.

38 For more on the relationship between reason, responsibility and political agency, see Hester, Helen. (2019) 'Sapience + Care: Reason and Responsibility in Posthuman Politics', *Angelaki: Journal of the Theoretical Humanities* 24 (2): 67–80.

39 Weeks (2011), p. 22.

40 Ibid., p. 168.

41 Ibid., p. 22.

42 Srnicek and Williams, *Inventing the Future*, p. 80.

43 Weeks, Kathi (2009) "Hours for What We Will': Work, Family, and the Movement for Shorter Hours', *Feminist Studies* 35 (1): 101–27, 118.

44 Wolfendale, Peter (2016) 'Prometheanism and Rationalism'. *Academia.edu*. Available at: https://www.academia.edu/26816420/Prometheanism_and_Rationalism.

45 Galloway, Alexander R. (2017) 'Brometheanism'. *Culture and Communication*. Available at: http://cultureandcommunication.org/galloway/brometheanism

46 Brassier, Ray (2014) 'Prometheanism and Its Critics'. in Robin Mackay and Armen Avanessian (eds) *#Accelerate: The Accelerationist Reader*. Falmouth: Urbanomic, pp. 467–87, p. 470.

47 Brassier, Ray (2014) 'Prometheanism and Real Abstraction,' in Robin Mackay, Luke Pendrell, and James Trafford. (eds) *Speculative Aesthetics.* Falmouth: Urbanomic, pp. 73–7, p. 77.

48 Ibid., p. 77.

49 Hester, Helen 'Promethean Labors and Domestic Realism'. e-flux, 2017. https://www.e-flux.com/architecture/artificial-labor/140680/promethean-labors-and-domestic-realism/.

50 Galloway (2017).

51 Hester (2017).

52 Marx (1971), p. 820.

53 Postone (1993), p. 380.

54 Ibid., p. 3812.

55 Ibid., p. 382.

56 Ibid., p. 380.

57 Ibid., p. 382.

58 Ibid.

59 This pushing back against the idea of immutable natural necessity will become increasingly important as the climate catastrophe deepens and the question of environmental constraints on human activity is navigated. See our discussion of 'Green Prometheanism' in the final chapter.

60 Rather, a more fruitful conceptual direction might be via the notion of 'natureculture'. Haraway, D. (2003) *The Companion Species Manifesto.* Chicago: Prickly Paradigm Press. See discussion in Wark, M. (2016) *Molecular Red: Theory for the Anthropocene.* London: Verso Books.

61 Firestone, Shulamith (1979) *The Dialectic of Sex: The Case for Feminist Revolution.* London: Women's Press, p. 182.

Chapter 5

1 Power, Nina (ed) (2018) *Why Work?* London: Freedom Press; Krisis Gruppe (1999); Robert Kurz *The Substance of Capital.* California: AK Press; Amelia Horgan's *Lost in Work;* Blanchflower, Danny (2019) *Not Working.* Princeton: Princeton University Press; Komlosy, A. (2018) *Work: The Last 1,000 Years.* London: Verso; Snyder, B. (2016) *The Disrupted Workplace.* Oxford: Oxford University Press; Pettinger's Lynne

(2019) *What's Wrong with Work?* Bristol: Policy Press; Spencer, D. *Making Light Work* (2021) Cambridge: Polity Press.

2   More (2016) *Utopia*. London: Verso Books.

3   Forrester, K. (2022), 'Feminist Demands and the Problem of Housework', *American Political Science Review* 1–15, p. 1.

4   Ibid., p. 9.

5   Ibid., p. 1.

6   For example, in our discussion at the end of Chapter 2.

7   Robin, Corey (2011) *The Reactionary Mind*. Oxford: Oxford University Press, p. 99.

8   Kathi Weeks (2011) *The Problem with Work: Feminism, Marxism, Antiwork Politics, and Postwork Imaginaries.* Durham, NC: Duke University Press, pp. 175–226.

9   Fisher, Mark (2009) *Capitalism Realism*. London: Zero Books.

10   Indeed, there are convincing arguments that position capitalism itself is in part powered by promises, expectations and visions of future states, which refract back upon present day economic activities. See Beckert, J. (2016) *Imagined Futures*. London: Harvard University Press.

11   Cooper, Melinda (2017) *Family Values: Between Neoliberalism and the New Social Conservatism*. New York: Zone Books.

12   Hall, S. (1988) *The Hard Road to Renewal*. London: Verso Books, p. 164.

13   Konings, M. (2018) *Capital and Time*. SUP: Stanford, p. 30.

14   Cockett, 1995 *Thinking the Unthinkable*. Mirowski and Plehwe, eds, *The Road from Mount Pelerin*. Glasgow: Fontana Press, (2009).

15   Hayek's use of 'socialism' here appears to be very broad, and most likely includes adjacent political-economic perspectives such as the Keynesianism he virulently opposed.

16   Hayek, F. (1960) 'The Intellectuals and Socialism', in George B. de Huszar (ed.), *The Intellectuals: A Controversial Portrait*. Glencoe, Illinois: the Free Press, pp. 371–84.

17   Ibid.

18   Srnicek, Nick and Williams, Alex (2015) *Inventing the Future: Postcapitalism and a World Without Work*. London: Verso, Weeks (2011).

19   Kwarteng et al (2012) *Britannia Unchained* (Basingstoke: Palgrave Macmillan).

20   For a gloss on contemporary versions of this, see Traverso (2019) *The New Faces of Fascism: Populism and the Far Right*. London: Verso.

21   Critiqued heavily by Srnicek and Williams (2015), pp. 5–50.

22 Milburn (2019) *Generation Left*. London: Polity Books. This shift from anti-utopian movement strategy towards utopian 'Hail Mary' electoralism in the UK and United States was noted in the expanded edition of *Inventing the Future*, where the authors acknowledge that their criticism of the hegemony of folk politics on the left required revision. Given the fate of Corbynism and Sanders' campaign for the Democrat Party candidacy, the subsequent debriefing on the left has resulted in slight residues of utopian ambition as well as plenty of anti-utopian expression.

23 Mark Fisher's concept, in response to capitalist realism's malaise, is Acid Communism. See Fisher (2021) *Post-Capitalist Desire*. London: Repeater.

24 Brassier, R. (2014) 'Prometheanism and Real Abstraction', in R. Mackay, L. Pendrell and J. Trafford (eds) *Speculative Aesthetics*. Falmouth: Urbanomic, p. 77.

25 Ruth Levitas (1990) *The Concept of Utopia*. London: Philip Allan.

26 Ibid.

27 The following draws on Peter Beilharz's (1992) succinct reconstruction in his *Labour's Utopias*. London: Routledge, as well as Vincent Geoghegan's (1987) *Utopianism & Marxism*. London: Methuen.

28 Marx, K. (1975) 'Excerpts from James Mill's *Elements on Political Economy*', in L. Colletti (ed.), *Marx – Early Writings*. London: Harmondsworth, p. 278.

29 Marx and Engels (1976) 'The German Ideology', in Marx and Engels, *Collected Works*, vol. 5. London: Lawrence and Wishart, p. 47.

30 Marx, K. (1973). *Grundrisse*. Harmondsworth: Penguin, p. 706.

31 Marx, K. *Capital: A Critique of Political Economy. Vol.3*. Translated by David Fernbach. London: Penguin, p. 959.

32 Bloch, E. (1986) *The Principle of Hope*. Oxford: Basil Blackwell. See also Greenaway, J. (2024) *A Primer on Utopian Philosophy*. London: Zero Books.

33 Weeks (2011), p. 196.

34 Lenin, V. I. (1975), *What Is to Be Done?* Peking: Foreign Languages Press: Peking, p. 211.

35 Lenin would also famously claim that 'Marxists … are hostile to any and every Utopia' and that there is 'no trace of utopianism in Marx'. Cited in Vincent Georgheagan (1987) *Utopianism & Marxism*. London: Methuen, p. 54. For more detailed discussion on Marxism and utopianism, see Levitas, Ruth (2010) *The Concept of Utopia*. Oxford: Peter Lang.

36 Bahro, R. (2011) *The Alternative in Eastern Europe*. London: Verso. See also the rare praise that Perry Anderson gives to Bahro in Anderson, P. (1980) *Arguments Within English Marxism*. London: Verso.

37 Bahro, R. (1978) *The Alternative in Eastern Europe*. London: New Left Books, p. 253.

38 Kant also uses the example of 'pure water' or 'pure earth': we never experience pure water – only water mixed with other things – but we can successfully identify it *as* water thanks to the regulating ideal. Thanks to Steve Howard for this Kant insight.

39 Pfannebecker, M and Smith, J. A. (2018) *Work Want Work: Labour and Desire at the End of Capitalism*. London: Zed, p. 141–2.

40 We might refer to this as the gap between the 'is' and the 'ought'. As Laboria Cuboniks puts it, 'The project of untangling what ought to be from what is, of dissociating freedom from fact, will from knowledge, is, indeed, an infinite task' – and one with critical links to utopian speculation. https://laboriacuboniks.net/manifesto/xenofeminism-a-politics-for-alienation/

41 Frase (2015) *Four Futures*. London/New York: Jacobin/Verso.

42 Notable mention has to be given to Ernst Bloch, whose work on utopianism is vast and rich (though not without limitations of course). Bloch, *The Principle of Hope*. (MIT, 1995).

43 The similarity (aside from content) between Horkheimer's advocacy of 'fidelity' to an ideal and Hayek's demand for the 'will' to fight for a utopia's realization is noteworthy in this discussion.

44 Marx, K., trans by Livinston and Benton (1975) *Early Writings. London*: Penguin Books, p. 423.

45 Raymond Williams (1983) *Towards 2000*. London: Penguin Books, pp. 91–2.

46 Weeks (2011), p. 204.

47 There is a kind of mirrored relationship here between utopianism and genealogy as methodologies of disruption. For Michel Foucault, like Friedrich Nietzsche before him, knowledge is a tool for cutting – a kind of weapon. Genealogy is a method for disassembling the past, deconstructing accounts of the self and society – thereby making possible new formations, new ways of being and thinking. Utopianism's method shakes the present from the other direction: rewriting the *future* in detail, forcing us to ask questions of the present. If this is where we *could* go, then the present configuration seems arbitrary and ripe for renewal. Foucault, M., Edited by James D. Faubion, Translated by Robert Hurley and Others (2020) *Aesthetics, Method, and Epistemology: Essential Works of Foucault 1954–1984*. See also Week's use of Nietzsche (2011), pp. 198–203.

48 Weeks (2011), p. 204.

49 Thompson, E. P. (1977) *William Morris: Romantic to Revolutionary*. New York: Pantheon, p. 791. Post-work authors Weeks (2011) and Pfannebecker and Smith (2020) each utilize this concept in different ways.

50 Bastani (2019) *Fully Automated Luxury Communism*. London: Verso, p. 243.

51 Lewis, S. (2019) *Full Surrogacy Now*. London: Verso; (2022) *Abolish the Family*. London: Verso. Firestone, S. (2015) *The Dialectic of Sex*. London: Verso. Xenofeminism https://laboriacuboniks.net/manifesto/xenofeminism-a-politics-for-alienation/

52 Lewis (2022) *Abolish the Family*. London: Verso, p. 18.

53 Srnicek and Williams (2015), p. 46.

54 Ibid.

55 Ibid.

56 Weeks (2011), p. 85.

57 Rodgers (2014) *The Work Ethic in Industrial America, 1850–1920*. Chicago: University of Chicago Press, p. 242.

58 We see a grim return of the apron iconography (this time as farce?) in the images of work that we are confronted with today in 2022, with cafes, online banks and barbers all using craft imaginaries to present authenticity. See Gandini, *Zeitgeist Nostalgia, on populism, work and the good life* (2020). We also note similar imagery, being used by Jon Cruddas – a contemporary proponent of modern work ethic tropes – for the front cover of his book *The Dignity of Work*. The book pictures what appears to be a white man's oily hands and blue overalls: a nod to post-war industrial Britain – another backwards utopia of work.

59 Marx (1973), p. 162. Quoted in Weeks (2011), p. 92.

60 Gorz (1992) *Farewell to the Working Class*. London: Pluto Press, p. 9; Gorz (1985) *Paths to Paradise: on the Liberation from Work*. London: Pluto Press, p. 68.

61 Clarke (2016), 'Prospects for Utopia in Space', in *The Ethics of Space Exploration*. https://link.springer.com/chapter/10.1007/978-3-319-39827-3_5. Yorke is drawing explicitly on Ernst Bloch here. The quote is a summary of Yorke by Danaher, J. (2019) *Automation and Utopia*. London: Harvard University Press, p. 153.

62 Of course, there is still much to be done on all of these fronts: better taxation, higher standards of education everywhere, ending child labour globally, greater regulation and ownership of banks and so on. Nonetheless none of these initiatives would seem to be as 'utopian' today as they did in Marx's time.

63 Hence, also, the difficulty with which critics try to narrowly define the field.

64 We caveat this sketch of Gorz by noting that this is only one set of utopian images that he provides. Across his work there are many concrete utopias – which speak to different scales of intervention (e.g. government, town, or workplace).

65 Illich (1973) *Tools for Conviviality*. (San Francisco: Harper Row).

66 Gorz, A. (1999) *Reclaiming Work*. Cambridge: Polity Press, p. 100.

67 Gorz (1985), p. 63. Wording added.

68   Gorz, A. (1982) *Farewell to the Working Class*. London: Pluto, p. 145.

69   Pankhurst, S. (1920) 'Cooperative Housekeeping'. *Workers' Dreadnought*. Available at: https://libcom.org/library/co-operative-housekeeping-sylvia-pankhurst [accessed on 25/11/2022].

70   Ibid.

71   See, for example, Siravo et al's report *Working Nights* (2021). Available at: https://autonomy.work/portfolio/workingnights/

72   Pankhurst (1920).

73   David Frayne's work, for example, is heavily influenced by Gorz (2015). See also Apostolidis' work for the demand for 'worker centers for all' (2019), p. 247. For policy work that readdresses Gorz's 'end of cars' theme, see Common Wealth: https://www.common-wealth.co.uk/reports/away-with-all-cars-redux

74   Soper, Kate (2020) *Post-Growth Living: Towards an Alternative Hedonism*. London: Verso, p. 108.

75   Ibid.

76   Gorz falls short here, lamenting the Wages for Housework campaign for, in his view, seeking to monetize an autonomous zone that should not be accounted for in this way. However, Gorz misunderstands the critical thrust of these movements – which seek not the marketization of everything but rather the economic recognition of the vast amount of unpaid work carried out, in order to refuse its imposition.

77   To address this would be to challenge what we have elsewhere called 'domestic realism'. See Hester, H. (2017) 'Promethean Labors and Domestic Realism'. e-flux. Available at: https://www.e-flux.com/architecture/artificial-labor/140680/promethean-labors-and-domestic-realism/

78   Once again, we can see how single versus dual realm utopianism rearing its head and dividing opinion amongst post-work thinkers.

79   Pankhurst (1920).

80   Pankhurst, S. (1920) 'Workers' Memory'. Available at: https://www.marxists.org/archive/pankhurst-sylvia/1920/resolutions.htm

81   We can also reflect on the national system of kitchens that emerged out of the First World War One and then the Second World War in Britain: Evans, B. (2022) *Feeding the People in Wartime Britain*. London: Bloomsbury.

82   Hester and Srnicek (2023) *After Work: A History of the Home and the Fight for Free Time*. London: Verso.

83   Claeys (2022) *Utopianism for a Dying Planet: Life after Consumerism*. Princeton: University Press.

84   Hester and Srnicek (2023).

85 Ibid. See also: Monbiot, 'How Labour Could Lead the Global Economy Out of the 20th Century'.

86 Hester and Srnicek (2023).

87 O'Brien, M. (2023) *Family Abolition Capitalism and the Communizing of Care*. London: Pluto Press.

88 Weeks, K. (2023) 'Abolition of the Family: The Most Infamous Feminist Proposal', *Feminist Theory*, 24 (3): 433–53.

89 Aprahamian, Francis and Swann, Brenda (eds) (2017) *J. D. Bernal A Life in Science and Politics*. London: Verso Books.

90 Bernal, J. D. (2010) *The Social Function of Science*. London: Faber.

91 Bernal, J. D. (2017) *The World, the Flesh and the Devil*. London: Verso Books.

92 Philipps, Leigh (2015) *Austerity, Ecology and the Collapse-Porn of Addicts: a Defence of Growth, Progress, Industry and Stuff*. London: Zero Books. We consider Philipps to be adjacent to post-work discourse: while he does not explicitly discuss shorter hours – and we understand that he stands against basic income – his writing on Promethean economic planning is consonant with many post-work authors' own perspectives.

93 As we've argued, it makes little sense to be 'anti-technology' – given the cyborg, that is, deeply technologically coupled, nature of our existence.

94 Ehrenreich, Barbara and English, Deirdre (2011) *Complaints and Disorders: The Sexual Politics of Sickness*. New York: Feminist Press, p. 156.

95 For a good introduction to this possible field, see Maja Hoffmann & Roland Paulsen (2020) Resolving the 'jobs-environment dilemma'? The case for critiques of work in sustainability research, *Environmental Sociology*, 6:4, 343–54. For a politics of temporal freedom couched in our 'left climate realism', see Chaudhary, A. S. (2024) *The Exhausted of the Earth*. London: Repeater Books. We should also note that Bastani (2019) devotes a chapter to the future of clean energy.

96 Srnicek and Williams (2016) *Inventing the Future (expanded edition)*. London: Verso Books, p. 191.

97 See, for example, Schmeler, Vetter and Vansintjan (2022) *The Future of Degrowth: A Guide to a World Beyond Capitalism* (London: Verso). Lewis, Kyle (2022) 'Beyond Caring?' *Social Reproduction, Post-Work and Green Futures*'. Available at: https://autonomy.work/portfolio/beyond-caring-green-futures/. See also Chaudhary, A. S. (2024) *The Exhausted of the Earth*. London: Repeater Books.

98 See: Frey and Schneider (2019) 'The Shorter Working Week: A Powerful Tool to Drastically Reduce Carbon Emissions'. *Autonomy*. Available at: http://autonomy.work/wp-content/uploads/2019/05/Fridays4FutureV2.pdf

99 Hoffmann and Paulsen (2020).

100 Aronoff, K., Battistoni, A., Aldana Cohen, D. and Riofrancos, T. *A Planet to Win: Why We Need a Green New Deal* (London: Verso, 2019). In their arguments for a GND, these authors also draw on the original New Deal as we have here.

101 Ibid., p. 7.

102 Ibid., p. 91.

103 Duncombe, J. and Marsden, D. (1995) 'Women's Triple Shift (Gender and Emotional Work in Families)', Sociology review, [Online], 4 (4): 30.

104 Harper, A. and Stronge, W. (eds) *The Shorter Working Week: A Radical and Pragmatic Proposal*. Autonomy. Available at: https://autonomy.work/portfolio/the-shorter-working-week-a-report-from-autonomy-in-collaboration-with-members-of-the-4-day-week-campaign/

105 Srnicek and Williams (2016), p. 190.

106 Standing, Guy (2020) *Battling Eight Giants: Basic Income Now*. London: I. B. Tauris, p. 35.

107 Standing, Guy (2020) *Battling Eight Giants: Basic Income Now*. London: I. B. Tauris, p. 37. See also: Boyce, James K (2019) *The Case for Carbon Dividends*. London: Polity Press.

108 Frey and Garcia (2022) *Toll Gates and Money Pumps: Why Carbon Taxation Could Be a Simple, Fair and Transformative Policy Instrument. Autonomy*. Available at: https://autonomy.work/portfolio/carbon-tax-dividend/

109 Buck, H. (2019) *After Geoengineering: Climate Tragedy, Repair and Restoration*. London: Verso.

110 Benjamin Bratton makes a similar argument in his book on lessons we can learn from the Covid-19 pandemic. Bratton, B. (2021) *The Revenge of the Real*. London: Verso.

111 Buck, H. (2021) *Ending Fossil Fuels: Why Net Zero Is Not Enough*, pp. 152–3.

112 Firestone, S. (1979) *The Dialectic of Sex: The Case for Feminist Revolution*. London: Women's Press, p. 165.

113 See also: Rabinbach (1992) *The Human Motor*. California: University of California Press.

114 See also: Blayney, S. (2022) *Health and Efficiency: Fatigue, the Science of Work, and the Making of the Working-Class Body*. Massachusetts: University of Massachusetts Press.

115 Cara New Daggett (2019) *The Birth of Energy*. Durham: Duke University Press, p. 192.

116 This narrative is strong despite evidence that suggests that gas and oil actually employ far fewer workers than previously thought. See Food and Water

Watch (2022). Available at: https://www.foodandwaterwatch.org/wp-content/uploads/2022/01/FSW_2201_FrackingJobsUpdate-FINAL2.pdf

117 Daggett (2019), p. 205.

118 Ibid.

119 Cara New Daggett (2019) *The Birth of Energy*. Durham: Duke University Press, p. 196.

120 As the brief comments from Srnicek and Williams quoted above show, however, it is inaccurate to paint their text as an unequivocally pro-productivist, pro-growth manifesto.

121 Ibid.

122 Hester and Srnicek (2023).

123 Ibid., p. 195.

124 Bataille, G. (1992) *The Accursed Share, Vol. 1*. New York: Zone Books.

125 Bataille, G. (1992) *The Accursed Share, Vols 2 and 3*. New York: Zone Books.

126 See Stronge, W. (2017) *Introduction*, in W. Stronge (eds) *Georges Bataille and Contemporary Thought*. London: Bloomsbury; Bataille, (1992); see also our discussion of Martin Hägglund in the previous chapter.

127 Firestone, Shulamith (1970) *The Dialectic of Sex: The Case for Feminist Revolution*. New York: Bantam Books, p. 226.

Conclusion

1 Mumford, Lewis (1922) *The Story of Utopias*. New York: Boni and Liveright.

2 All of these are, of course, effects of the general socio-economic damage of neoliberal policymaking over the past three decades.

3 On this feature of anti/post-work thought, Pfannebecker and Smith write 'the dream of a post-scarcity future has often been invoked from positions of very great scarcity', and 'the habitual disparity between present famine and demanded feast in anti-work writing is even more pronounced in this latest wave, because it comes in the context of impending climate catastrophe'. Pfannebecker, M. and Smith, J. A. (2018) *Work Want Work: Labour and Desire at the End of Capitalism*. London: Zed, p. 118.

4 This strategy explicitly refers to the neoliberal tactic of 'never letting a good crisis go to waste'. See Mirowski (2013).

5 Stratford, B. (2020) 'Green Growth vs Degrowth: Are We Missing the Point?' *openDemocracy*. Available at: https://www.opendemocracy.net/en/oureconomy/green-growth-vs-degrowth-are-we-missing-point/

6   This is also why post-work's critics often tend to miss the mark in their characterizations of what post-work texts are up to.

7   In contrast to the suggestion made by Gourevitch, Alex and Stanczk, Lucas (2018). 'The Basic Income Illusion', *Catalyst*, 1 (4).

8   It is therefore unsurprising that the first unemployment insurance schemes in Britain were initiated by trade unions for their members. Hay, J. R. (2016) *Origins of the Liberal Welfare Reforms, 1906–14*. Basingstoke: Palgrave Macmillan.

9   Trade union leaders such as Andy Stern in the United States and various others across the globe have been voices for basic income from a labour movement perspective. Stern, Andy (2016) *Raising the Floor*. New York: Public Affairs. See Van Parijs and Vanderbought (2017) *Basic Income: A Radical Proposal for a Free Society and a Sane Economy*. Cambridge MA: Harvard University Press. for an overview.

10 This phrase is discussed in many places, for example ACFM episode 'Trip 31: Strikes' on *Novara Media*. Available at: https://novaramedia.com/2023/02/05/acfm-trip-31-strikes/

11 Federici, 2012. *Revolution at Point Zero: Housework, Reproduction, and Feminist Struggle*. Oakland, CA: PM Press, p. 20.

12 Weeks, K. (2020) 'Anti/Postwork Feminist Politics and a Case for Basic Income', *tripleC*, 18 (2): 583. Some of the original theorists of the Wages for Housework movement saw guaranteed incomes also as a way to encourage a *redistribution* of reproductive labour.

13 Rathbone, E. (1986) *The Disinherited Family*. Bristol: Falling Wall Press, p. 336.

14 Labour Party and TUC (1930) *Report on Family Allowances by a Special Joint Committee*. In another context, in 1971 the chairman of the Federal Reserve Arthur Burns would explicitly argue that strong welfare policy effectively acted as material support – some form of strike fund – for public sector strikes: Melinda Cooper (2017) *Family Values: between Neoliberalism and the New Social Conservatism*. New York: Zone Books, p. 29. See also Panitch, L., and Gindin, S. (2012) *The Making of Global Capitalism: The Political Economy of American Empire*. London: Verso, pp. 164–72.

15 A famous 2015 survey revealed that over one-third of the British workforce felt that their job made no meaningful contribution to the world. Available at: https://yougov.co.uk/topics/society/articles-reports/2015/08/12/british-jobs-meaningless. This is part of Graeber's argument for basic income in *Bullshit Jobs* (2018).

16 Weeks (2020), p. 586.

17 In the United States, for example, there are millions of people not participating in the labour force (not in a job and not looking for one), the majority of them men. Eberstadt, N. (2022) *Men Without Work: Post-pandemic Edition*. Vancouver Canada: Templeton Press.

18 Esping-Anderson (1990) *The Three Worlds of Welfare Capitalism*. Cambridge: Polity Press, p. 22.

19 Pfannebecker and Smith (2018), p. 64; Joseph Rowntree Foundation (2015) 'The Low Pay, No-Pay Cycle'. Available at: https://www.jrf.org.uk/report/low-pay-no-pay-cycle

20 TUC (2021) '"Fire and Rehire" Tactics have become Widespread during Pandemic – Warns TUC'. Available at: https://www.tuc.org.uk/news/fire-and-rehire-tactics-have-become-widespread-during-pandemic-warns-tuc

21 Cohen, M. (1978) *I Was One of the Unemployed*. London: EP Publishing Ltd. Van Parijs notes a few similar unemployed movements where a demand for some form of basic income emerged, such as the *Syndicat des chômeurs* in France 1982. Van Parijs and Vanderbought (2017).

22 Mowat, C. L. (1968) *Britain Between the Wars*. London: Routledge, p. 128. Fleming, S. introduction to Rathbone, E. (1986) *The Disinherited Family*. Bristol: Falling Wall Press, p. 336.

23 Mowat (1968), pp. 484–7; Fleming, (1986), p. 62.

24 We can take further inspiration from the activities and demands of, for example the Claimant Unions who emerged in the late 1960s and 1970s. The minimum agreed programme of one such group included 'a commitment to an adequate income being available to all, without a means test, and an opposition to any distinction being made between the deserving and the undeserving'. Hilary Rose (1973) 'Up Against the Welfare State: The Claimant Unions', *Socialist Register,* 10. *1973*. Available at: https://socialistregister.com/index.php/srv/article/view/5354

25 For the US context, for example, see Whittle H. J., Palar K., Ranadive N. A., Turan J. M., Kushel M., Weiser S. D. 'The land of the sick and the land of the healthy': Disability, bureaucracy, and stigma amongst people living with poverty and chronic illness in the United States. *Soc Sci Med.* 2017 Oct;190:181–9. doi: 10.1016/j.socscimed.2017.08.031.

26 Oliver (1990) *The Politics of Disablement*. London: Springer; Clifford, E. (2022) *The War on Disabled People*. London: Bloomsbury; Ryan, F. (2020) *Crippled: Austerity and the Demonization of Disabled People*. London: Verso.

27 Withers, A. J. (2012) *Disability, Politics & Theory*. Winnipeg: Fernwood Publishing, pp. 13–57; Oliver (1990), pp. 43–60.

28 Oliver (1990), p. 78; Withers (2012), p. 81; Clifford (2022).

29 Frayne, D. (ed) (2019) *The Work Cure*. Monmouth: PCCS Books.

30 Finkelstein, V. (1993). 'The Commonality of Disability'. in J. Swain, V. Finkelstein, S. French, and M. Oliver (eds) *Disabling Barriers – Enabling Environments*. Maidenhead Berkshire: Open University Press, pp. 9–16; Sage Publications, Inc. p. 12.

31 ONS (2022) 'Outcomes for Disabled People in the UK: 2021'. Available at: https://www.ons.gov.uk/peoplepopulationandcommunity/healthandsocialcare/disability/articles/outcomesfordisabledpeopleintheuk/2021#employment

32 Compared to around 60 per cent of non-disabled people being employed. BLS (2022) 'Persons With a Disability: Labor Force Characteristics – 2021'. Available at: https://www.bls.gov/news.release/pdf/disabl.pdf

33 ONS (2022).

34 Taylor (2004).

35 Abberley, P. (1999) 'The Significance of Work for the Citizenship of Disabled People'. Paper presented at University College, Dublin. Available at: https://disability-studies.leeds.ac.uk/wp-content/uploads/sites/40/library/Abberley-sigofwork.pdf

36 Ibid.; Gleeson, B. (1999) *Geographies of Disability*. London: Routledge Press.

37 Abberley (1999).

38 In this way, we should note, they dovetail with the radical feminist perspectives of Federici and Weeks discussed above. Abberley himself notes a similar overlap (1999).

39 Withers (2012), p. 109.

40 Abberley, P. (1996). 'Work, Utopia and Impairment', in L. Barton (ed.), Disability and society: Emerging issues and insights. London: Longman, pp. 76–7.

41 Sunny Taylor (2004) 'The Right Not to Work: Power and Disability' *Monthly Review*. https://monthlyreview.org/2004/03/01/the-right-not-to-work-power-and-disability/

42 Ibid.

43 Ibid. Such value assumptions, and their rejection, have lessons not just for our attitudes regarding today's profit-driven labour market, but also for progressive movements and ultimately post-capitalist arrangements of work too. Withers writes that: 'Frequently, people who are organising or agitating for social justice retain this core capitalist value. We often view other people's value through their contributions to the struggle, through how much work they do or how productive they are. If we truly want to create a just society, we must value people as people, not as producers'. Withers (2012), p. 108.

44 Taylor (2004).

45 Health and Safety Executive, 'Mental Health Conditions, Work and the Workplace'. Accessed 1 June 2023. https://www.hse.gov.uk/stress/mental-health.htm

46 Social policy expert Helen Barnard, for example, focuses on how costly UBI schemes would be and how the idea will require daunting levels of public support: 'I am not convinced that the gains would be worth the additional cost or that it would help with the battles for funding and dignity that we need to win anyway'. Barnard, H. (2022) *Want*. Newcastle: Agenda Publishing, p. 96. As we have argued here, the demand for a basic income is as much a catalyst for building public support as it is the outcome; the 'gains' of such a shift in public debate would of course be huge. Barnard's preference for 'better funding for further education' and for a system that maintains sanctions is indicative of how timid, myopic, and indeed ethically dubious the welfare debate has become (p. 97).

47 Weeks (2020), pp. 575–94, p. 580.

48 Wright, E. O. (2019) *How to Be an Anticapitalist in the Twenty-first Century*. London: Verso.

49 This debate between 'reform' and 'revolution' has been raging for over a century. See Esping-Anderson (1990): ' … socialism could also defend the gradualist strategy against the more apocalyptic scenario presented in revolutionary communist dogma. Where the latter believe that the roots of revolution lay in crisis and collapse, the reformists realised that the human misery that crises bred would only weaken the socialist project'. p. 45. For their part, the xenofeminists state that 'XF is not a bid for revolution, but a wager on the long game of history, demanding imagination, dexterity and persistence'. (2018).

50 Hall (1988) 'The Great Moving Right Show', in *The Hard Road to Renewal*. London: Verso Books, p. 158.

51 Weeks (2020) plots a similar strategy, noting the unhelpful but common dichotomy between reform and revolution.

52 Nancy Fraser makes a similar argument in 'Social Justice in the Age of Identity Politics: Redistribution, Recognition, and Participation', in Redistribution or Recognition? A Political-Philosophical Exchange, by Nancy Fraser and Axel Honneth (2003). London: Verso. See also: Mary Lawhon & Tyler McCreary (2023).

53 Federici, Silvia (1995) 'Wages Against Housework', in *The Politics of Housework*, New Edition, edited by Ellen Malos, 187–94. Cheltenham: New Clarion Press, p. 191.

54 Cox, Nicole and Federici, Silvia (1976). *Counter-Planning from the Kitchen: Wages for Housework, A Perspective on Capital and the Left*. Brooklyn: New York Wages for Housework Committee, p. 3.

55 Weeks (2020), p. 581.

56 For that we would recommend books such as Bhargava, D. and Luce, S. (2023) *Practical Radicals: Seven Strategies to Change the World*. London/New York: The New Press; Gilbert, J. and Williams, A. (2022) *Hegemony Now*. London: Verso; Schneider, J. (2022) *Our Bloc*. London: Verso; Nunes, R. (2021) *Neither Vertical or Horizontal*. London: Verso Books.

Abberley, P. (1999) 'The Significance of Work for the Citizenship of Disabled People'. *Paper presented at University College*, Dublin. Available at: https://disability-studies.leeds.ac.uk/wp-content/uploads/sites/40/library/Abberley-sigofwork.pdf

Abberley, P. (1996) 'Work, Ytopia and Impairment'. Barton, L. (ed.) *Disability and Society: Emerging Issues and Insights*. London: Longman, pp. 76–7.

Abello, O. P. (2021) 'Guaranteed Income in Jackson Designed by Black Moms for Black Moms, Showing Results for Black Moms'. *Next City*. Available at: https://nextcity.org/urbanist-news/guaranteed-income-in-jackson-designed-by-black-moms-for-black-moms

Amira, D. (2010) '"Jobs, Jobs, Jobs": The Allure, and Danger, of a Favorite Political Mantra'. *New York Mag*. Available at: https://nymag.com/intelligencer/2010/02/jobs_jobs_jobs_the_allure_and.html

Andersen, K. (2023) *Welfare That Works for Women?* Bristol: Policy Press.

Anderson, E. (2023) *Hijacked: How Neoliberalism Turned the Work Ethic against Workers and How Workers Can Take It Back*. Cambridge: Cambridge University Press.

Anderson, E. (2017) *Private Government: How Employers Rule Our Lives (and Why We Don't Talk about It)*. Princeton: Princeton University Press.

Anderson, P. (1980) *Arguments within English Marxism*. London: Verso.

Apostolidis, P. (2019) *The Fight for Time: Migrant Day Labourers and the Politics of Precarity*. Oxford: Oxford University Press.

Aprahamian, F., and Swann, B., eds (2017) *J. D. Bernal: A Life in Science and Politics*. London: Verso Books.

Aristotle. (1987) *De Anima (On the Soul)*. London: Penguin.

Aristotle. (1981) *Politics*. London: Penguin.

Arendt, H. (1998) *The Human Condition*. London: University of Chicago Press.

Aronoff, K., et al. (2019) *A Planet to Win: Why We Need a Green New Deal*. London: Verso.

Aronowitz, S., et al. (1998) 'The Post-Work Manifesto'. Aronowitz, S., and Cutler, J. (eds) *Post-Work: The Wages of Cybernation*. London: Routledge.

Autonomy. (2024) *Autonomy*. Available at: https://autonomy.work/

Autonomy. (2023) 'The Results Are in: The UK's Four-day Week Pilot'. *Autonomy*. Available at: https://autonomy.work/portfolio/uk4dwpilotresults/

Autonomy. (2020) 'Long Term Care Centres'. *Autonomy*. Available at: https://autonomy.work/wp-content/uploads/2020/11/LTCCv7.pdf

Badiou, A. (2016) 'Nick Srnicek and Alex Williams in Conversation with Alain Badiou'. *Vimeo*. Available at: https://vimeo.com/193993130

Bahro, R. (2011) *The Alternative in Eastern Europe*. London: Verso.

Barnard, H. (2022) *Want*. Newcastle: Agenda Publishing.

Barnes, C. (2012) 'Re-Thinking Disability, Work and Welfare: Disability at Work'. *Sociology Compass* 6:6, pp. 472–84.

Barnes, P. (2021) *Ours: The Case for Universal Property*. London: Polity.

Bassett, C., Kember, S., and O'Riordan, K. (2020) *Furious: Technological Feminism and Digital Futures*. London: Pluto Press.

Bastani, A. (2019) *Fully Automated Luxury Communism: A Manifesto*. London: Verso.

Bastani, A. (2015) 'Britain Doesn't Need More Austerity, It Needs Luxury Communism'. *Vice*. Available at: https://www.vice.com/en/article/ppxpdm/luxury-communism-933.

Bastani, A. (2014) 'Fully Automated Luxury Communism'. *Novara Media*. Available at: https://novaramedia.com/2014/11/10/imo-w-aaron-bastani-e003/

Bastani, A., Sarkar, A., and Butler, J. (2015) 'Fully Automated Luxury Communism'. *Novara Media*. Available at: https://novaramedia.com/2015/06/19/fully-automated-luxury-communism/

Bataille, G. (1992a) *The Accursed Share, Vol.* 1. New York: Zone Books.

Bataille, G. (1992b) *The Accursed Share, Vols* 2 and 3. New York: Zone Books.

Beckert, J. (2016) *Imagined Futures*. London: Harvard University Press.

Benanav, A. (2021) 'Overcapacity and Post-Scarcity'. *3:AM Magazine*. Available at: https://www.3ammagazine.com/3am/overcapacity-and-post-scarcity-an-interview-with-aaron-benanav-part-i/

Benanav, A. (2020a) *Automation and the Future of Work*. London: Verso.

Benanav, A. (2020b) 'How to Make a Pencil'. *Logic Magazine*. Available at: https://logicmag.io/commons/how-to-make-a-pencil/

Berg, H. (2021) *Porn Work: Sex, Labor, and Late Capitalism*. Chapel Hill, NC: University of North Carolina Press.

Bernal, J. D. (2017) *The World, the Flesh and the Devil*. London: Verso Books.

Bernal, J. D. (2010) *The Social Function of Science*. London: Faber.

Beveridge, W. (1949) 'Epilogue'. Rathbone, E. *Family Allowances: A New Edition of The Disinherited Family*. London: Allen & Unwin.

Bhargava, D., and Luce, S. (2023) *Practical Radicals: Seven Strategies to Change the World*. New York: New Press.

Bianchi, S. (2011) 'Family Change and Time Allocation in American Families'. *The ANNALS of the American Academy of Political and Social Science* 638:1, pp. 21–44

Bivens, J., and Kandra, J. (2021) 'CEO Pay Has Skyrocketed 1,460% since 1978'. *Economic Policy Institute*. Available at: https://www.epi.org/publication/ceo-pay-in-2021/

Black Panther Party. (1966) 'Ten-Point Program'. *Marxists Internet Archive*. Available at: https://www.marxists.org/history/usa/workers/black-panthers/1966/10/15.htm

Blanchflower, D. (2019) *Not Working*. Princeton: Princeton University Press.

Blayney, S. (2022) *Health and Efficiency: Fatigue, the Science of Work, and the Making of the Working-Class Body*. Massachusetts: University of Massachusetts Press.

Bloch, E. (1995) *The Principle of Hope*. Cambridge, MA: MIT Press.

BLS. (2022) 'Persons with a Disability: Labor Force Characteristics – 2021'. *Bureau of Labor Statistics*. Available at: https://www.bls.gov/news.release/pdf/disabl.pdf

Boggs, J. (2009) *The American Revolution: Pages from a Negro Worker's Note-book*. New York: Monthly Review Press.

Boland, T., and Griffin, R. (2023) *The Reformation of Welfare: The New Faith of the Labour Market*. Bristol: Bristol Policy Press.

Boltanski, L., and Chiapello, E. (2018) *The New Spirit of Capitalism*. London: Verso.

Bowring, F. (1999) 'Job Scarcity: The Perverted Form of a Potential Blessing'. *Sociology* 33:1, pp. 69–84.

Boyce, J. K. (2019) *The Case for Carbon Dividends*. London: Polity Press.

Brassier, R. (2014a) 'Prometheanism and Its Critics'. Mackay, R., and Avanessian, A. (eds) *#Accelerate: The Accelerationist Reader*. Falmouth: Urbanomic, pp. 467–87.

Brassier, R. (2014b) 'Prometheanism and Real Abstraction'. Mackay, R., Pendrell, L., and Trafford, J. (eds) *Speculative Aesthetics*. Falmouth: Urbanomic, 2014, pp. 73–7.

Bratton, B. (2021) *The Revenge of the Real*. London: Verso.

Braverman, H. (1974) *Labour and Monopoly Capital. The Degradation of Work in the Twentieth Century*. New York: Monthly Review Press.

Bregman, R. (2016) *Utopia for Realists*. Amsterdam: De Correspondent.

Buck, H. (2021) *Ending Fossil Fuels: Why Net Zero Is Not Enough*. London: Verso.

Buck, H. (2019) *After Geoengineering: Climate Tragedy, Repair and Restoration*. London: Verso.

Calnitsky, D. (2017) 'Debating Basic Income'. *Catalyst* 1:3. Available here: https://catalyst-journal.com/2017/12/debating-basic-income#ch-0

Cant, C. (2019) *Riding for Deliveroo*. Cambridge: Polity Press.

CDC. (2023) 'Disability Impacts All of Us'. *Center for Disease Control and Prevention*. Available at: https://www.cdc.gov/ncbddd/disabilityandhealth/infographic-disability-impacts-all.html#:~:text=26%20percent%20

Chadwick, E. (1837) *An Article on the Principles and Progress of the Poor Law Amendment Act*. London: C. Knight.

Chamberlain, J. (2017) *Undoing Work*. New York: Cornell Press.

Chandler, D. (2023) *Free and Equal*. London: Penguin.

Charmes, J. (2022) 'Variety and Change of Patterns in the Gender Balance between Unpaid Care-Work, Paid Work and Free Time across the World and Over Time: A Measure of Wellbeing?' *Wellbeing, Space and Society* 3:2, pp. 1–19.

Charmes, J. (2019) 'The Unpaid Care Work and the Labour Market: An Analysis of Time Use Data Based on the Latest World Compilation of Time-Use Surveys'. *International Labour Organization*. Available at: http://www.ilo.org/gender/Informationresources/Publications/WCMS_732791/lang–en/index.htm

Chaudhary, A. S. (2024) *The Exhausted of the Earth: Politics in a Burning World*. London: Repeater Books.

Cholbi, M. (2018) 'The Duty to Work'. *Ethical Theory and Moral Practice* 2:1, pp. 1119–33.

Christophers, B. (2021) *Rentier Capitalism: Who Owns the Economy, and Who Pays for It?* London: Verso Books.

Churchill, W. (1909) *Parliamentary Debates*. House of Commons, 5th series, 19 May 1909, vol. 5, col. 503.

Claeys, G. (2022) *Utopianism for a Dying Planet: Life after Consumerism*. Princeton: Princeton University Press.

Clark, A. (2011) *Supersizing the Mind*. Oxford: Oxford University Press.

Clark, A. (2003) *Natural-Born Cyborgs: Minds, Technologies, and the Future of Human Intelligence*. Oxford: Oxford University Press.

Cleaver, H. (2000) *Reading Capital Politically*. Chico, CA: AK Press.

Clifford, E. (2020) *The War on Disabled People: Capitalism, Welfare and the Making of a Human Catastrophe*. London: Zed Books.

Cloward, F. F., and Piven, R. (2010) 'The Weight of the Poor: A Strategy to End Poverty (1966)'. *The Nation*. Available at: https://www.thenation.com/article/archive/weight-poor-strategy-end-poverty/

Cockett, R. (1995) *Thinking the Unthinkable: Think-tanks and the Economic Counter-revolution, 1931–83*. London: HarperCollins.

Cockshott, P., and Cottrell, A. (1993) *Towards a New Socialism*. Nottingham: Spokesman Books.

Cohen, M. (1978) *I Was One of the Unemployed*. London: EP Publishing.

Compass. (2024) *Compass Online*. Available at: https://www.compassonline.org.uk/

Cooper, M. (2017) *Family Values: Between Neoliberalism and the New Social Conservatism*. New York: Zone Books.

Coote, A., and Percy, P. (2020) *The Case for Universal Basic Services*. London: Polity.

Cootes, R. J. (1966) *The Making of the Welfare State*. London: Longmans, Green and Co.

Cowan, R. S. (1989) *More Work for Mother: The Ironies of Household Technology from the Open Hearth to the Microwave*. London: Free Association Books.

Cowan, R. S. (1979) 'From Virginia Dare to Virginia Slims: Women and Technology in American Life'. *Technology and Culture* 20:1, pp. 51–63.

Cox, N., and Federici, S. (1976) *Counter-Planning from the Kitchen: Wages for Housework, a Perspective on Capital and the Left*. Brooklyn: New York Wages for Housework Committee.

Cremin, C. (2011) *Capitalism New Clothes: Enterprise, Ethics and Enjoyment in Times of Crisis*. London: Pluto Books

Cummine, A. (2016) *Citizen's Wealth: Why (and How) Sovereign Funds Should be Managed by the People for the People*. Llandysul: Gomer Press.

Daggett, C. N. (2019) *The Birth of Energy: Fossil Fuels, Thermodynamics, and the Politics of Work*. Durham, NC: Duke University Press.

Dahlgreen, W. (2015) '37% of British Workers Think Their Jobs Are Meaningless'. *YouGov*. Available at: https://yougov.co.uk/society/articles/13005-british-jobs-meaningless

Danaher, J. (2019) *Automation and Utopia*. London: Harvard University Press.

Davies, M. L. (1918) 'The Claims of Mothers and Children'. Phillips, M. (ed.) *Women and the Labour Party, by Various Women Writers*. London: Headley Bros.

Davis, J. C. (1983) *Utopia and Ideal Society: A Study of English Utopian Writing 1516–1700*. London: Cambridge University Press.

Davis, L. J. (2002) *Bending Over Backwards: Disability, Dismodernism and Other Difficult Positions*. New York: New York University Press.

De Grazia, V. (1981) *The Culture of Consent: Mass Organisation of Leisure in Fascist Italy*. Cambridge: Cambridge University Press.

Dean, M. (1991) *The Constitution of Poverty: Toward a Genealogy of Liberal Governance*. London: Routledge.

Delfanti, A. (2021) *The Warehouse: Workers and Robots at Amazon*. London: Pluto Books.

Design Collective. (1985) *Very Nice Work If You Can Get it: The Socially Useful Production Debate*. Nottingham: Spokesman Books.

Dinerstain, A., and Pitts, F. H. (2018) 'From Post-Work to Post-Capitalism? Discussing the Basic Income and Struggles for Alternative Forms of Social Reproduction'. *Journal of Labour and Society* 21, pp. 471–91.

Douglass, F. (1883) 'Address Delivered before The National Convention of Colored Men, at Louisville, KY', September 24. Available at: https://omeka.coloredconventions.org/items/show/554

Dowling, E., and Hester, H. (2021) 'The Future of Care: Helen Hester in Conversation with Emma Dowling'. *Autonomy*. Available at: https://autonomy.work/portfolio/ffp-hester-dowlingconvo/

Duncombe, J., and Marsden, D. (1995) '"Workaholics" and "Whingeing Women": Theorising Intimacy and Emotion Work – The Last Frontier of Gender Inequality?' *Sociological Review* 43, pp. 150–69.

Dwyer, P., et al. (2023) *The Impacts of Welfare Conditionality: Sanctions Support and Behaviour Change*. Bristol: Policy Press.

Dyer-Witheford, N. (2015) *Cyber-Proletariat: Global Labour in the Digital Vortex*. London: Pluto Books.

Eberstadt, N. (2022) *Men without Work*. West Conshohocken, PA: Templeton Foundation Press.

Eby, M. (2020) 'The Lost History of Socialism's DIY Computer'. *Jacobin*. Available at: https://jacobin.com/2020/08/computer-yugoslavia-galaksija-voja-antonic

Ehrenreich, B., and English, D. (2011) *Complaints and Disorders: The Sexual Politics of Sickness*. New York: Feminist Press.

Esping-Anderson, G. (1990) *The Three Worlds of Welfare Capitalism*. Cambridge: Polity Press.

Evans, B. (2022) *Feeding the People in Wartime Britain*. London: Bloomsbury.

Fahmy, E., Pemberton, S., and Sutton, E. (2012) 'Public Perceptions of Poverty and Social Exclusion: Final Report on Focus Group Findings'. *Poverty and Social Exclusion in the UK*. Available at: https://www.poverty.ac.uk/system/files/WP_Analysis_No3_Focus-groups_Fahmy-Pemberton-Sutton.pdf

Fairlie, S. (2009) 'A Short History of Enclosure in Britain'. *The Land* 7. Available at: https://www.thelandmagazine.org.uk/articles/short-history-enclosure-britain

Farrar, E. (1974) 'The Invisible Woman'. *The Power of Women* 1:1 (March/April), pp. 8–12.

Federici, S. (2012) *Revolution at Point Zero: Housework, Reproduction, and Feminist Struggle*. Oakland, CA: PM Press.

Federici, S., and Austin, A., eds (2017) *Wages for Housework, The New York Committee 1972–1977: History, Theory, Documents*. New York: Autonomedia.

Finkelstein, V. (1993) 'The Commonality of Disability'. Swain, J., et al. (eds) *Disabling Barriers – Enabling Environments*. London: Sage, pp. 9–16.

Finland Toolbook. (2018) 'Finland's Basic Income Experiment 2017–2018'. *Finland Toolbook*. Available at: https://toolbox.finland.fi/life-society/finlands-basic-income-experiment-2017-2018/

Firestone, S. (1979) *The Dialectic of Sex: The Case for Feminist Revolution*. London: Women's Press.

Fisher, M. (2021) *Post-Capitalist Desire: The Final Lectures*. London: Repeater.

Fisher, M. (2009) *Capitalism Realism*. London: Zero Books.

Fishwick, A., and Kiersey, N. (2021) *Post-capitalist Futures: Political Economy beyond Crisis and Hope*. London: Pluto Books.

Fleming, S. (1986) 'Eleanor Rathbone: Spokewoman for a Movement'. Rathbone, E., *The Disinherited Family*. Bristol: Falling Wall Press.

Fones-Wolf, K. (1981) 'Boston Eight Hour Men, New York Marxists and the Emergence of the International Labor Union', *Historical Journal of Massachusetts* 9, pp. 47–59.

Food and Water Watch. (2022) 'More Oil and Gas Production = Fewer Jobs'. *Food and Water Watch*. Available at: https://www.foodandwaterwatch.org/wp-content/uploads/2022/01/FSW_2201_FrackingJobsUpdate-FINAL2.pdf

Forget, E. L. (2011) 'The Town with No Poverty: The Health Effects of a Canadian Guaranteed Annual Income Field Experiment'. *Canadian Public Policy* 37:3, pp. 283–305.

Forrester, K. (2022) 'Feminist Demands and the Problem of Housework'. *American Political Science Review* 116:4, pp. 1278–92.

Fortunati, L. (2007) 'Immaterial Labor and Its Machinization'. *Ephemera* 7:1, pp. 139–57.

Foucault, M. (2020) *Aesthetics, Method, and Epistemology: Essential Works of Foucault 1954–1984*. New York: New Press.

Foucault, M. (2008) *The Birth of Biopolitics: Lectures at the Collège de France, 1978–1979*. Basingstoke: Palgrave Macmillan.

Frase, P. (2015a) *Four Futures: Life after Capitalism*. London: Verso.

Frase, P. (2015b) 'Ours to Master'. *Jacobin*. Available at: https://jacobin.com/2015/03/automation-frase-robots/

Fraser, N. (2022) *Cannibal Capitalism*. London: Verso.

Fraser, N. (2003) 'Social Justice in the Age of Identity Politics: Redistribution, Recognition, and Participation'. Fraser, N., and Honneth, A. (eds) *Redistribution or Recognition? A Political-Philosophical Exchange*. London: Verso.

Fraser, N., and Gordan, L. (2020) 'Dependency: A Genealogy'. Fraser, N. (ed) *Fortunes of Feminism: From State-Managed Capitalism to Neoliberal Crisis*. London: Verso.

Frayne, D. (2017) 'Is Work in Crisis?' *Autonomy*. Available here: https://autonomy.work/portfolio/david-frayne-response/

Frayne, D. (2015) *The Refusal of Work: The Theory and Practice of Resistance to Work*. London: Zed Books.

Frayne, D., and Maher, M. (2021) 'Jobs and Wellbeing: Re-Opening the Debate'. *Autonomy*. Available at: https://autonomy.work/portfolio/jobswellbeing/

Frey, P., and Garcia, L. (2022) 'Toll Gates and Money Pumps: Why Carbon Taxation Could Be a Simple, Fair and Transformative Policy Instrument'. *Autonomy*. Available at: https://autonomy.work/portfolio/carbon-tax-dividend/

Frey, P., and Schneider, C. (2019) 'The Shorter Working Week: A Powerful Tool to Drastically Reduce Carbon Emissions'. *Autonomy*. Available at: http://autonomy.work/wp-content/uploads/2019/05/Fridays4FutureV2.pdf

Galloway, A. R. (2017) 'Brometheanism.' *Culture and Communication*. Available at:http://cultureandcommunication.org/galloway/brometheanism

Gandini, A. (2020) *Zeitgeist Nostalgia: On Populism, Work and the Good Life*. Cambridge: Zero Books.

Germain, J. (2021) 'The National Welfare Rights Organization Wanted Economic Justice for Black Americans'. *Teen Vogue*. Available at: https://www.teenvogue.com/story/national-welfare-rights-organization-black-women

Gershon, L. (2017) 'Why Do We Take Pride in Working for a Paycheck?' *JSTOR Daily*. Available at: https://daily.jstor.org/why-do-we-take-pride-in-working-for-a-paycheck/

Gilbert, J., and Williams, A. (2022) *Hegemony Now: How Big Tech and Wall Street Won the World (And How We Win It Back)*. London: Verso.

Gill, M., and Burrow, R. (2018) 'Fear in Haute Cuisine: The Interplay of Emotions and Institutions'. *Organization Studies* 39:4, pp. 445–65.

GiveDirectly. (2024) 'About GiveDirectly'. *GiveDirectly*. Available at: https://www.givedirectly.org/about/

Gleeson, B. (1999) *Geographies of Disability*. London: Routledge.

Gollancz, V., ed. (1917) *The Making of Women: Oxford Essays in Feminism*. London: Allen and Unwin.

Goodin, R. E., et al. (2008) *Discretionary Time: A New Measure of Freedom*. Cambridge: Cambridge University Press

Gorz, A. (1999) *Reclaiming Work: Beyond the Wage Based Society*. Cambridge: Polity.

Gorz, A. (1989) *The Critique of Economic Reason*. London: Verso Books.

Gorz, A. (1985) *Paths to Paradise: On the Liberation from Work*. London: Pluto.

Gorz, A. (1982) *Farewell to the Working Class: An Essay on Post-Industrial Socialism*. London: Pluto Books.

Gough, I. (1979) *The Political Economy of the Welfare State*. London: Macmillan Press.

Gourevitch, A. (2013) 'Labor Republicanism and the Transformation of Work'. *Political Theory* 41:4, pp. 591–617.

Gourevitch, A., and Stanczk, L. (2018) 'The Basic Income Illusion'. *Catalyst* 1:4, pp. 151–77.

Graby, S. (2015) 'Access to Work or Liberation from Work? Disabled People, Autonomy, and Post-Work Politics'. *Canadian Journal of Disability Studies* 4:2, pp. 132–61.

Graeber, D. (2018) *Bullshit Jobs: A Theory*. London: Allen Lane.

Graeber, D., and Frank, T. (2014) 'The More Your Job Helps Others, The Less You Get Paid'. *Z Network*. Available at: https://znetwork.org/znetarticle/the-more-your-job-helps-others-the-less-you-get-paid/

Grünberg, M. (2023) 'The Planning Daemon: Future Desire and Communal Production'. *Historical Materialism* 31:4, pp. 115–59.

Hägglund, M. (2019) *This Life: Secular Faith and Spiritual Freedom*. New York: Pantheon Books.

Hall, S. (1988) *The Hard Road to Renewal: Thatcherism and the Crisis of the Left*. London: Verso Books.

Hansard. (1945) Family Allowances Bill, Volume 411, 11 June 1945. Available at: https://hansard.parliament.uk/Commons/1945-06-11/debates/117f1481-7ae3-4f85-834c-065d1b9b7529/FamilyAllowancesBill

Hansard. (1942) National Scheme of Family Allowances, Volume 380, 23 June 1942. Available at: https://api.parliament.uk/historic-hansard/commons/1942/jun/23/national-scheme-of-family-allowances

Haraway, D. (2016) *Staying with the Trouble: Making Kin in the Chthulucene*. Durham, NC: Duke University Press.

Haraway, D. (2003) *The Companion Species Manifesto*. Chicago: Prickly Paradigm Press.

Haraway, D. (1985) 'A Manifesto for Cyborgs: Science, Technology, and Socialist Feminism in the 1980s'. *Socialist Review* 80, pp. 65–108.

Harper, A., and Stronge, W., eds (2019) 'The Shorter Working Week: A Radical and Pragmatic Proposal'. *Autonomy*. Available at: https://autonomy.work/portfolio/the-shorter-working-week-a-report-from-autonomy-in-collaboration-with-members-of-the-4-day-week-campaign/

Hay, J. R. (2016) *Origins of the Liberal Welfare Reforms, 1906–14*. Basingstoke: Palgrave Macmillan.

Hayek, F. (2006) 'The Meaning of the Welfare State'. Pierson, C., and Castles, F. (eds) *The Welfare State Reader*. Cambridge: Polity Press, pp. 90–95.

Hayek, F. (1986) *The Road to Serfdom*. London: Routledge.

Hayek, F. (1960) 'The Intellectuals and Socialism'. de Huszar, G. B. (ed.) *The Intellectuals: A Controversial Portrait*. Glencoe, IL: Free Press, pp. 371–84.

Hester, H. (2024) 'The Automated Heart: Digital Domesticity and Emotional Labour Saving'. *New Vistas* 10:2. Available at: https://uwlpress.uwl.ac.uk/newvistas/issues/

Hester, H. (2020) 'Why Women Deserve a Four-Day Week'. *International Politics and Society*. Available at: https://www.ips-journal.eu/regions/europe/why-women-deserve-a-four-day-week-4610/

Hester, H. (2019) 'Sapience + Care: Reason and Responsibility in Posthuman Politics'. *Angelaki: Journal of the Theoretical Humanities* 24:2, pp. 67–80.

Hester, H. (2018) *Xenofeminism*. Cambridge: Polity.

Hester, H. (2017) 'Promethean Labors and Domestic Realism'. *e-flux*. Available at: https://www.e-flux.com/architecture/artificial-labor/140680/promethean-labors-and-domestic-realism/

Hester, H., and Srnicek, N. (2023) *After Work: A History of the Home and the Fight for Free Time*. London: Verso.

Hester, H., and Stronge, W. (2020) 'Towards Post-Work Studies: Identifying Misconceptions in an Emerging Field'. *Autonomy*. Available at: https://autonomy.work/portfolio/post-workmisconceptions2/

Hochschild, A. (1983) *The Managed Heart: The Commercialization of Human Feeling*. Berkeley: University of California Press.

Hoffmann, M., and Paulsen, R. (2020) 'Resolving the "Jobs-Environment Dilemma"? The Case for Critiques of Work in Sustainability Research'. *Environmental Sociology* 6:4, pp. 343–54.

Horgan, A. (2021) *Lost in Work: Escaping Capitalism*. London: Pluto Books.

HSE. (n.d.) 'Mental Health Conditions, Work and the Workplace'. *Health and Safety Executive*. Available at: https://www.hse.gov.uk/stress/mental-health.htm

Huberman, M., and Minns, C. (2007) 'The Times They Are Not Changin': Days and Hours of Work in Old and New Worlds, 1870–2000'. *Explorations in Economic History* 44:4, pp. 538–67.

Hung, L., et al. (2019) 'The Benefits of and Barriers to Using a Social Robot PARO in Care Settings: A Scoping Review'. *BMC Geriatrics* 19:1, pp. 232–42.

Hunnicutt, B. (1988) *Work without End*. Philadelphia: Temple University Press.

Idle, N., Gilbert, J., and Milburn, K. (2023) 'Trip 31: Strikes'. *Novara Media*. Available at: https://novaramedia.com/2023/02/05/acfm-trip-31-strikes/

IFS. (2023) 'Remote Working Is Probably Here to Stay, and These Are the Reasons Why'. *IFS*. Available at: https://ifs.org.uk/articles/remote-working-probably-here-stay-and-these-are-reasons-why

Illich, I. (1981) *Shadow Work*. London: Marion Boyars.

Illich, I. (1973) *Tools for Conviviality*. San Francisco: Harper Row.

ILO. (2022a) 'Working Time and Work-Life Balance around the World'. Available at: https://www.ilo.org/wcmsp5/groups/public/—dgreports/—dcomm/documents/publication/wcms_864222.pdf

ILO. (2022b) 'Violence and Harassment at Work Has Affected More than One in Five People'. *ILO*. Available at: https://www.ilo.org/global/about-the-ilo/newsroom/news/WCMS_863177/lang—en/index.htm

Jaffe, S. (2021) *Work Won't Love You Back: How Devotion to Our Jobs Keeps Us Exploited, Exhausted and Alone*. London: Hurst.

Jäger, A., and Zamora, D. (2023) *Welfare against Markets*. Chicago: Chicago University Press.

Jakic, B. (2014) 'Galaxy and the New Wave: Yugoslav Computer Culture in the 1980s'. Alberts, G., and Oldenziel, R. (eds) *Hacking Europe. History of Computing*. London: Springer, pp. 107–128.

James, S. (2020) 'I Founded the Wages for Housework Campaign in 1972 – And Women Are Still Working for Free'. *Independent*. Available at: https://www.independent.co.uk/voices/international-womens-day-wages-housework-care-selma-james-a9385351.html

James, S. (2016) 'Child Benefit has Been Changing Lives for 70 Years. Let's Not Forget the Woman behind It'. *The Guardian*. Available at: https://www.theguardian.com/commentisfree/2016/aug/06/child-benefit-70-years-eleanor-rathbone

James, S. (2012) *Sex, Race, and Class: The Perspective of Winning: A Selection of Writings, 1952–2011*. Oakland, CA: PM Press.

Jameson, F. (2014) *Representing 'Capital': A Reading of Volume One*. London: Verso.

JFI. (2024) 'Initiative Area: Guaranteed Income.' *Jain Family Institute*. Available at: https://jainfamilyinstitute.org/initiatives/guaranteed-income/

Johnson, B. (2019) 'We Can Improve Mental Health, Save Money and Boost the Economy All in One Go'. *The Telegraph*. Available at: https://www.telegraph.co.uk/news/2019/07/14/can-improve-mental-health-save-money-boost-economy-one-go/

Johnston, A. (2015) 'Robotic Seals Comfort Dementia Patients but Raise Ethical Concerns'. *KALW*. Available at: https://www.kalw.org/show/crosscurrents/2015-08-17/robotic-seals-comfort-dementia-patients-but-raise-ethical-concerns

Jones, J. (2020) 'Campaigns around Working Time Have Always Been about Freedom'. *Autonomy*. Available at: https://autonomy.work/portfolio/workingtimerepublicanism/

Jones, K., and Kumar, A. (2022) *Idleness*. Newcastle: Agenda Publishing.

Jones, P. (2019) 'Employability in the New Economy'. *Autonomy*. Available at: https://autonomy.work/portfolio/employability-in-the-new-economy-brand-you/

JRF. (2015) 'The Low Pay, No-Pay Cycle'. *Jospeh Rowntree Foundation*. Available at: https://www.jrf.org.uk/report/low-pay-no-pay-cycle

JRF. (2020) 'A Minimum Income Standard for the UK in 2022'. *Jospeh Rowntree Foundation.* Available at: https://www.jrf.org.uk/report/minimum-income-standard-uk-2022

Kamerade, D., et al. (2019) 'A Shorter Working Week for Everyone: How Much Paid Work Is Needed for Mental Health and Well-Being?' *Social Science and Medicine* 241, pp. 1–9.

Kautsky, K. (1903) *The Social Revolution.* Chicago: Charles Kerr and Co.

Kenedy, J. F. (1960) 'Speech of Senator John F. Kennedy, United Steelworkers of America Convention, Convention Hall, Atlantic City, NJ'. *The American Presidency Project.* Available at: https://www.presidency.ucsb.edu/documents/speech-senator-john-f-kennedy-united-steelworkers-america-convention-convention-hall

Kenway, E. (2023) *Who Cares: The Hidden Crisis of Caregiving, and How We Solve It.* London: Wildfire.

Keynes, J. M. (2013) *The Collected Writings of John Maynard Keynes: Volume X: Essays in Biography.* Cambridge: Cambridge University Press.

King, D. (1995) *Actively Seeking Work? The Politics of Unemployment and Welfare Policy in the United States and Great Britain.* Chicago: Chicago University Press.

King, M. L. (2010) *Where Do We Go from Here: Chaos or Community?* Boston: Beacon Press.

Kleiner, D. (2016) 'Universal Basic Income Is a Neoliberal Plot to Make You Poorer'. *OpenDemocracy.* Available at: https://neweconomics.opendemocracy.net/universal-basic-income-is-a-neoliberal-plot-to-make-you-poore/

Knibbs, K. (2020) 'There's No Cure for Covid-19 Loneliness, but Robots Can Help'. *Wired.* Available at: https://www.wired.com/story/covid-19-robot-companions/

Komlosy, A. (2018) *Work: The Last 1,000 Years.* London: Verso.

Konings, M. (2018) *Capital and Time: For a New Critique of Neoliberal Reason.* Stanford: Stanford University Press.

Krisis Group. (1999) 'Manifesto against Labour'. *Krisis.* Available at: http://www.krisis.org/1999/manifesto-against-labour

Kurz, R. (2016) *The Substance of Capital.* Chico, CA: AK Press.

Kwarteng, K., et al. eds (2012) *Britannia Unchained: Global Lessons for Growth and Prosperity.* Basingstoke: Palgrave Macmillan.

Laboria Cuboniks. (2018) *The Xenofeminist Manifesto: A Politics for Alienation.* London: Verso Books.

Lambert, C. (2015) *Shadow Work.* Berkeley: Counterpoint.

Lansley, S., and Mack, J. (2015) *Breadline Britain: The Rise of Mass Poverty.* London: Oneworld Publications.

Lawhon, M., and McCreary, T. (2023) 'Making UBI Radical: On the Potential for a Universal Basic Income to Underwrite Transformative and Anti-Kyriarchal Change'. *Economy and Society* 52:2, pp. 349–72.

Lazar, S. (2024) 'Frontier AI Ethics: Anticipating and Evaluating the Societal Impacts of Generative Agents'. *Arxiv.* Available at: https://arxiv.org/abs/2404.06750

Levitas, R. (1990) *The Concept of Utopia.* Oxford: Peter Lang.

Lewis, K. (2022) 'Beyond Caring? Social Reproduction, Post-Work and Green Futures'. *Autonomy.* Available here: https://autonomy.work/portfolio/beyond-caring-green-futures/

Lewis, S. (2022) *Abolish the Family: A Manifesto for Care and Liberation.* London: Verso.

Lewis, S. (2019) *Full Surrogacy Now: Feminism against Family.* London: Verso.

Longmate, N. (2003) *The Workhouse: A Social History.* London: Pimlico.

Mandel, B. (2007) *Labor, Free and Slave*. Chicago: University of Illinois Press.

Mandelson, P., and Liddle, R. (1996) *The Blair Revolution: Can New Labour Deliver?* London: Faber and Faber.

Mann, E. (1987) *Taking on General Motors: A Case Study of the Campaign to Keep Gm Van Nuys Open*. Los Angeles: Institute of Labor Relations.

Marson, D. (1973) *Children's Strikes in 1911*. History Workshop Pamphlets 9.

Marx, K. (1996) *Wages, Price and Profit*. 1st edition, 1975. Peking: Foreign Languages Press.

Marx, K. (1976) *Capital vol. 1*. London: Penguin.

Marx, K. (1975a) 'Draft of an Article on Friedrich List's Book Das nationale System der politischen Oekonomie'. *Marx/Engels, Collected Works, Vol. 4*. New York: International Publishers, pp. 265–94.

Marx, K. (1975b) *Early Writings*. London: Penguin Books.

Marx, K. (1973) *Grundrisse*. New York, Penguin

Marx, K. (1971a) *Capital vol. III*. Moscow: Progress Publishers.

Marx, K. (1971b) *Critique of the Gotha Programme*. Moscow: Progress Publishers.

Mau, S. (2023) *Mute Compulsion: A Marxist Theory of the Economic Power of Capital*. London: Verso Books.

Mayors for a Guaranteed Income. (2023) *Mayors for a GI*. Available at: https://www.mayorsforagi.org/

Mazzucato, M. (2011) *The Entrepreneurial State: Debunking Public vs. Private Sector Myths*. London: Penguin.

mcm_cmc. (2015) 'Fully Automated Luxury Communism: A Utopian Critique'. *Libcom*. Available at: https://libcom.org/article/fully-automated-luxury-communism-utopian-critique

Medina, E. (2014) *Cybernetic Revolutionaries: Technology and Politics in Allende's Chile*. Cambridge, MA: MIT Press.

Meiksins Wood, E. (2017) *The Origins of Capitalism: A Longer View*. London: Verso.

Milburn, K. (2019) *Generation Left*. London: Polity Books.

Miliband E. (2021) *Go Big: How to Fix Our World*. London: Penguin.

Mingay, G. (1997) *Parliamentary Enclosure in England: An Introduction to Its Causes, Incidence and Impact, 1750–1850*. London: Routledge.

Mirowski, P. (2013) *Never Let a Serious Crisis Go to Waste: How Neoliberalism Survived the Financial Meltdown*. London: Verso.

Mirowski, P., and Plehwe, D. eds (2009) *The Road from Mont Pelerin: The Making of the Neoliberal Thought Collective*. London: Harvard University Press.

Monbiot, G. (2017) 'How Labour Could Lead the Global Economy out of the 20th Century'. *Guardian*. Available at:https://www.theguardian.com/commentisfree/2017/oct/11/labour-global-economy-planet

Moore, P. (2010) *The International Political Economy of Work and Employability*. Basingstoke: Palgrave.

More, T. (2016) *Utopia*. London: Verso Books.

Morris, W. (2008) *Useful Work vs. Useless Toil*. London: Penguin.

Morris, W. (1993) *News from Nowhere and Other Writings*. London: Penguin.

Mothers Uncovered. (2020) 'Mothers and Basic Income'. *Mothers Uncovered*. Available at: https://mothersuncovered.com/2020/05/17/mothers-and-basic-income/

Mowat, C. L. (1968) *Britain between the Wars, 1918–1940*. London: Routledge.

Mullainathan, S., and Shafir, E. (2013) *Scarcity: Why Having Too Little Means So Much*. New York: Times Books.

Mumford, L. (1922) *The Story of Utopias*. New York: Boni and Liveright.

Murphy, M. (2023) *Creating an Ecosocial Welfare Future*. Bristol: Policy Press.

Murray, L. (2019) 'Away with All Cars.' *Common Wealth*. Available at: https://www.common-wealth.org/publications/away-with-all-cars-redux

Nadasen, P. (2012) *Rethinking the Welfare Rights Movement*. London: Routledge.

Nanda, S., and Parkers, H. (2019) 'Just Tax'. *IPPR*. Available at: https://www.ippr.org/files/2019-09/just-tax-sept19.pdf

NEF. (2019) 'Average Weekly Hours Fell Faster between 1946 and 1979 than post-1980'. *New Economics Foundation*. Available at: https://neweconomics.org/2019/03/average-weekly-hours-fell-faster-between-1946-and-1979-than-post-1980

Neville, R., Speke A., and Hildyard, L. (2023) 'Analysis of UK CEO Pay in 2022: High Pay Centre'. *High Pay Centre*. Available here: https://highpaycentre.org/ftse-100-ceos-get-half-a-million-pound-pay-rise/

Nunes, R. (2021) *Neither Vertical or Horizontal: A Theory of Political Organization*. London: Verso Books.

O'Brien, M. (2023) *Family Abolition: Capitalism and the Communizing of Care*. London: Pluto Press.

Offe, C. and Wiesenthal, H. (1980) 'Two Logics of Collective Action: Theoretical Notes on Social Class and Organizational Form'. *Political Power and Social Theory* 1:1, pp. 67–115.

Oliver, M. (1996) *Understanding Disability: From Theory to Practice*. New York: St. Martin's Press.

Oliver, M. (1990) *The Politics of Disablement*. London: Springer.

ONS. (2022a) 'Economic Inactivity by Reason (seasonally adjusted)'. *Office for National Statistics*. Available at: https://www.ons.gov.uk/employmentandlabourmarket/peoplenotinwork/economicinactivity/datasets/economicinactivitybyreasonseasonallyadjustedinac01sa

ONS. (2022b) 'The Employment of Disabled People 2021'. *Office for National Statistics*. Available at: https://www.gov.uk/government/statistics/the-employment-of-disabled-people-2021/the-employment-of-disabled-people-2021

ONS. (2022c) 'National Population Projections 2020-Based Interim'. *Office for National Statistics*. Available at: https://www.ons.gov.uk/peoplepopulationandcommunity/populationandmigration/populationprojections/bulletins/nationalpopulationprojections/2020basedinterim#changing-age-structure

ONS. (2022d) 'Outcomes for Disabled People in the UK: 2021'. *Office for National Statistics*. Available at: https://www.ons.gov.uk/peoplepopulationandcommunity/healthandsocialcare/disability/articles/outcomesfordisabledpeopleintheuk/2021#employment

ONS. (2019) 'Long-Term Trends in UK Employment: 1861 to 2018'. *Office for National Statistics*. Available at: https://www.ons.gov.uk/economy/nationalaccounts/uksectoraccounts/compendium/economicreview/april2019/longtermtrendsinukemployment1861to2018#womens-labour-market-participation

ONS. (2016) 'Women Shoulder the Responsibility of Unpaid Work'. *Office for National Statistics*. Available at: https://www.ons.gov.uk/ employmentandlabourmarket/peopleinwork/earningsandworkinghours/articles/ womenshouldertheresponsibilityofunpaidwork/2016-11-10#

Paine, T. (1974) 'Agrarian Justice'. Foner, P. S. (ed.) *The Life and Major Writings of Thomas Paine*. New York: Citadel Press, pp. 605–23.

Panitch, L., and Gindin, S. (2012) *The Making of Global Capitalism: The Political Economy of American Empire*. London: Verso.

Pankhurst, S. (1920a) 'Cooperative Housekeeping'. *Workers' Dreadnought*. Available at: https://libcom.org/library/co-operative-housekeeping-sylvia-pankhurst

Pankhurst, S. (1920b) 'Workers' Memory'. *Workers' Dreadnought*. Available at: https:// www.marxists.org/archive/pankhurst-sylvia/1920/resolutions.htm

Peck, J. (2001) *Workfare States*. New York: Guildford Press.

Perelman, M. (2000) *The Invention of Capitalism: Classical Political Economy and the Secret History of Primitive Accumulation*. Durham, NC: Duke University Press.

Pettinger, L. (2019) *What's Wrong with Work?* Bristol: Policy Press.

Pettit, P. (1997) *Republicanism: A Theory of Freedom and Government*. Oxford: Oxford University Press.

Pew Research Centre. (2015) 'Raising Kids and Running a Household: How Working Parents Share the Load'. *Pew Social Trends*. Available at: http://www.pewsocialtrends. org/2015/11/04/raising-kids-and-running-a-household-how-working-parents-share-the-load/.

Pfannebecker, M., and Smith, J. A. (2018) *Work Want Work: Labour and Desire at the End of Capitalism*. London: Zed.

Philipps, L. (2015) *Austerity, Ecology and the Collapse-Porn Addicts: A Defence of Growth, Progress, Industry and Stuff*. London: Zero Books.

Phillips, L., and Rozworski, M. (2019) *The People's Republic of Walmart*. London: Verso.

Pickett, K., and Wilkinson, R. (2019) *The Inner Level: How More Equal Societies Reduce Stress, Restore Sanity and Improve Everyone's Well-Being*. London: Penguin.

Pickett, K., and Wilkinson, R. (2009) *The Spirit Level: Why More Equal Societies Almost Always Do Better*. London: Allen Lane.

Piepzna-Samarasinha, L. (2022) *The Future Is Disabled*. Vancouver: Arsenal Pulp Press.

Piketty, T. (2021) 'From Basic Income to Inheritance for All'. *Le Monde*. Available at: https://www.lemonde.fr/blog/piketty/2021/05/18/from-basic-income-to-inheritance-for-all/

Polanyi, K. (2002) *The Great Transformation*. Boston: Beacon Press.

Portes, J., Reed, H., and Percy, A. (2017) 'Social Prosperity for the Future: A Proposal for Universal Basic Services'. *UCL*. Available at: https://www.ucl.ac.uk/bartlett/igp/ news/2017/oct/igps-social-prosperity-network-publishes-uks-first-report-universal-basic-services

Postone, M. (1993) *Time, Labor, and Social Domination*. Cambridge: Cambridge University Press.

Prescient and Strategic Intelligence. (2020) 'Personal Robots Market Research Report: By Offering (Hardware, Software), Type (Cleaning Robots, Entertainment & Toy Robots, Educational Robots, Handicap Assistance Robots, Companion Robots, Personal

Transportation Robots, Security Robots) – Global Industry Analysis and Growth Forecast to 2030'. *PS Market Research*. Available at: https://www.psmarketresearch. com/market-analysis/personal-robot-market

Rabinbach, A. (1992) *The Human Motor: Energy, Fatigue, and the Origins of Modernity*. Oakland, CA: University of California Press.

Rathbone, E. F. (1986) *The Disinherited Family*. Bristol: Falling Wall Press.

Rathbone, E. F. (1924) 'Family Endowment in Its Bearing on the Question of Population'. *Eugenics Society*, 12 November 1924.

Read, J. (2003) *The Micro-Politics of Capital*. New York: SUNY Press.

Reed, H., et al. (2022) *Tackling Poverty: The Power of a Universal Basic Income*. London: Compass.

Reeves, R. (2019) 'Eleanor Rathbone, the Forgotten MP Who Changed Women's Lives by Pioneering Child Benefits'. *The i*. Available at: https://inews.co.uk/opinion/comment/ eleanor-rathbone-mp-family-allowances-international-womens-day-266610

Reform Committee of the South Wales Miners. (1970) 'The Miners' Next Step'. Coates, K., and Topham, T. (eds) *Workers' Control*. London: Panther Books.

Roberts, W. C. (2016) *Marx's Inferno: The Political Theory of Capital*. Princeton: Princeton University Press.

Robeyns, I. (2001) '*An Income of One's Own: A Radical Vision of Welfare Policies in Europe and Beyond*'. *Gender and Development* 9:1, pp. 82–9.

Robin, C. (2011) *The Reactionary Mind*. Oxford: Oxford University Press.

Robin, V., and Dominguez, J. (2008) *Your Money or Your Life*. London: Penguin.

Rodgers, D. (2014) *The Work Ethic in Industrial America, 1850–1920*. Chicago: University of Chicago Press.

Roediger, D. (2007) *The Wages of Whiteness*. London: Verso Books.

Roediger, P. S., and Foner, D. R. (1987) *Our Own Time: A History of American Labor and the Working Day*. London: Verso.

Rose, H. (1973) 'Up against the Welfare State: The Claimant Unions'. *Socialist Register* 10, p. 186. Available at: https://socialistregister.com/index.php/srv/article/view/5354

Rose, N. (1989) *Governing the Soul: The Shaping of the Private Self*. London: Routledge.

Rowan, R. (2015) 'Extinction as Usual? Geo-Social Futures and Left Optimism'. *e-flux*. Available at: http://supercommunity.e-flux.com/authors/rory-rowan/

Russell, B. (2004) *In Praise of Idleness*. London: Routledge.

Russell, B. (1966) *Roads to Freedom*. London: Unwin

Ryan, F. (2020) *Crippled: Austerity and the Demonization of Disabled People*. London: Verso.

Samman, E., Presler-Marshall, E., and Jones, N. (2016) 'Women's Work: Mothers, Children and the Global Childcare Crisis'. *Overseas Development Institute*. Available at: https:// odi.org/en/publications/womens-work-mothers-children-and-the-global-childcare- crisis/

Samuel, S. (2020) 'You Can Buy a Robot to Keep Your Lonely Grandparents Company. Should You?' *Vox*. Available at: https://www.vox.com/future- perfect/2020/9/9/21418390/robots-pandemic-loneliness-isolation-elderly-seniors

Sanchis, J. (2021) *Quatre Dias*. Valencia: Sembra Libres.

Sayer, L. (2005) 'Gender, Time and Inequality: Trends in Women's and Men's Paid Work, Unpaid Work and Free Time'. *Social Forces* 84:1, pp. 285–303.

Schmeler, M., Vansintjan, A., and Vetter, A. (2022) *The Future of Degrowth: A Guide to a World beyond Capitalism*. London: Verso.

Schneider, J. (2022) *Our Bloc*. London: Verso.

Seabrook, J. (2016) *Cut Out: Living without Welfare*. London: Pluto Books.

Seabrook, J. (2013) *Pauperland: A Short History of Poverty in Britain*. London: C Hurst and Co.

Seabrook J., and Stronge, W. (2018) 'In and out of Work: An Interview with Jeremy Seabrook'. *Autonomy*. Available at: https://autonomy.work/wp-content/uploads/2018/08/Jeremy-Seabrook-interview-V3.pdf

Seccombe, W. (1995) *Weathering the Storm: Working-Class Families from the Industrial Revolution to the Fertility Decline*. London: Verso.

Sheffey, A. (2021) 'Elon Musk Says We Need Universal Basic Income because "In the Future, Physical Work Will Be a Choice"'. *Business Insider*. Available here: https://www.businessinsider.com/elon-musk-universal-basic-income-physical-work-choice-2021-8?r=US&IR=T

Sheppard, E. (2021) 'Cripping Queer Futurities'. *YouTube*. Available at: https://www.youtube.com/watch?v=uzfnkAKIuiE

Shilliam, R. (2018) *Race and the Undeserving Poor*. Newcastle upon Tyne: Agenda Publishing.

Siravo, J., et al. (2021) 'Working Nights'. *Autonomy*. Available at: https://autonomy.work/portfolio/workingnights/

Smith, A. (2014) 'The Lucas Plan: What Can It Tell Us about Democratising Technology Today?' *Guardian*. Available at: https://www.theguardian.com/science/political-science/2014/jan/22/remembering-the-lucas-plan-what-can-it-tell-us-about-democratising-technology-today

Smith, J. (2020) *Smart Machine and Service Work: Automation in an Age of Stagnation*. London: Reaktion Books.

Smith, J. (2016) *Imperialism in the Twenty-First Century: Globalization, Super-Exploitation, and Capitalism's Final Crisis*. New York: New York University Press.

Snyder, B. (2016) *The Disrupted Workplace: Time and the Moral Order of Flexible Capitalism*. Oxford: Oxford University Press.

Soper, K. (2020) *Post-Growth Living: Towards an Alternative Hedonism*. London: Verso.

Spargo, J. (1912) *Applied Socialism: A Study of the Application of Socialist Principles to the State*. New York: B.W. Huebsch.

Spencer, D. (2021) *Making Light Work: An End to Toil in the Twenty-First Century*. Cambridge: Polity Press.

Srnicek, N., and Williams, A. (2015) *Inventing the Future: Postcapitalism and a World without Work*. London: Verso.

Standing, G. (2020) *Battling Eight Giants: Basic Income Now*. London: I. B. Tauris.

Standing, G. (2019) *The Plunder of the Commons: A Manifesto for Sharing Public Wealth*. London: Penguin.

Standing, G. (2017) *The Corruption of Capitalism: Why Rentiers Thrive and Work Does Not Pay*. London: Biteback Books.

Standing, G. (2014) *The Precariat Charter: From Denizens to Citizens*. London: Bloomsbury.

Standing, G. (2011) *The Precariat: The New Dangerous Class*. London: Bloomsbury.

Stern, A. (2016) *Raising the Floor*. New York: Public Affairs.

Stiglitz, J. (2018) 'From Manufacturing Led Export Growth to a 21st Century Inclusive Growth Strategy: Explaining the Demise of a Successful Growth Model and What to Do about It'. *United Nations University: Think Development – Think WIDER*. Available at: https://www.wider.unu.edu/sites/default/files/Events/PDF/Papers/Draft-paper-Juseph-Stiglitz-Sept2018.pdf

Stratford, B. (2020) 'Green Growth vs Degrowth: Are We Missing the Point?' *OpenDemocracy*. Available at: https://www.opendemocracy.net/en/oureconomy/green-growth-vs-degrowth-are-we-missing-point/

Strauss, D. (2022) 'Rise in Long-Term Sickness Poses Threat to UK Economic Growth'. *Financial Times*. Available at: https://www.ft.com/content/8eb63de7-6b08-4714-9435-d3c42d2e4ba2

Stronge, W. (2020) 'What Counts as Basic?' *Autonomy*. Available at: https://autonomy.work/portfolio/incomenotservices/

Stronge, W. (2017) 'Introduction'. Stronge, W. (ed.) *Georges Bataille and Contemporary Thought*. London: Bloomsbury, pp. 1–7.

Stronge, W., et al. (2021) 'A Future Fit for Wales: A Basic Income for All'. *Autonomy*. Available at: https://autonomy.work/portfolio/walesubi/

Stronge, W., and Murray, N. (2021) 'Claim the Commute'. *Autonomy*. Available at: https://autonomy.work/portfolio/claimthecommute/

Suwandi, I. (2019) *Value Chains: The New Economic Imperialism*. New York: Monthly Review Press.

Taylor, S. (2004) 'The Right Not to Work: Power and Disability'. *Monthly Review*. Available at: https://monthlyreview.org/2004/03/01/the-right-not-to-work-power-and-disability

Thompson, E. P. (1977) *William Morris: Romantic to Revolutionary*. New York: Pantheon.

Thompson, E. P. (1967) 'Time, Work-Discipline, and Industrial Capitalism'. *Past and Present* 38, pp. 56–97.

Thompson, P. (2018) 'The Refusal of Work: Past, Present and Future'. *Futures of Work*. Available at: https://futuresofwork.co.uk/2018/09/05/the-refusal-of-work-past-present-and-future/

Tillmon, J. (2010) 'From the Vault: "Welfare Is a Women's Issue" (Spring 1972)'. *Ms Magazine*. Available at: https://msmagazine.com/2021/03/25/welfare-is-a-womens-issue-ms-magazine-spring-1972/

Tilly, L. A., and Scott, J. W. (1989) *Women, Work, and Family*. New York: Routledge.

Traverso, E. (2019) *The New Faces of Fascism: Populism and the Far Right*. London: Verso.

Trott, B. (2007) 'Walking in the Right Direction?' *Turbulence* 1. Available at: http://www.turbulence.org.uk/turbulence-1/walking-in-the-right-direction/index.html

TUC. (2023) 'New TUC Poll: 2 in 3 Young Women have Experienced Sexual Harassment, Bullying or Verbal Abuse at Work'. *Trades Union Congress*. Available at: https://www.tuc.org.uk/news/new-tuc-poll-2-3-young-women-have-experienced-sexual-harassment-bullying-or-verbal-abuse-work#:~:text=The%20TUC%20poll%20found%20that,three%20incidents%20of%20sexual%20harassment

TUC. (2021) '"Fire and Rehire" Tactics Have Become Widespread during Pandemic – Warns TUC'. *Trades Union Congress*. Available at: https://www.tuc.org.uk/news/fire-and-rehire-tactics-have-become-widespread-during-pandemic-warns-tuc

TUC. (2019) 'Sexual Harassment of LGBT People in the Workplace'. *Trades Union Congress*. Available at: https://www.tuc.org.uk/research-analysis/reports/sexual-harassment-lgbt-people-workplace#:~:text=Main%20findings,report%20it%20to%20 their%20employer

TUC. (2017) 'Average Worker Now Spends 27 Working Days a Year Commuting, Finds TUC'. *Trades Union Congress*. Available at: https://www.tuc.org.uk/news/average-worker-now-spends-27-working-days-year-commuting-finds-tuc#

UBI Labs. (2021) *UBI Lab Network*. Available at: https://www.ubilabnetwork.org/

UK Parliament. (2022) 'UK Disability Statistics: Prevalence and Life Experiences'. *Commons Library*. Available at: https://commonslibrary.parliament.uk/research-briefings/cbp-9602/#:~:text=How%20many%20people%20have%20a,22%25%20of%20 the%20total%20population

UNODC. (2018) 'Home, the Most Dangerous Place for Women, with Majority of Female Homicide Victims Worldwide Killed by Partners or Family, UNODC Study Says'. *United Nations Office on Drugs and Crime*. Available at: https://www.unodc.org/unodc/ en/press/releases/2018/November/home–the-most-dangerous-place-for-women–with-majority-of-female-homicide-victims-worldwide-killed-by-partners-or-family–unodc-study-says.html

Van der Linden, M. (2008) *Workers of the World: Essays toward a Global Labor History*. Leiden: Brill.

Van Parijs, P., and Vanderborght Y. (2017) *Basic Income: A Radical Proposal for a Free and Sane Society*. London: Harvard University Press.

Walsh, M., and Wrigley, C. (2001) 'Womanpower: The Transformation of the Labour Force in the UK and the USA since 1945'. *Recent Findings of Research in Economic and Social History* 30. Available at: https://ehs.org.uk/womanpower-the-transformation-of-the-labour-force-in-the-uk-and-usa-since-1945/

Wark, M. (2016) *Molecular Red: Theory for the Anthropocene*. London: Verso Books.

Weber, M. (1958) *The Protestant Ethic and the Spirit of Capitalism*. New York: Charles Scribner's Sons.

Weber, M. (1946) 'Science as Vocation'. Weber, M., *From Weber: Essays in Sociology*. New York: Oxford University Press, pp. 129–56.

Weeks, K. (2023) 'Abolition of the Family: The most Infamous Feminist Proposal'. *Feminist Theory* 24:3, pp. 433–53.

Weeks, K. (2020) 'Anti/Postwork Feminist Politics and a Case for Basic Income'. *tripleC* 18:2, pp. 575–94.

Weeks, K. (2011) *The Problem with Work: Feminism, Marxism, Anti-work Politics and Post-Work Imaginaries*. Durham, NC: Duke University Press.

Weeks, K. (2009) '"Hours for What We Will": Work, Family, and the Movement for Shorter Hours'. *Feminist Studies* 35:1, pp. 101–27.

Whiteside, N. (1991) *Bad Times: Unemployment in British Social and Political History*. London: Penguin.

Whittle, H. J., et al. (2017) '"The Land of the Sick and the Land of the Healthy": Disability, Bureaucracy, and Stigma among People Living with Poverty and Chronic Illness in the United States'. *Soc Sci Med* 190, pp. 181–9.

WHO. (2023) 'Disability'. *World Health Organisation*. Available at: https://www.who.int/news-room/fact-sheets/detail/disability-and-health

Williams, A., and Srnicek, N. (2013) '#Accelerate: Manifesto for an Accelerationist Politics'. *Critical Legal Thinking*. Available at: https://criticallegalthinking.com/2013/05/14/accelerate-manifesto-for-an-accelerationist-politics/

Williams, R. (2015) *A Short Counter-Revolution: Towards 2000 Revisited*. London: Sage.

Withers, A. J. (2012) *Disability, Politics and Theory*. Winnipeg: Fernwood Publishing.

Wolfendale, P. (2016) 'Prometheanism and Rationalism'. *Academia.edu*. Available at: https://www.academia.edu/26816420/Prometheanism_and_Rationalism

Womak, A. (2018) 'How a Universal Basic Income Could Help Women in Abusive Relationships'. *Independent*. Available at: https://www.independent.co.uk/voices/domestic-violence-abuse-bill-theresa-may-financial-independence-a8260736.html

Wood, A. (2022) *Despotism on Demand: How Power Operates in the Flexible Workplace*. New York: Cornell University Press

Wright, E. O. (2019) *How to Be an Anticapitalist in the Twenty-First Century*. London: Verso.

Wright, J. (2023) *Robots Won't Save Japan: An Ethnography of Eldercare Automation*. Ithaca: Cornell University Press.

Wright, S. (2023) *Women and Welfare Conditionality: Lived Experiences of Benefit Sanctions, Work and Welfare*. Bristol: Policy Press.

Wright, S. (2011) 'Relinquishing Rights? The Impact of Activation on Citizenship for Single Parents in the UK'. Betzelt, S., and Bothfeld, S. (eds) *Activation and Labour Market Reform in Europe: Challenges to Social Citizenship*. Basingstoke: Palgrave Macmillan, pp. 59–78.

Wright, S., and Dwyer, P. (2022) 'In-Work Universal Credit: Claimant Experiences of Conditionality Mismatches and Counterproductive Benefit Sanctions'. *Journal of Social Policy* 51:1, pp. 20–38.

Wright, S., and Patrick, R. (2019) 'Welfare Conditionality in Lived Experience: Aggregating Qualitative Longitudinal Research'. *Social Policy and Society* 18:4, pp. 597–613.

Yorke, C. C. (2016) 'Prospects for Utopia in Space'. Schwartz, J., and Milligan, T. (eds) *The Ethics of Space Exploration*. New York: Springer, pp. 61–71.

YouGov. (2017) '45% of Working Brits Would Retire on the Spot for £1m'. *YouGov*. Available at: https://yougov.co.uk/topics/politics/articles-reports/2017/10/16/how-much-money-would-you-want-to-retire

Zachariah, D., and Härdin, T. 'Cybernetic Planning and Climate Change Reversal'. *YouTube*. Available at: https://www.youtube.com/watch?v=65LjjIQdNw8&list=LL&index=2

Index